FIERCE V...

Letters Home from a Canadian Journalist in postwar England 1949–1954

OUIDA MacLELLAN

Abridged and Edited

BAYEUX

FIERCE VIRGIN: LETTERS HOME FROM A CANADIAN JOURNALIST IN POSTWAR
ENGLAND 1949–1954
© Copyright 2012 Bayeux Arts
119 Stratton Crescent SW,
Calgary, Canada T3H 1T7

www.bayeux.com

Cover and Book design: PreMediaGlobal

Portrait of the author by A.K. Browning, 1953, who titled it *Fierce Virgin*.

Library and Archives Canada Cataloguing in Publication

MacLellan, Ouida, 1927-2009
    Fierce virgin : letters from a Canadian journalist in post-war England, 1949-1954 / Ouida MacLellan.

ISBN 978-1-897411-39-1

    1. MacLellan, Ouida, 1927-2009. 2. MacLellan, Ouida, 1927-2009 —Correspondence.
3. Journalists—Canada—Biography.
4. Journalists—Canada—Correspondence. 5. England—Description and travel. I. Title.

PN4913.M33A3 2012   070.4082   C2012-902872-X

Printed in Canada

Books published by Bayeux Arts are available at special quantity discounts to use premiums and sales promotions, or for use in corporate training programs. For more information, please write to Special Sales, Bayeux Arts, Inc., 119 Stratton Crescent SW, Calgary, Canada T3H 1T7.

All rights reserved. No part of this publication may be reproduced, stored in a retrieval system, or transmitted, in any from or by any means, electronic, mechanical, recording, or otherwise, without the prior written permission of the publisher, except in the case of a reviewer, who may quote brief passages in a review to print in a magazine or newspaper, or broadcast on radio or television. In the case of photocopying or other reprographic copying, users must obtain a license from the Canadian Copyright Licensing Agency.

The ongoing publishing activities of Bayeux Arts, under its "Bayeux" and "Gondolier" imprints, are supported by the Canada Council for the Arts, the Alberta Foundation for the Arts, and the Government of Canada through the Book Publishing Industry Development Program.

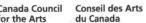

CONTENTS

Introduction   v

A Note on the Editing   viii

"Sitting here Fuming"
  February–March 1949   1

"He Greeted Me Like an Old Pal"
  April–May 1949   11

"Men Make Me Sick"
  June–August 1949   20

"If You had a Brain You'd be Dangerous"
  September–November 1949   33

"I've Just Got to Get this Job"
  December 1949   44

"Tickled Pink . . . I Have My First Story"
  January–March 1950   51

"Urgently Wanted at the Savoy by the Beaver"
  April–July 1950   65

"I Want to Say Yes"
  August–December 1950   77

"I'll Do as I Please When I Please"
  January–March 1951   92

"Fired by the Sunday Express"
  April–July 1951   104

"Perhaps I Have at Last Grown up"
  August–December 1951   117

"Most Men Think Female Journalists are Tarts"
   January–February 1952   124

"Flat Behaviour"
   March–May 1952   134

"Either a Feast or a Famine"
   June–August 1952   148

"Good Fun with no Seriousness Thrown in"
   September–December 1952   155

"Getting Scoops"
   January–July 1953   165

"A Canadian and an Englishman"
   August 1953–August 1954   176

"Yes"
   September–December 1954   188

Afterword   199

INTRODUCTION

Rodney Touche

Ouida MacLellan was twenty-one years old in February 1949 when she set off from Canada to work for six years in London's Fleet Street. From age fourteen, Ouida never wanted to be anything other than a newspaper reporter, with her sights set on London. This was an unusual ambition for a young girl born in Moncton, New Brunswick, in 1927, and especially for a girl whose father and mother had very limited literary interests.

Moncton in those days was a railway town where Canadian National Railways managed its Maritime operations. Ouida's father, Gerald, was born in New Brunswick in 1893 and worked all his life for CNR as a civil engineer. He was a devout Catholic. He might have had a career as a baseball player, having been invited to a tryout by the Boston Red Sox. He went to Boston for the weekend, where it rained both days. He would have had to stay over to Monday for the tryout. He refused rather than not show up for work. No calling in sick for him. He was not invited again.

Ouida's mother, Miriam Gibson, was brought up as a Methodist and converted to Catholicism on marriage. Ouida was their first child, named for a woman Miriam had met on holiday in Florida. She did not know that this was the pen name of an English writer, Louisa de la Ramée (1839–1908), for whom it was the babyhood version of her name. Neither did she know that Louisa's novels about the social life of guards' officers were considered scandalous.

Miriam could not have chosen a better name as an icebreaker for a daughter with a journalistic career ahead of her. However, when Ouida was asked for the origin of her name she always explained how her mother had come across it. Accuracy was instinctive. She was too honest to attribute it to the novelist, perhaps also not wanting to imply that her mother might have read scandalous novels.

Ouida's career as a journalist started in 1941 at the age of fourteen, writing for her Moncton school paper, *The High News*. She spent the summer vacations of 1943 and 1944 as the first female reporter on the *Moncton Times*. She had been recommended by the Superintendent of Moncton Schools.

After one year at St. Francis Xavier University, in Antigonish, Nova Scotia, where she wrote for the *Xaverian*, she became a full-time member of the editorial staff of the *Moncton Times* (now amalgamated with the *Transcript*). Her hours of work could go as late as two a.m., when she would bicycle home, sometimes watched by a police car—such was the nature of small-town Moncton.

One of her assignments was to interview returning veterans of World War II for a weekly column called "Back to Civvie Street." For another ongoing column called "Towns of the Maritimes," she travelled throughout the province, usually staying overnight and meeting local residents. These columns were later published as four booklets.

By 1949, she had acquired radio experience with a weekly program on a Moncton station. She had also been a member of a choir and a piano accompanist; and had played badminton, tennis, and basketball.

All of this activity broadened her social life and the number of her boyfriends. She resisted marriage proposals, one of which was from a high school friend with whom she kept in touch all her life. Although dear to her, he was a homeboy who had no intention of leaving Moncton. Another was the scion of a local brewing family whose car was always stocked with beer. Ouida did not drink then, and never beer, and was not impressed by her suitor's wealth.

Ouida grew up with two much younger sisters, Miriam and Joan, and two surrogate "brothers," Bernard and Ged Mooney, evacuees from England whom the MacLellans took into their family during the war. In 1947, the parents of the North American evacuees formed the Kinsman Trust as a form of partial repayment. The Trust awarded one-year scholarships to a British school or university and also a "grant-in-aid" to continue, in England, a course of education already embarked upon. Ouida was among the recipients. She had no wish to continue in university. She wanted to continue her education as a reporter. The "grant-in-aid" was just what she needed until she was accepted by an English newspaper.

She set off alone on February 19, 1949, from New York to Southampton on RMS *Queen Elizabeth* and that day she wrote to her mother the first of some 400 letters that described the next six years that she spent in London. Most of the letters are typed on flimsy Air Letter forms, which had a lower postal rate (sixpence). Ouida wrote, noting the time, on both sides, leaving no empty space, sometimes twice in one day, and always one or more times a week.

These blue Air Letter forms, along with some letters for full-priced mail, were kept by her parents and filled a shoebox found in Ouida's office after her death at the age of eighty-two. Only a very few letters in response have survived.

Her style was flowing and outspoken. Although she was addressing her mother, she said what she thought, even telling her off. Such candour and openness were unusual in a mother/daughter relationship in that period. Her mother read selections to her father, who wrote to her every Sunday.

Day-to-day management of the Trust was provided by Thomas Riley. His wife, Louise, was honorary secretary and met Ouida at Southampton when the ship docked. The Rileys, with their daughter Pat, were a great help to Ouida, inviting her to their home, giving her money, and finding her lodgings with a Mrs. Bennett near Kew Gardens in Richmond, a thirty-minute train ride to central London.

Ouida started at once writing a series of columns called "In Britain Today" for use by the *Moncton Times*. She sent them to her mother to submit and collect payment, five dollars per column. Her mother was told off if she tried to edit them in any way. These columns were kept up for the first three years but ended when negotiations for a higher fee broke down.

At first, the columns were her only income to supplement grants from the Trust. She had applied immediately, without success, to two Fleet Street newspapers, the *Sunday Express* and the *Evening Standard*, both owned by Lord Beaverbrook. She had met Lord Beaverbrook in November, 1948, and introduced herself as the granddaughter of Angus MacLellan, the guard on a train who had found Beaverbrook, aged twelve, running away from home, and sent him back.

Beaverbrook was among the distinguished guests at the Winter Fair in Amherst, Nova Scotia. She told him of her ambition. He wrote to her on Nov 12, 1948, saying, "When I see you again I will offer some advice on journalism," and telling her to "send me your reporting stories for a few days to the Royal York Hotel, Toronto."

His advice was to wait until he sent for her, which she ignored. In March 1949, she got a job for two days on the *Sunday Express*, which needed extra staff prior to the weekend. She told Lord Beaverbrook's secretary what she had done, and on April 15, 1949, he sent a car to bring her to Cherkley Court, his 375-acre estate some twenty miles from London. She met him again at his London flat in October, and the next year she got a full-time job at the *Evening Standard*, a job that she kept until April 30, 1955.

That was the date of her marriage to me, a colleague on the *Evening Standard*, and the end of her full-time career as a journalist. She and I moved to Canada in 1956, living first in Toronto, and later, from 1961, in Calgary. Her experience reporting on the art world in London, for which she had received the advice of her landlady, a Royal Academician, enabled her to present a weekly program with the CBC reviewing gallery openings and to prosper as an art consultant, building collections for companies. She was a volunteer with the Allied Arts Centre, which rented pieces of art by the month to its members.

By the early 1980s, when her four children had left home, Ouida had achieved a prominent position in Calgary's art world and was appointed chairman of the Calgary Region Arts Foundation, a board of forty volunteers who controlled the distribution of some $800,000 of civic funds to about sixty arts organizations.

Extracts from the letters that she wrote to "Dear Mum," describing her life from 1949 to 1955, follow.

A NOTE ON THE EDITING

This project would not have been carried out without the considerable amount of work done by Philip McCoy, who was a close friend of Ouida's during the last thirty-seven years of her life. He made the initial selection of excerpts from the 393 letters. We agreed that the focus should be on four major areas: her adjustment to life in post-war England, her friendships and romances, her work and development as a journalist, and her state of mind emotionally and intellectually.

Throughout, we have tried to portray the remarkably candid, volatile, and complicated relationship of Ouida with her mother. Inevitably, much has been omitted, especially references to friends and extended family in New Brunswick. Most of the letters start with "Dear Mum" and end with "Love, Ouida." These words have been left out unless the excerpt is also the first paragraph or the last paragraph of the letter. We have wanted to maintain the narrative flow of the letters, but not at the expense of meaning or intention. My editorial comments appear throughout in square brackets or footnotes. The manuscript was well prepared for publication by Jane Karchmar, a professional editor.

Rodney Touche

"SITTING HERE FUMING"
February–March 1949

Saturday, Feb. 19, 1949, RMS Queen Elizabeth

Dear Mum,

Just covered a good part of the boat, and believe you me, my feet hurt but good! Even walked into the first-class section without knowing it.

My cabin mate is an "Aunt Sis" someone—about 60, and boy are her relatives celebrating hard right now!!! Hope they calm down soon! So far as I know, we are sailing about ten and it is now 8:38 p.m.

Wednesday, Feb. 23, 1949, RMS Queen Elizabeth

Dear Mum,

Guess my good habits are slipping already, for I haven't written you a word since sailing, but honestly it has been wonderful just to relax and enjoy things without a worry in the world—or at least none that bother me too much. Have written two columns . . . and am forwarding the results. [For the *Moncton Times and Transcript*.]

Have met some very nice people—only one really interesting and I did not meet him until last night. He is Dick DeLuce, brother of the famous AP [Associated Press] war correspondent, Daniel DeLuce. A very nice chap my own age who is going to join Dan in Paris. Leo Peterson in New York gave me some UP [United Press] names in London—all single men, he said—and I should manage all right.

The voyage has been very nice, nothing too exciting, but restful, which is evidently what I needed. Today a little chap from India kept running around behind me snapping a picture every time I turned around. Felt like Betty Grable!

Want to get this stuff off at Cherbourg so shall have to close. Shall write at length when settled, which should be a day or two.

Love, Ouida

Friday, Feb. 25, 1949, London

Dear Mum,

Well, Mrs. Riley [from the Kinsman Trust], a very nice person indeed, met me at Southampton. In fact, she came on board the boat for me, so we had no trouble whatsoever. Customs wasn't too bad, and I made it through with the cigars for Mr. Mooney.[1] The customs officer I got was a tall, handsome "pretty" man who evidently thought he was as good looking as I thought he was. He had me open my trunk and thrust his hand in the top drawer. You should have seen his face when he quickly hauled his hand out again and disgustedly said, "Something must have broken." It was one of the bottles of shampoo, but luckily enough little damage was done. It discouraged him, however, for he said, "Oh, it's all right" and promptly marked my other bags without opening them at all. He was going to charge me duty on my typewriter but I must have looked very sorrowful for he said he would let it go this time. The trip to London was pleasant and uneventful.

Mrs. Riley had already found me a place to live, and I like it fine. She said she thought I would like it better in a private house with a nice family and tried to find me a nice, pleasant, homey one. She did a very good job, for certainly these people are nice. It is a double house, with the daughter, her husband and twin sons (age 6) living downstairs and Mrs. Bennett and at present a nephew (age 27) living up. I live up and have a rather small room but quite bright. After George (the nephew) leaves for St. Helena Island in April, I am to have his room, which is much bigger. The house has a nice garden, and I am told this is a lovely area. Guess the Kew Gardens are quite famous as well as beautiful and it is near Richmond, in case you are scanning a map. It is about 25 minutes from Piccadilly Circus, and evidently I shall be working right in London. A bit like living in the Bronx and working in N.Y., I believe . . . Haven't met Mr. Riley yet but shall tomorrow, I think . . . will call at the UP office on Monday.

One of the twins is here now leaning on me. I seem to fascinate them—I'm queer!!

Love, Ouida

Monday, Feb. 28, 1949

Mum, about parcels. Food parcels come in between two to three weeks, I guess. In fact everything does . . . Food is the most necessary thing here, and as for clothing, put a cleaner's label on things and wash out a pair of stockings and there is no trouble. Mark things "used clothing." As for food, if you could, I would appreciate some of those packages of

---

[1] Mr. Mooney was the father of the evacuees Bernard and Ged who stayed with the MacLellans during the war.

hot chocolate . . . Then tinned things are great—especially the meat. Butter is also most acceptable and is easily sent in a coffee tin and wrapped in salt paper. Sugar is very handy, and if possible, stick in a bit of brown sugar, as theirs over here is extremely coarse and not too good for porridge. Rating very high among tinned goods is salmon. It costs about three dollars a pound fresh here. Powdered eggs and tinned bacon . . . are also very welcome . . . Oh yes, Kleenex is handy. Perhaps you could pack things in it, as it is unobtainable here, and my nose runs continually.

You were right about the hot water bottle; it is impossible to live without one. I use one of Mrs. Bennett's every night and would probably die without it. Really the only time I am comfortably warm is when in bed with the covers pulled up over my head. Oh well, perhaps summer will come soon! Oh, stick in a few cookies; they are wonderful too, even if people here don't consider them "cookies." Boy! I'm going to run you in debt sure with all these suggestions.

There was considerable frost here this morning, but I see now the man next door is out working his garden, tell Dad.

Bye for now.

Love, Ouida

March 3, 1949, Ash Wednesday afternoon

Just got a fantastic brainwave and decided I had better jot it down immediately or probably the thought would take the next slow boat for China and I would be left.

What would you think of writing the columns in the form of letters? It would enable me to put in all the funny little incidents that really don't belong in a regular news article. Perhaps I can send you a sample of both and you could send the same to the papers or else just send them the one you think they would like best.

Then the heading could be, "Letters from Britain" by me and start off "Dear Mike"; or even leave the heading as it is now, "In Britain Today," and still start them "Dear Mike" or some better name if you can think of one . . . Somehow writing things in the form of a letter seems to come much easier for me, and after I start work I don't want to be tied down too much by the columns. Also, if you can picture one person in particular rather than hundreds in general, it is easier to write.

When the column is started, it could be explained that the author is writing home her impressions of things in England to Mike, a lifelong pal, who is still in the Maritimes. Also, in this manner, the columns could be easily reprinted in book form if they merit it, whereas just plain articles wouldn't make as interesting reading.

You may think this brainwave is all wet, but it was just an idea that came while I was sitting here writing letters anyway trying to catch up. Previously I had been labouring over a column and it seemed to come so hard . . . Oftentimes when a person reads a letter they can imagine the situations much more easily. Suppose this sounds like a sales talk on the letter-column idea but you must admit it doesn't sound too bad. Will send samples anyway.

[All of the above is lightly marked out in the original letter, and on the same sheets, the following is added.]

Friday, March 5, 1949

Hi!
Have had a complete change of mind since starting this letter but since I've already paid for the stamp, will use the paper anyway. Last night Danny Gilmore [journalist for United Press] took me to dinner at the American Embassy and I met his bureau chief, Roger Titrarian, and UP's Bill Williams. A number of well-known AP and New York Herald men were also around. Anyway, I talked the idea of the letter over with the UP boys and they claim people will tire of a letter sometimes too quickly. Have also decided on my own that letters can slip into the juvenile bracket if one isn't careful. The straight news story will be much better and rate me higher in the end I'm sure. That was a good talk I gave you, though!!!

Also your letter arrived today, telling me Marg [family friend] had liked the first column I sent you, and it seemed to throw me into my regular stride—which I have been out of for some time. Was a bit worried about those first columns because they HAVE to be good, but your OK reinstated me and I'm fine again. Have been puttering around ever since arriving, trying to settle down. After talking to the boys last night, several good ideas came, then your letter today put the cap on and I hit the typewriter hard. Corrected a previous mess and turned out two more I feel better about. Will send along others shortly, but you can start sending these out to editors now with the assurance others will follow regularly. By the way, your airmail letters are arriving here in three days flat . . . Still haven't received anything by straight mail so am not taking any chances on the boats at all. Will send all columns by airmail to make sure they arrive in time.

Tuesday, March 8, 1949

Dear Mum,
Well, I was to see Miss Lorimer [who worked for The Kinsman Trust] yesterday. Mrs. Riley has been saying they thought three months on a publication like "Woman's Own," then I would be ready for a daily. I didn't think so, however, and neither did Miss Lorimer.

She was very nice and said she truthfully thought it would be a waste of both my time and theirs to put me on the weekly. It wasn't what I wanted at all. She said she had no doubt, however, that a place can be found for me on one of the big international dailies. It seems I am just the type of person they are looking for. She is arranging several interviews for me with editors of the Express (Beaverbrook) and the Daily Mail, and said she is sure I'll be working by Saturday.

On top of that, the minute she heard I had radio experience, she said she thought I should do a program on The Woman's Hour, and perhaps a regular spot could be arranged for me. I could hardly believe my ears, and even though it is a woman's program, anything is good for a start. The Woman's Hour is a daily program at 2 p.m. on the BBC Light Programme series . . . The sooner my name becomes familiar over here, the better it will be for me—this, Miss Lorimer also mentioned.

Your suggestions for the column weren't bad, but you don't seem to catch onto my ideas at all. The column isn't going to be anything like the high school pieces; that was too childish for now. Each column will be entirely on the same subject, as you will see from the ones I mailed Sunday. Also there will be no opportunity to include names of actual people from home unless I bring them into the story. Such as the Shelbourne girl [an evacuee] I intend to work into the piece about a visit to Roedean School at Brighton, which is one of England's top girls' schools, and during the war Roedean students went to Edgehill in Nova Scotia. That is, unless I meet a person who is a real character and worth a story on their own, then they shall have it. Once in a while I may work in a column of all little items about the queer things that happen, but ordinarily, they will be straightforward news stories woven around one particular theme.

You know, if I could wrangle the time—and the money—I would like to study dramatics and dancing a bit. Have always wanted to, and certainly there are plenty of opportunities here.

Golly, Mum, if I could manage a radio job in addition to the newspaper work, it might afford me enough pocket money to take short trips on holidays. Would love to spend Easter in Paris and I certainly want to see as much of Europe as possible before returning home. Might even try for a trip home by way of India and the Far East. Too bad I'm a girl, because a boy could work his passage.

If you manage to sell columns to the Saint John paper, you put the money in my account, and not yours!!! You are not my researcher: a researcher digs up all the material and information for a writer and certainly you don't do that. I have something in mind for your pay, so leave my moola alone and go make some of your own. I hope you are sending a copy of the column to The Charlottetown Guardian and The Fredericton Gleaner. Might even try The Truro Daily News. I'm not grabby, but I like a lot, and so long as I'm going to write the column, it might as well pay the most. I'm going to need it.

Wednesday, March 9, 1949

I go tomorrow to meet John Gordon who is one of the big lights in English journalism. He's editor of the Express, and Miss Lorimer is very confident.

[One of the first purchases Ouida made in London was an expensive hat, which she came to regard as her lucky hat. She wore it for the first time on March 11 for her job interview with John Gordon of the Express Group. Although she didn't mention the hat in letters home during March, she described it and its magical effect in a column published a month later in the *Moncton Times and Transcript*, April 16, 1949. For the rest of her life, Ouida liked wearing hats and, in later years, organized a series of lunches for "Women Who Wear Hats." Invitees might even include strangers whose hats she admired.]

IN BRITAIN TODAY by Ouida MacLellan

The hat manufacturers in Britain are staging a comeback, and the posters in all the eye-catching places tell you that "You look better in a hat." Under one picture of a handsome young man embracing a lovely girl wearing a large, beautiful hat, is the caption, "A hat made all the difference!" Now, many people will say that is a lot of tomfoolery, but let me tell you a story.

Last week I bought a hat. Not just any hat, but one I fell in love with in a little shop near Oxford Circus. For several days I passed that window until I got up enough courage to walk in, right behind two ladies, one wearing a gorgeous mink coat, while the other was the possessor of smart fox furs. The interior of the shop and casual attitude of the other shoppers were enough to scare anyone. After the hat (a lovely creation of black satin with a flowing ostrich plume on one side) had been lifted from the window and placed on my head, I gingerly asked the price: £5:15:6—fast figuring made that, in my Scotch-Canadian father's language, about $23. In a meek voice I explained it was a bit higher than I expected to pay, and the clerk queried, "Could you manage five pounds?" I left with the hat.

Then the week really started. Wearing my hat, I had an interview with an important company official, which went off with flying colours. Next, I kept my final appointment with a dentist, and when he completed his work, I enquired about the bill; he surveyed my hat, smiled, and commented that he too being a Canadian would be pleased to add his fee to my scholarship. When I made the rounds of the hotels, the uniformed men outside as well as inside opened the doors with a flourish and a very pleasant greeting—I wasn't a bit fooled. I knew it was the hat.

Two United Press men, without doubt impressed by my headgear, took me to dinner. The first, to the American Embassy, where one feels at once she is back in America. Everything is American style, the music, the food (imported), and even the good old-fashioned Cokes. The second newsman found a quaint little Italian restaurant in the Soho district. It is called the Isola Bella. The waiters, all in formal dress, gave excellent service; the menu was handwritten in Italian. Needless to say, I left the ordering to my escort, and although I did not know what we ate, I do know it was good.

The week ended with a friend, the wife of a Harley Street physician, taking me to the theatre, and did I ever feel good to be properly garbed when I discovered she had seats in the orchestra centre stalls, from where I thoroughly enjoyed the play "Annie Get Your Gun." Looking over my shoulder and straight up to the third gallery, I knew where I would have been, had I come alone. Now, I leave it to my readers. Are those posters right?

Friday, March 11, 1949

Dear Mum,
Yesterday I had an appointment with John Gordon at 11:30. He was very nice and said one couldn't depend on what Beaverbrook might do when he returns in April, but at present I shall work on Saturdays only, reporting for the Sunday Express. Since it is a weekly paper, they take on a staff of reporters for Saturday only. He said he thought this would give me a chance to get used to the routine of a British newspaper and still have some free time. Sounds wonderful to me because today I have an appointment with a Miss Rowley of the BBC and if it is possible to work up something in that department too and still have some free time I'll be happy. Also any ideas for stories I get, I'm to tell the Express people.

Tomorrow I go to work at 11 a.m. John Gordon asked if that was too early. Imagine!!!

[Ouida was hired by the *Sunday Express* on March 10, 1949. The following account of her first day at the newspaper appeared in her column for the Moncton paper on April 9.]

IN BRITAIN TODAY by Ouida MacLellan

Fleet Street! The home of British journalism and regarded by many as the heart of the entire journalistic world. It is the fond dream and the ambition of many aspiring journalists to one day work on London's famous Fleet Street, and small wonder.

A better setting for a Walt Disney cartoon could not be found, was the first impression of a reporter from a small city paper when she arrived at the foot of Fleet Street. The towering buildings seemed to come alive, bearing the names of famous newspapers from all parts of the world . . . Facing them alone was a mighty big task, so much so, one got the shakes as Mickey Mouse does when he starts out on a new adventure,

There are two extra-large buildings which seem to hold sway over the entire street. Standing side by side, they are Lord Beaverbrook's Daily Express and Lord Camrose's Daily Telegraph, both with circulations well up in the millions. The most important structure from our point of view, however, is the Daily Express building, for it was from a very pleasant News Editor here, that the first London assignment was received.

The first day at work will not be forgotten in a hurry. One of the "grand old men of Fleet Street," who turned out to be 45 years old and with the name of Lewis, was assigned to show us the ropes. The Library, where clippings and information on every article are filed, was the first step, followed by a whirlwind call at everyone's desk—the editorial staff number about fifty. Names went in one ear and out the other as we tried frantically to keep up to the pace set by Mr. Lewis.

At lunch hour we were escorted to one of Fleet Street's famous eating places or "pubs," the Cock; this one, along with the Cheshire Cheese pub, were the favorite hangouts of the writer Samuel Johnson.

The afternoon brought my first assignment. According to the invitation, a reception was being held at the Waldorf Hotel in Aldwych by the Atomic Energy Association and one Dr. Bankoff was to be the guest speaker. Speeches can be so dull and the statistics complicated, but what a surprise!

One minute you were in the midst of a group of chattering men and women; the next, you thought you had joined Buck Rogers on a trip into the 30th century. Dr. Bankoff's statements were amazing and difficult to believe. He claimed that within the next fifty years, medical science will have progressed in such a manner that all parents will be assured of the birth of healthy normal children; deficiencies and disease of both body and mind will be curable prior to birth, thus assuring the world of useful citizens. Even the bad traits in a person's character will be destroyed and the good traits or talents given aid. These fantastic statements left one deep in thought, but suddenly the meeting broke up for tea and it was time to return to the office.

Now, came the discovery that the reporting of a story in England is quite different from that of one in Canada. To begin with, no English paper ever has more than six pages and all stories must be brief. In fact, many stories never make the paper at all, and reporters have introduced the phrase "Writing one for the Spike," which means he is sure that particular story will never get past the spike of the Editor. A person has to be very important indeed, to rate even one paragraph over here, whereas in the Maritimes, he would in all probability be given at least half a column . . . Yes, my life on Fleet Street is going to be both interesting and instructive.

Friday, March 25, 1949

Dear Mum,

Mum, I was furious when I received your letter! You should know by now that your suggestions that you write my columns drive me mad. I shall stop writing altogether if you try any stunts like that. I hate to growl like this, but you must realize I have to be completely independent, and besides, if your efforts are to be anything like that sample you sent over here, you'll ruin me in no time. Don't worry about me not getting the columns to you in time, for I happen to have a head on my shoulders—small as it may be! I'll manage all right here, just don't you try any of your funny little angles. I'm too far away to have a say, but think you know what I mean all right. The next columns are almost ready and will follow immediately.

For heaven sake, send me copies of the Sydney and Halifax papers. You must realize they are far more important than the Moncton ones: they are in territories where I am unknown. It is the results of the columns in them that counts. Moncton is a mighty small place, don't forget, and one can't always stick there. Please send me copies of the columns from both papers and tell me what pages they are from.

Tonight I go to a cocktail party in Kensington [an up-market area of London] after work. Last night (Friday) I started ballet lessons. I sure felt awkward, but think I'll like it all right.

Monday, March 28, 1949, 3 p.m.

You know, Mum, I've been sitting here fuming! You know how much work I had to do at home for the editors. Well, Saturday my pay for the Sunday Express job amounted to £6:7:0, that is $25.40 Canadian. That was my take-home pay AFTER the taxes were deducted. That was for all day Saturday and the little bit I do on Thursday at the hotels[2] and a couple of other small calls I have forgotten about. Imagine!! I'm making as much here doing nothing as I did at home working like a slave!

---

[2] Her Thursday job was to visit the five-star hotels, such as The Dorchester, Grosvenor House, Claridge's, and The Savoy, looking for newsworthy guests.

Out of the lot, I bank some and keep some, enough to live on. At that rate, if I manage anything with the BBC, which looks like a possibility, I'll be able to bank that entirely.

Tuesday, March 29, 1949, evening

Dear Mum,

The big box of hot chocolate arrived this morning, and Mrs. Bennett immediately made a cup for Mollie [Mrs. Bennett's daughter], herself, and me with milk. It tasted wonderful, and both Mrs. Bennett and Mollie said they have never tasted anything like it since before the war.

The news about the "Food for Britain" box sounds wonderful, for only today we received word the meat ration is to be cut again. At present we receive 10 pence worth per person per week—that is about 20 cents worth. Altogether that's about two chops with about two slices of corn meat thrown in for good measure. With the three rations (Mrs. Bennett, George, and I), we had a bit of steak and kidney (awful small) which with vegetables was made into a pie for Sunday, then two chops last night, and the remaining chop (George is not here) made a small stew for two today. That is our rations for the whole week, so you can see how slim the pickings are . . . Honestly, Mum, you can't imagine the pleasure I get out of sharing your boxes with the folks here. They are so tickled with the extra bits that mean so very much.

Ugh! Ugh! That Joe Foley [an acquaintance from New York] just called about a date I thought he had forgotten about. I don't mind him too much but I'll be darned if I'm going to enjoy listening to the ex-editor of the Communist Daily Worker, who has since turned Catholic. If the poor guy only knew how I hate lectures! Maybe I can break a leg between now and 7:30.

You know, Mum, I wish someone was around to give me a good shaking up. I see lots of nice-looking young men, think they look interesting, then lose interest immediately when I have to be bothered talking to them. Dates just don't seem too exciting any more, no matter how hard I try to be good company. Even when the boys seem interested, I can't keep it up . . . Joan Riley wrote that she has received a proposal from a very nice chap from Nantucket . . . she wonders if she will be able to change from a big city to a small place. It started me thinking and although this life is very nice, I'm afraid I'd still prefer a small place—like Antigonish. Sometimes I think I'm cheating by taking things like this trip when possibly others would get more of a kick out of things. Maybe I'm just in a queer mood but if so, it's lasting a darn long time . . . I keep waiting for someone to thrill or even interest me, but so far it looks like a hopeless case. Surely there is something you can say to jar me out of this!!

Love, Ouida

"HE GREETED ME LIKE AN OLD PAL"
April–May 1949

Friday, April 1, 1949, morning

This morning I received a fancy looking airmail letter with a Paris postmark and the name DeLuce on the back. Dick has come through and I've an idea he has a bit of his brother's writing ability in him, too, for his description of Paris is really good. He is at Cite Universitaire, rooming at Maison Canadiens (Canada House) and studying French for 20 hours per week. He's going to Italy for the Easter holidays and says plans call for a visit to England the latter part of June. However, if I go to France before then he'll be glad to show me as much of Paris as he knows, but I shan't be in France for a year or more, so that ends that!

Sunday, April 3, 1949, 10:00 a.m.

I'm not getting discouraged, but it is hard going out on assignments, meeting people, getting interviews, etc. and yet nothing ever makes the paper. I haven't managed a word in yet and it rather gets you down. Suppose if I live through this I'll be a bigger man (or woman) for it, but it's mighty hard to take. Like yesterday, I went to the Savoy, met this Herbert L. Miskend who is president of the Yolande Corporation in New York, got an interview which I consider quite good. The facts were interesting, particularly to women— you see, his company makes handmade lingerie, and he told me what the latest colours, styles, and fabrics are and what fashion trends indicate etc. I really thought it was good, and when writing the story I kept it short yet pithy. Not a word got in. I'm afraid people will think I'm rather a prefabricator or imposter or something. I told Mr. Miskend about the paper shortage, etc., but he'll still wonder why he spent half an hour talking to me for nothing. He even said he would like to send me a Yolande garment and asked for my home address. Now I suppose I shall never see the garment, for I certainly could never afford to buy anything like that. [3]

I also suppose that could have been taken as a bribe for a good story, and of that I gather the newspaper people don't approve over here, but I credit myself with enough intelligence

---

[3] Beaverbrook policy was that when what was written was critical, it was news; if the subject liked it, it was advertising. Yolande lingerie would have been spiked.

not to be taken in by that. Gifts have never influenced my writing opinions yet and I don't see why they should now—especially since what I write doesn't yet get in anyway. Mum, I can't say anything or ask why, but I almost hate to go on assignment when I know full well it will never make the paper. I was on one story yesterday which did get in, but then we just phoned in the information and someone in the office wrote the story. John Prebble and I went to visit the mother of a soldier who had been condemned to death by a court martial. The court martial was not confirmed, so the boy is to be released and sent home. It was quite exciting, for we were given a staff car and driver, and as we arrived on the scene, so did reporters from four other papers. As it was, the story got a single column head on an inside page and they used 172 words. NUFF said!!

One of the reporters on the Daily Express has just started off on a round-the-world trip, and I think his writing is very stupid. I'm sure I could do better myself but evidently no one over here thinks so. Also, Mr. Head, the editor, asks me if there is anything I'd like to write on my own—not that it would ever get in! However, everything I think of has usually been covered already at some time and it is so difficult trying to hunt up something different or new in a strange country. For the readers at home, I know what they haven't seen or heard of, but over here it is impossible.

Thursday, April 7, 1949

Last night was most interesting. George [Mrs. Bennett's nephew] and Joan (his fiancée) and two other couples took me to the Prospect of Whitby pub, famous in Dickens and used in movies too. It was a very old and fascinating place and the most amazing thing was, it was the only place I have yet found where I ordered milk and got it in England. You see, milk was taken off the ration about a week ago and you can get it occasionally. You should have seen the looks on the faces of the heavy drinkers in the pub when I got my milk. Also upstairs is a quaint little room where we got a very delicious meal with fresh salmon. Believe I shall use the place in a column, as it is really a sightseeing spot.

Monday, April 11, 1949, morning

Had a story to do in the afternoon last Friday. It entailed tramping around to the larger stores to see what effect the new budget had on buying. It rained and I had to dash between showers, the managers were harder to find than nylons, and my feet hurt, but I managed to get the information. As a result I wrote and rewrote the story several times, was told the editor was very pleased with it AND two little tiny paragraphs got in the first edition of the paper and was left out of the later ones!!! Such a life.

Anyway, I raced back from town and went to my dancing lesson. Miss Webber says I'm improving, but I can't see it!

Mrs. Bennett and I were invited over to the Brittons across the street for the evening. They have some young people—Tim, age 26, Wendy, age 23, Christopher, age 17, and a nephew John, age 28. It was a very pleasant evening, and evidently the Brittons are in quite a few things, for they belong to a very nice tennis and cricket club—a person has to be recommended by another member to join—which they want me to join, and Tim belongs to a Shakespeare group and to an amateur theatrical company. Tim also owns a car, which I suppose makes up for the fact that he is no Tyrone Power.

Anyway, I was invited to visit Hampton Court on Sunday and thought it would be with the family, or at least Wendy and Tim, but Tim alone came to take me. We had a very pleasant day, and he seems quite nice. On the way back we drove through Richmond Park, then over to look at the tennis club—the courts are grass!!! Anyway, we drove back to the Brittons about seven and Tim asked me to come in and meet those I had not already met. He also asked me about a play up in town for Wednesday night and a club dance on Saturday and possibly Monday night. It puzzled me that he should ask me before going in the house, for I fully expected to be seen home, but I soon learned why. I had not met the cousin John [Osborne] before, and Tim did not give him a terrifically big buildup. John is not too bad looking . . . rather serious, but nice, and fun, too. He is a Catholic—the Brittons are high Anglican—and while we were joking about the church socials, John asked me to attend the next one on April 29 at our own church with him. Guess maybe that is why Tim got his two bits in first, as he probably knows his cousin better than I do. As neither one makes any difference to me, I'll jolly well date them both—not a pig, but I like a lot!!!

Tim also asked about attending some dances at some of the big clubs in town. It seems he travels with a gang, which is always much more fun than just one person, BUT how come an eligible young man in a crowd is unattached so much he can immediately date a new girl up? There must be a catch somewhere!!!!! Leave it to me to think of something queer EH?? Guess only time will tell.

Monday, April 11, 1949, 6:30 p.m. [second letter that day]

I have opened a post office savings account. You see, there is no interest on a chequing account at the bank but you get 2½% on a post office savings account. The bank manager suggested I take both and just keep enough in the bank to keep ahead of my cheques then deposit the remainder in the post office and let it gather interest until I want it. Thought I could let the post office one ride until a year from now then draw it all out in time for my European jaunt. Put in £3 to start with, which is $12.00, so that's not too bad.

Easter Sunday Morning, April 17, 1949

Dear Folks,

So many things have happened the last few days, I hardly know where to begin! Wednesday Isabel Greene [Moncton friend, a singer] and I went walking in Kew Gardens in the morning, then I saw "School for Scandal" in the afternoon, and Tim Britton took me to see Gertrude Lawrence in "September Tide" in the evening. In the evening Thursday I went to communion then wrote that parliament column before going to town to do the hotels . . . While in at the office I met a female secretary of Lord Beaverbrook's and gave her my card . . . Didn't think anything more about it.

Friday I went to the church service at nine o'clock, then the Greens invited me back to their house for a while . . . In the afternoon Pat Riley and I went to Hyde and Regents parks, as Mr. Head had instructed me to see what my impressions would be. I thought I wrote a fairly good article.

It looked like another good day yesterday so I wore the little silk high-necked blouse, the grey suit (thank heavens!), and my green shoes, gloves, and purse to go in to work. Wasn't in the office half an hour before Beaverbrook's secretary called and asked me if I were free that afternoon. I said it would depend on Mr. Head and when I asked him he said "Certainly." The next message was for me to take the 3:07 train to Leatherhead, and I would be met there with the car. To say I was rather shaking was putting it mild but I made it and took along a couple of gramophone records for the old boy. (His secretary gave them to me.)

The rest reads like a story! (I'll do a column on it.) The chauffeur met me at the station and off I went, sitting in the back—glass separates the back from the front seats—through the most beautiful country! We came to a private road and in we turned, and after close to a mile or more came to a lovely mansion-like place nestled among the trees. It is an old stone house that one sees so often on large country estates. The rooms are immense and beautifully furnished and the main sitting room opened through huge French doors onto a spacious verandah which overlooks a terraced lawn, fountain, etc. etc. etc. and a valley thrown in.

Lord Beaverbrook was sitting in his library with an old engineer's cap—like the railway men wear—perched on his head. He greeted me like an old pal and we went walking on the lawn. He then had the butler bring out some soft drinks—lemon squash—and his nurse, an attractive Irish girl of 24 and a Captain something-or-other (millionaire) joined us. After the drinks he asked if I'd like to go swimming and ordered a swimming suit—red wool—which would have covered me twice. The pool is at lawn level and also has several French doors separating it from outside. The water was a beautiful blue and we all went in for a dip, then stretched out on the lawn in the sun to dry off. Imagine, April!!

A little red convertible car was then ordered (after we had dressed), and the nurse and I climbed in the back while the Captain with Lord Beaverbrook at the wheel sat in front, and off we went all over his estate, which stretches for miles. He drives the car as though it were a jeep and we went flying along narrow little roads, bridle paths, over fields and down hills. Lord Bennett's land is right next. Then we went through a little cluster of houses which Lord Beaverbrook owns but his gardeners etc. occupy. The country is beautiful, and Lord B. got the biggest kick out of me knowing the names of many of the trees etc.—thanks to Daddy's careful training when I was a kid! I used the New Brunswick names for Hackmatack, etc. and he loved it.

Some Braden fellow—an MP—joined us for cocktails (lemon squash again) then I went off with the chauffeur to the station. Lord B. wants my columns and asked if I would like to come down and stay a while in the near future. You bet I would! He also said he would see that I worked every day, but don't think I'd like that so well. Oh, well, he may forget completely, so we'll let it ride.

Oh yes, he asked about my ancestors and I mentioned grandfather and he said he knew him well. He nearly fainted when he found out I was a granddaughter.[4]

Monday, April 25, 1949

John's name is Osborne... Went with the Britton gang to Tag Island[5] for dancing last Saturday night and it was grand. There were three professional couples who were a pleasure to watch and it made me wish I could do the same.

Shall send along some pictures Tim and I took at Hampton Court. It's this Friday night I go to the church social with his cousin. It seems my friend Joe Foley was away or something for a time. Am wondering what he will do when next we meet!

Last night when I got home Tim Britton had called and asked for me to call him back. This I did and we went tearing off to see "A Yankee in King Arthur's Court" with Bing Crosby. Today I make the round of the hotels and tomorrow comes the church social with John Osborne. Imagine Tim will ask me out again on Saturday—I hope, 'cause it's fun with the whole gang.

---

[4] Ouida liked recounting the invitation from Lord Beaverbrook. "I told him I was working and this was my only day; he said: 'Go and ask your editor.' I went up to Mr. Head and said that Lord Beaverbrook wants me... He yelled, 'GO!' pointing at the door."

[5] Actually Taggs Island, a private resort on the river Thames near Hampton Court.

Thursday, April 28, 1949

Received my clippings back from Lord Beaverbrook and he said he found them most interesting, and hopes I'll continue to improve my style and strengthen my reporting genius until I become a leader in my profession. Am rather thinking of writing him again and thanking him for the encouragement and asking him what suggestions he had to offer for this advice. Would that be too bold?

Sunday, May 1, 1949

Things went along fine at the office yesterday, but still haven't a single comma in the paper this morning. Oh, well, I have a year yet! Max Caulfield (a Catholic) asked me to go dancing last night but I said I already had a date even though I didn't. He was just trying to be friendly, but he is married! Junor, Prebble, and Max Caulfield had lunch with me and I also met Milton Shulman, the Evening Standard movie critic who hails from Toronto. He's considered quite good.

[These three senior journalists on the Express took her under their wing and often to lunch in Fleet Street. John Junor was a political columnist and became editor of the *Daily Express*; John Prebble was writing his best-selling series on the Highland Clearances; Max Caulfield, an Irishman, later wrote books on the uprisings in Ireland.]

Wednesday, May 4, 1949

Don't worry, Mum, I haven't written Lord Beaverbrook again . . . Rather figured myself it would be forward, and besides, I'd like him to forget about me until the latter part of June, as I want some free time when Dick DeLuce comes over, and want to work in at least one visit to Marie's before starting hard work.

Went to church at 9:15 this morning and John Osborne walked me home. Osborne is strange, he puzzles me almost as much as I puzzle him, I think. I think I told you he walked me home from the theatre Tuesday night, and did I add that the technique of English boys is no different from that of an American or Canadian?

Tuesday, May 10, 1949, morning

Had a letter from David Ross at Cambridge this morning and he's determined I'm going up to visit him. Am rather looking forward to seeing Cambridge, as it would make a good article comparing it with Xavier [St. Francis Xavier University, Nova Scotia] and Mt. Allison [University, New Brunswick] as I know both campuses. Oh yes, David is a very sweet guy as you probably have guessed, but I met him through Tim and if Tim can't stand his cousin as competition what will he say to a third party??? Not that I care particularly.

Wednesday, May 11, 1949, 4:10 p.m.

In the mail this morning was a letter from the Richmond Cricket Club saying I have been elected a member and please forward my subscription (dues, to you) which is £3:3:0—about $12.60. It seems rather a lot, for we have to supply our own balls and the courts aren't terrific. John Greene claims I'm crazy to pay that much, but then all this "gang" of Tim's belong and as John Osborne always points out—it's chiefly for the social side a person joins. Besides, I'd be a complete social outcast if I didn't join—at least with this "gang."

About John Osborne—can't quite describe him except that he's very little taller than I am, medium build, dark hair, protruding chin, smokes a pipe, darn sarcastic, difficult to understand, never can tell what he's thinking and when you do think you have him placed, he's gone again. Don't expect he'll ever ask me out unless Tim Britton ups and dies, but he'll continue to walk me home from church on Sunday, and if we meet anywhere, like after the theatre, he'll walk me home. Otherwise he's quite liable to say little or nothing to me when we are with the gang or he might be perfectly sweet, depending which way the wind is blowing.

Sunday, May 15, 1949, morning

Just back from 9:15 mass with John Osborne—or at least I got there first and he joined me, then walked me home. Next week there is a mission at the church with a Redemptorist father, and John says we are going. It's a queer situation, during the week I'm with Tim, or whenever the crowd is around I'm sort of with Tim, then Sunday morning and at other odd times, it's John. As for me, I don't know which way I prefer to be. Oh yes, before I forget . . . Tim called me "sweetie-pie" the other night and I near crowned him.

Thursday, May 19, 1949

[She was visiting family friends, Marie and Bill Fraser, in Melbourne, Hertfordshire, near the air force base where Bill Fraser was stationed. The village is near Cambridge.]

2 p.m. in Cambridge: I met David Ross and we walked for miles all over the campuses, which are beautiful. Then took a boat out and went "punting" on the river which flows through the campus.

We had dinner at a quaint place in the east end of Cambridge and the food was wonderful! One thing that did shock me, was that the students entertain their friends in their rooms. David laughed at me being embarrassed but I kept trying to imagine such a thing at Xavier.

We walked some more then stopped on one of the bridges, and the surrounding view was breathtaking. Such a romantic spot—only we weren't romantic. Such a pity for a perfectly wonderful setting to go to waste. Why, even I might have melted in such a place, but David didn't try. Drat Englishmen!!!

Wednesday, May 25, 1949, 2:30 p.m.

Saturday I met some Canadian agriculture experts at the Dorchester and got quite a yarn, but nothing in the paper. They were quite pleasant and one of them wanted to take me dancing but I was conveniently busy.

Thursday, May 26, 1949, 5:50 p.m.

Dear Daddy,
Your regular Sunday letter came this morning so decided it was about time I wrote you again . . . To begin with I'll answer your questions about Bill and Marie's cottage. They have pump water which is rather lousy. Then they heat with coal which is brought by the bag load every two weeks. They have the same as we do here in Kew, small fireplaces in each room. In the kitchen she uses a small oil stove with two places for pans. In the mornings Marie used to bring up a pitcher of hot water to my room (I slept in a large feather bed—not so hot!!) and I would pour it into the large bowl, cool it with water in my own pitcher (big and pink), and wash. The thatched roofs are composed of what is called a thatching grass—it is a dried straw—and the average life of the roof is 20 years. The only trouble is birds nest in them and all sorts of mice, rats, and insects find them a wonderful place for a home. There was one roof just being re-covered when I was in Melbourne.

Better not tell Mum, but I have an offer for a flight in a jet plane my next trip to Melbourne. This Sgt. Gillen said he thought he could arrange it for me and since he suggested it and not I, am rather hoping it will come off. The only thing is, in case of an accident, the pilot is the only one who has even a slight chance of getting out alive, the speed is so terrific, and I believe only two pilots have ever lived to tell of a jet plane escape and even they don't know how it was done. There is really little danger though and I'm sure the risk would be worth the trip.

Monday, May 30, 1949, afternoon

Dear Mum,

... Went to the Brittons on Saturday night to listen to "Oklahoma" on the radio ... Tim came in about eleven and walked me home. Since he had the dog with him we took it for a walk first BUT I'm afraid now, Tim's cruising for a bruising. Despite his three years in the navy, I'm certain that he is inexperienced with girls—in particular, that is, not in general. Don't believe he has ever fallen for any one in particular—yet—and I hope I'm not asking for trouble. Why is it I always get a guy who is just trying out his wings or is a one-woman man? I tormented the life out of Tim Saturday night, then suddenly realized the darn goose seemed to be taking me seriously and after all, I intend to be free when Dick De Luce comes to London and also promised David Ross a couple of dates. Always troubles!

Wednesday, June 8, 1949, morning

By the way, I placed second in the ladies in an American tennis tournament conducted at the club on Monday. It is one where you start out with a partner, then change partners and opponents each set. A set is the best of five games [normally six games] and the number of games won by each side is awarded as points to both the man and the woman. I won seven shillings and sixpence, then had to have my racquet restrung yesterday and that cost me 38/6 so I lost, on the whole ... After tennis all morning and afternoon, we danced all evening. Had a perfectly lovely time. At intermission John DeLanghe and I went for a walk all around the cricket grounds—me in bare feet most of the way—had several dances with Delanghe (he's very good), never saw John Osborne in better mood—he was absolutely sweet—and Tim held my hand coming home in the car then bid me a very FOND goodnight. Pleasant, but not too much style, but then I was too tired to notice or care.

Am having trouble with Mr. Riley again. He casually asked the other day, how long it would be before I could support myself. I said I had come for a year, hadn't I, then he said there isn't too much money in the Canadian fund (more in the American) and he thought if I could support myself it would be nice. But if I wanted any money for a trip to the continent etc. that could be arranged of course. I can't make them out, but have no intention of working every day now, as I'm having a perfectly lazy time and if more work means less money from the Trust, then the devil with it.

Love, Ouida

"MEN MAKE ME SICK"
June–August 1949

Monday, June 13, 1949, 10:10 p.m.

Had the queerest thing happen Saturday. When I ate lunch at The Cock alone on Thursday, I dropped a sixpence. Saturday, when Junor and Caulfield arrived for dinner, the waitress (with whom we have made friends) asked them to tell "Madam" she had found the sixpence. A few minutes later John Prebble arrived and the waitress gave him the sixpence to give me. The other two put up a howl demanding to know why Prebble should be trusted and not them. The reply was, "Well, why shouldn't I trust her own husband?" The three, (seeing as how they are all married) nearly dropped! It's become a standing joke, and they took great delight in breaking the news to me when I arrived about 1:55 p.m. The funny thing is, had I a choice I also would have picked Prebble—he's exceptionally nice! Believe there is some figuring going on at the office, as the three of them are usually with me. Prebble never misses a few minutes' chat each Saturday, Caulfield's desk is next to mine, and Junor usually comes down for tea with me. The only trouble is, all the guys seem to try to offer me either a drink or tea at some time during the day and if I didn't keep refusing, I'd float home each Saturday. Great to be a female among so many males—so long as they keep their distance!!!

Had Nixon the photographer with me on a wedding assignment Saturday afternoon and I'll be darned if didn't both the picture and the story make the paper!!! Am sending a copy along. Don't know what happened (except that I gave Nixon my cocktails at the reception after the wedding), but he has now graduated to the group who always wink as they go by. I'll probably be fired for distraction, but even the senior editors don't seem to mind my presence, and I'll admit to being extra sweet at times. Such a life!

Tuesday, June 21, 1949, 10:17 p.m.

I met David Ross this morning at ten in Richmond and we went by bus to Wimbledon. Had to queue for a time then went into the park about 11:30. First we got five-shilling tickets then discovered that this provided standing room only in the centre court. We wanted to sit, so had to go and pay in addition 10 shillings and sixpence. Then we got some food before the matches began at 2:00 p.m. and spent time watching the crowds, styles, and queer freaks. It was wonderful!

[Ouida described her first visit to Wimbledon in her column for the Moncton paper published on July 2, 1949. In subsequent years, she went with Fred Perry, Britain's three-time winner in the 1930s, and contributed to his reports for the *Evening Standard*. She had a lifelong interest in tennis as a player, spectator, and in later life as a member of the board of Tennis Canada. She played her last game of doubles just two days before her death in November 2009.]

IN BRITAIN TODAY by Ouida MacLellan

Wimbledon was recently defined as "another and more popular name for the sport known as lawn tennis." It is a word that is on everyone's tongue these days and certainly does mean lawn tennis at its very best. A forty-five minute bus ride from Richmond Park takes one to this famous meeting place for title-seekers of the British championship in tennis.

On our arrival at ten o'clock in the morning, there was a lengthy queue at the entrance gates, some of whom had been there all night. The one-and-a-half hour wait before the gates are opened is taken up by watching various entertainers and people selling newspapers and books . . .

Such a transformation once you get inside! From the top of the main building, an ivy-covered structure, there is a splendid view of the scene below. In one corner of these beautifully constructed grounds were huge sun umbrellas shading a number of tea tables with "serve yourself" counters back of them set up under a large canopy. The whole picture here took on the appearance of a very "posh" garden party. The clothes of the women were stylish and quite exciting, there being so many different costumes, including taffetas, satins, as well as dainty cottons—backless, strapless, and with plunging necklines. Numerous cartwheel straw hats and multi-colored glasses gave additional dashes of colouring to the moving scene.

Around the main competitors' entrance, a number of people gathered to watch the stars arrive, and despite the big black-and-white sign saying, "Autograph hunting is prohibited," there were several books in sight.

The like of the grass courts at Wimbledon is hard to compare except with that of velvet: When one player slid during the afternoon play, it left a dark green mark like velvet has when rubbed the wrong way. There are 15 courts in all, with the centre court drawing the largest crowd. However, throughout the day, or after playing starts at 2 p.m., one moves from court to court in order to watch for a time the playing of as many stars as possible . . .

The highlights appear to be the Americans, both on the courts and off them. Ted Schroeder, 28 years old, is the favourite and a rather amazing person; he is a refrigerator engineer who plays tennis on Sundays and usually enters a tournament only once—rarely losing. He is a terrific pipe smoker, continually chewing on a corncob pipe. He is noted for his fairness in the game, greased-lightning action, and a disarming smile which spreads slowly all over his face. When playing in a match the other day at Queen's Club, he leaped in the air, expecting a drive on his forehand, when suddenly his opponent whipped it across on his backhand: Schroeder managed a back flip, got his racquet on the ball to return the drive, and won the game.

Gertrude Moran, 25, has been causing almost as much sensation as Schroeder but most of it off the courts, although her tennis is top grade. Nicknamed "Gorgeous Gussie," this player is an attractive outdoor-girl type and is considered the beauty of the courts and always draws big crowds. An English dress designer whipped up something new in tennis outfits for Miss Moran, with a bertha-like collar and lace-trimmed panties. This smart player wore the outfit in an exhibition match on Sunday but wisely returned to her neat white shorts and sweat shirt for the important matches . . .

Other interesting players included the minute F. Ampon from the Philippines, who hopped about like a huge grasshopper, the Australian John Bromwich, Czechoslovakia's J. Brobny, and the tiny Chinese ballet dancer Gem Hoahing.

Thursday, June 23, 1949, 3:30 p.m.

Life is once again treating me wonderfully . . . the party tomorrow night, tennis club dance Saturday night, semifinal tennis match Sunday afternoon, Marian Anderson concert Sunday night, the Royal Tournament with Princess Alice in the Royal Box Monday afternoon, Richmond theatre with Mrs. Bennett Monday night, reception at the Dorchester Hotel, Park Lane, for Anthony Eden Tuesday afternoon, "Oklahoma" with Wendy Britton Tuesday night, Victoria League Ball Wednesday night, and the hotel rounds again next Thursday. Also, this morning I received an invitation to tea with the Drapers' Guild on July 5; a fork luncheon at the Victoria League House on July 6, and the annual general meeting of the Victoria League at the Mansion House on July 8.

The only black spot in the whole thing is Mr. Riley, and today I went to see him and talked with his secretary, since he was out. She's a good head and can't stand the ground he walks on. Off the record, she told me Mr. Riley is the meanest man walking the face of the earth. She also told me how to handle him and said not to take one thing off him. Shall be as sweet as I can, but here it is four weeks again since Mrs. Bennett has had a cheque and Riley's out of town until Tuesday. The secretary also told me he is helping people who have no right to the [Kinsman Trust] money at all and also that there is plenty of money available.

John Osborne took me walking again last night. We get along great together now. The matter of an escort for the Victoria League Ball is still up in the air. So far I have only one ticket but the events director at The Dorchester did say she'd do her best to get me another so I can have an escort. It would be horrible without one, but they won't want to give away too many complimentary tickets. Then the problem would be who to ask. Tim's car, David's appearance, or John's company? Believe it will be Tim . . . because I think I would have the best time with him despite the fact we are a bit cooled off. David's all right, but am afraid I'm not that keen. Guess I like a great variety of moods and temperament, and David never changes. The girl phoned yesterday to see if I would care to join a larger party for a table at the ball or sit by myself. Of course I took the larger group, for every new acquaintance helps.

Monday, June 27, 1949, 6:10 p.m.

Dear Mum,
Well! Have just returned from the Royal Tournament and what a thrill. I was sitting next to Princess Alice in the Royal Box for the last part of the show—after tea, that is . . . I wore the pale pink silk dress with my £5 black hat, elbow-length black gloves, knee-length nylons, the black shoes I bought in New York, and a little black evening drawstring bag I finished at noon. It was a very effective costume and in perfect taste, as Princess Alice was wearing a similar outfit. It was a wonderful show, and I shall do a column on it tomorrow if possible, but Wednesday is more probable.

Tomorrow for Anthony Eden's reception I shall wear my green satin dress with the black hat, I guess. It is really more impressive, and on him I'd like to make an impression.

Had a wonderful time at the party on Friday and another grand evening at the tennis club dance on Saturday night. For the dance I wore the white gown you sent from home, black satin court shoes of Mrs. Bennett's, and carried a black evening bag of hers, too. Couldn't think of any jewellery that would do justice so decided on flowers. There are beautiful roses in the garden but with the heat we are now experiencing, they would wilt in no time. It so happens, however, there is an artificial flower shop in Richmond who make flowers even more natural looking than real ones. They do work for all the royal affairs and the film people and are terrific.

Anyway, I got two red roses and had Mollie adhesive tape them to my skin on the right shoulder by the throat. They were the subject of constant discussions at the dance and took more attention than a regiment of soldiers. In addition to looking stunning, Mollie had arranged the leaves so not a bit of tape showed—it was flesh-coloured anyway—and everyone wanted to know how on earth they stayed up. I told them it was willpower.

For the tennis club dance on Saturday, I wore that maroon and white frock I brought over here with my low black Antigonish shoes. Had to steer David Ross off the rocks during the evening as we went walking out around the cricket grounds and he was evidently in a romantic mood. I politely said "No thanks" and without being rude said I was quite too far away from home to get bitten. Didn't do any harm either, for he danced the remainder of the evening with me, then asked if he would see me the following day.

Wednesday, June 29, 1949, 4:45 p.m.

Dear Mum,
Well! Things are still happening to me! This morning the doorbell went, and there stood the mailman with a parcel for me . . . Would you believe it, inside was the most beautiful handmade nightgown I've ever laid eyes on! That Mr. Miskend, the president of Yolande Incorporated in New York, didn't forget!!! Had to pay 17/6 duty but that's nothing when you consider the cost of the garment. It is a lovely bluey-green colour with a deep inset of natural colour lace in the front. The entire nightie is handmade and you've never seen the like of the stitches . . . Mrs. Bennett says I'll have to save it for my honeymoon—I should live so long!!! Oh, yes, the material is a very fine rayon silk. Boy, it really is a beauty, but where on earth will I ever wear it???

The reception for Anthony Eden yesterday went off great but I missed the chance of a lifetime! I spoke to him, saying "I've been a fan of yours for a long time," (I was really thinking of your crush on him) and felt like a nut when he replied, "Judging from your appearance, it hasn't been that long." As I turned away, a dopey-looking guy stepped up and asked my name, saying he was from the Evening Standard (afternoon Beaverbrook paper). Like a dope I said I was Sunday Express and ruined a chance for some publicity. He had intended describing my outfit and hat as among the smartest at the reception, he said—but of course, reporters must never give a boost to other reporters.

Eden's hair is quite grey but he has bad teeth and a weak mouth. Also I have never seen such terrible hands. Not physically, but in expression. He moves them as though they were blocks of wood and looks more like Sinatra in a croon than a politician speaking. Outside of his mouth (which is very disappointing as he barely opens it when he speaks and his lips seem to move inward rather than outward with force), he is indeed very handsome but struck me as being a bit bored yesterday, as I would have been too for the place was lousy with chattering old dames and had I not been munching delicious sandwiches and eating wonderful strawberries with whipped cream on them, I too would have been bored.

Well, John and I will leave here about 7:30 for the Victoria League Ball. I'll change at The Dorchester in the room the press office girl is using, and we'll have to play Cinderella and leave early in order to catch the 1:30 train out of Waterloo station. The dance probably doesn't end until two. Then we shall probably have to walk from the Richmond station back, which is about a mile or so, at 2:15 a.m. John seems excited though, and since his manners are beautiful, I have nary a worry at all—except about my own manners, which I hope will do.

Saturday, July 9, 1949, morning

Dear Mum,

First about the Victoria League ball. I gather from the tone of your letter you were disappointed in my write-up. Here I've been thinking it was quite good! Anyway, it was Princess Alice who shook hands at the door, she's president of the Victoria League. We entered a small foyer which opened into the ballroom. The tables were situated around the dance floor, and that's where we ate. It was at the entrance of the foyer we were announced. The dance floor was just a cleared space in the middle of a huge chandelier-hung ballroom. Don't know what I could have said about my escort, John Osborne, at the ball. As for the men's formal dress, they wear it over here half the time so it's really not anything out of the ordinary except that there was a mixture of tails, single-breasted and double-breasted dinner jackets. All John did was bump me into Princess Margaret while we were dancing and when I looked foolish as we discovered who it was we were apologizing to, he said he guessed it wasn't every guy who could dance me into a princess.

[Ouida's description of the Victoria League Ball appeared in her column in the Moncton paper on July 16, 1949. The Victoria League was founded in 1901, the year of Queen Victoria's death, as a way to connect the people of the Commonwealth.]

IN BRITAIN TODAY by Ouida MacLellan

The Victoria League Ball was held at the Dorchester Hotel in Park Lane with H.R.H. Princess Margaret heading the list of important people present. A tall man in a red cutaway coat announced the guests as they entered into the reception room where you met a princess, a duchess, and several other distinguished persons. Hearing your own name announced in a full baritone voice was rather startling, but right behind came, "The Right Honorable Mr. So-and-So, the Ambassador of Saudi Arabia." We could not catch his correct name, but the sound of the title served to make us feel quite small and unimportant.

From the reception room we proceeded to the ballroom graced by royalty, movie queens, stage stars, lords and ladies, young debutantes, and society matrons. Truly, it was a setting for a Hollywood movie, making it difficult not only to believe it was real, but that we were in the midst of it.

First thing to note were the gowns—large hoops, little hoops, straps and strapless, some beautiful, some not quite so . . . There was a very lovely smoke gray chiffon creation trimmed with beautiful gray fox; imagine the surprise, when our eyes reached the top of this, to find the eyes of Ella Raines, the movie star, looking back at us.

Princess Margaret was wearing an off-white gown trimmed with silver sequins. She is very small in stature and gives evidence of a very lively personality, particularly the large blue eyes. The Princess danced most of the evening, either talking to or looking calmly at her partners. There were three of them, and while they may have very nice personalities, the dazzling importance of their partner must have thrown them out of character. However, as we saw them, one looked like a baby having gas pains, with that identical smile on his face continuously; another, while a very handsome chap, wore a very grim expression indeed, and the third was badly in need of a violin or a haircut

Also attracting much attention in the royal party was the daughter of the American ambassador, Sharman Douglas . . . A pleasant girl, she definitely danced the American style, which is quite noticeable at an English affair.

To go back to the beginning; after the reception, dinner was served. The menu called it "le saumon d'ecosse froid" and "le poussin en cocotte paysanne," but when it arrived it was really a cold salmon salad followed by an entire small chicken, beautifully done and very tender. Ice cream, strawberries, and coffee completed the meal, after consuming which, they expected us to dance! . . .

Dancing continued until 2 a.m. with a bit of time taken out for an auction with none other than Gertrude Lawrence acting as auctioneer. This popular actress, wearing a lovely pale mauve chiffon gown, spoke with such a coaxing voice the people hearing her could not refuse to buy—thus the Victoria League made money. Hoop-la and tombola were played in the foyer while dancing was in progress in the main ballroom.

Thursday, July 14, 1949, 5:55 p.m.

Dear Mum,

Guess I'm a real out-and-out skunk, but at least I do know it, so perhaps that doesn't make me so bad. You know they claim you should be able to learn something from everyone you meet. Well, David Ross has taught me one thing: I can't stand not having a sufficient amount of cash.

Suppose this sounds extremely small, but the other night after the theatre we had to examine the menus of three restaurants before we found one cheap enough, and the sausages we had were uneatable. Then today he asked me to have lunch with him and I had to read the price list before reading the food list to see what I wanted. When the man brought us two bottles of orange squash, it came to 1 shilling and sixpence. David gave the man two shillings and took back the sixpence change. Golly, I was so embarrassed I could have died, for tipping goes over here. Also the food is never too good when you have to eat according to price rather than taste. Everything is like that. I know he has to save, but for heaven's sake, why doesn't he leave me home rather than take me out and have to starve. I just can't do it. We've never been used to much money I know, but at least we don't go into places looking for cheap things. Either we have enough cash or we don't go at all, and I guess that's the system I'll have to stick to!

John Junor [then writing a weekly column on politics called Crossbencher] took me to tea at the Parliament buildings yesterday but it was a very crowded day and we didn't go into the Commons at all. Honestly, with John calling me "Ducky" and the Hon. Hugh Delargy MP calling me "Chicken" the people around must have thought I'd come straight from the barnyard! It was interesting though, and I'll be sending some column material along shortly. Hope the batch I sent off yesterday will do. I told you it's rather dry for news here right now.

The only parcel that never came through was the one with all the sugar and the maple sugar. That was a real loss . . . Strawberry jam would be most welcome indeed . . . The sugar ration has been cut to 8 ozs. per week again and the sweets (candy) are back on rations at 4 ozs. per week. That means it is impossible to do any jamming over here . . . the tinned meat parcel was wonderful and we've been feeding like kings. We always share with Mollie and the twins and they do love it. You can't imagine how maddening it is trying to think up something different to eat.

Friday, July 15, 1949

In my column about my Night Around London, my companion was Chris Dobson. He is John Junor's assistant on the paper and an exceptionally sweet guy. He's very nice-looking, with a cute twinkle to his face and a nice personality. Whether this was a one-night stand or not, I don't know, but I certainly wouldn't mind seeing more of him as he's fun. Afraid David [Ross] has gone a bit serious on me so that will probably have to end. These wretched men, why in heaven's name can't they control their feelings as I can?? It never does any good to go falling for people and it always cuts the fun! Men make me sick!!! Suppose it would be a queer world without them though!

Tuesday, July 26, 1949 [written from Melbourne, Hertfordshire, at the Fraser's]

Funny thing over here, the young people seem to feel they are all quite capable of looking after themselves. Like last night—Michael, a guy I met here, asked if I'd like to go to Switzerland skiing with them next February. He was over with a crowd last year and loved it. They think nothing of going off like that for holidays, and I have a hard time trying not to look shocked. After a while you begin to wonder who's right and who is crazy!!

Monday, Aug. 8, 1949

Dick DeLuce called about noon on Tuesday and I met him in Knightsbridge and we had dinner at Harrods. I returned home, then Dick picked me up about 7:15 and we went to the Richmond Theatre. It was great seeing him again. He's very good company, never lets me get away with anything, but I don't know how I feel—don't feel at all, in fact, just sort of numb. Wednesday I met him at 3 p.m. and we did some sightseeing, then met Osgood Carruthers, Carter Davidson of AP, and their wives and some others at the American Embassy for supper . . . Friday, Mrs. Levick took Dick and me to Knole and it was grand[6] . . . After work Saturday night, we went to "Annie Get Your Gun" and bickered most of the evening. Dick seemed in a mood, and as I was extremely tired, I had no patience . . . Tonight I have a date with Chris, we're going to a movie with Luke White and Dinah Hogarth (aristocracy). Dick said he would come out, but I said no I was busy . . . so I shan't see him again until Thursday when we'll have lunch at the Savoy, and his boat train leaves at eight that night.

Thursday, Aug. 11, 1949, morning

Monday night Chris Dobson and I went to the cinema with Luke White [the future Lord Annaly] and Dinah Hogarth. You know, it's funny but having a title doesn't improve manners any. Oh, I like Luke fine, he's a very nice guy, but I'll still take Chris for the little things like helping you on with your coat, care in crossing streets, opening doors etc. Also for

---

[6] Mrs. Levick was the wife of Harley Street physician C. B. Levick; Knole is one of England's largest country houses, with a famous garden.

eating spaghetti!!! We had a very good meal afterward in a restaurant in the square where Luke lives (Loundes Square) in Knightsbridge. Then Chris saw me home, all the way out on the train to Kew and back. He is the first chap to do that, and it was rather nice having company, although you really can't blame a guy for not doing so, as it makes it very late and you have to be careful of getting a train back into town. It must have been 12:01 or 12:17 before Chris got a train back. Everything closes down rather early over here, including the undergrounds, restaurants (11:00 p.m.), and just everything!

There is still no sign of the maple cream of April 16, so it looks as though I've lost that for sure. We finished off the last tin of chicken the other day and was it good! Oh yes, the butter and bacon arrived safely. The bacon couldn't have lasted too much longer but then the weather was very hot so probably in winter it would come easy. Mrs. Bennett washed and boiled it immediately and we ate it more like ham than bacon and it was lovely.

Friday, Aug. 12, 1949, 12:30 p.m.

Dear Mum,
Well, here I am, all muddled up again and not sure whether I'm happy or sad. Dick's boat was supposed to have left yesterday but it has been delayed. However, I guess I've seen the last of him. You see, he's now a man of the world and I'm still quite mid-Victorian. The silly ass, I could have told him that long ago without him wasting a week finding out. The guy I met on the ship didn't return, at least not all of him. Instead, we have a self-styled "lone wolf" whose tender age no woman is able to believe, since he has a rather "man of the world" air about him . . .

Anyway, you can probably guess the frame of mind I'm in—the old story, looking forward to a thing too much, then disappointed and not sure whether it's my fault or his. You see, I still don't drink, and sometimes it's hard to be sociable that way.—I'm told!

We parted company in Trafalgar Square and he said he'd call me before he leaves but that won't make any difference. I had a nice lump in my throat and certainly didn't feel like returning home since I had passed up a party to see Dick off. Thought for a bit and decided I had to do something, so phoned Chris and he was sweet. I spent an hour in a news cinema, then met Chris at seven and we went to the open air theatre in Regent's Park. They presented "Faust" and it was terrific. Will do something for the column on it. It was fairly cool outdoors but Chris brought along his trench coat for me. He's a strange guy, happy and carefree most of the time, yet works and studies most nights of the week, supports his mother and kid brother and seems very ambitious. He even mentioned that he often slips off to this open air theatre by himself to see Shakespeare. Last night we sat in the cheapest seats, and Chris wouldn't go to the play "Black Chiffon" as I suggested because he was short of cash and payday is today for him. Even at that he insisted on buying my ticket back to Kew and intended coming along with me until I insisted it was crazy, as he'd be very late, and I'd already put him to enough bother. Even though he's saving just as much as the next person, there's never been any hint of it during dates. He spares nothing to make them nice.

Have just read over all your recent letters and don't see anything I have to answer. Not sure whether I explained the money situation to you as you asked some time ago. I get £6:9:0 per week, 4 pounds for Saturday, and the rest for work during the week. That makes it just over $25—all my own, as there is no tax, and the room and board is taken care of by the Trust. However, things do add up, like the fare to the city and back, shoe repairs, etc. However, I do manage to save some.

Thursday, Aug. 18, 1949, night

Am in a terrible muddle today. There is a prospect of an interview with a temperamental old Chinese guy who is reputed to be the richest man in China. Only trouble is, his story is not too new, he's being a bit finickitey about giving out information. Mr. Head says to go ahead and get it and then the story will probably never be used. So help me, I'm going mad: the people at the hotels are getting so they hate to see me come, as nothing I get ever appears in print. It's so discouraging and I move in dead fear of meeting people I interview a second time. It's annoying to a person to talk to me for half an hour or more, then never hear another thing about it. I hate the Savoy Hotel the worst of all, for the females there make me feel like dirt under their feet. They're interested in no one except the big names and the Sunday Express just never uses those—unless it's something nasty about them. Why, Time magazine had something on Erskine Caldwell, the author, and over here, the Express wouldn't even use the story I got from him, which I think was better than Time's . . .

Chris told me today that Mike Smart phoned last night and is going ahead with plans for our visit to Odiham [RAF station] for the big air show and party on the September 17th weekend. Evidently we will be staying down there overnight, and that will mean I'll have to get out and find a church for myself the next morning . . . Sally [Cochran], the other girl who is going with Mike, is also a Catholic but whether she is a regular Sunday or a part-time one, I'm not quite sure.

Then, on top of that, I hate having to share Mike and Chris. I don't want Mike to be with someone else—yet I don't feel like sharing Chris, either. It's rather accepted that I'm Chris's property now, yet like the dog in the manger, Mike rather attracts me, too. Oh nuts!!!!!!!

Guess I'd better end this letter before I break out in a rash for no reason at all.

Monday, Aug. 22, 1949

Have decided to go in and see George Malcolm Thompson on the Daily Express (whom I met through Milton Shulman, another Canadian over here) about working every day. I'm not getting enough this way and have loafed quite long enough. Afraid I'll forget everything I ever knew if I'm not put to hard work soon. Will see about a holiday first, and then ask him what the prospects would be for the middle of September. Suppose if I do get something it will mean I shall have to pay my own board, but it would be worth it if I can get more work and experience. Maybe if I started by offering to pay half-board for a while, I could get away with it. Then perhaps I could even do both the Daily (if I get something) and the Sunday work and get a bit extra that way.

Tuesday, Aug. 23, 1949, afternoon

This morning I went into the office to take the story to Mr. Head about the interview with the richest man in China and he seemed quite pleased with it! I have a couple of changes to make and am to return the story tomorrow. Will hold my breath until Saturday to see if anything comes of it, as it may be the start I'm looking for.

Then he also said I might have two weeks off for the Wales trip with my friends the Middletons [a Canadian couple], only now they are thinking of going to Scotland instead of Wales, as they have obtained additional petrol. Was rather planning on a Wales trip, but suppose Scotland will be just as nice. Anyway, I can't grumble, as I'm mighty lucky to be getting anything!

[The article about Sir Robert Ho Tung, the richest man in China, did not appear in the Sunday Express, but was used in Ouida's Sept. 10 column in the Moncton newspaper.]

> IN BRITAIN TODAY by Ouida MacLellan
>
> Flat 28 at Grosvenor House, Park Lane, is occupied by one of the most charming old men I have ever had the pleasure of meeting. He is Sir Robert Ho Tung and known to be the richest man in China. His wealth has made no apparent difference to this little 96-pound man. At the age of 86, he is happy, keen, alert, and has the most wonderful brain for figures.
>
> In a second he divided one million Hong Kong dollars by 16 and told me it was £62,500; this sum, by the way, which in Canadian money comes to $250,000, is the amount Sir Robert recently gave to Hong Kong University for the purpose of erecting a women's hostel.
>
> When I met Sir Robert, he was dressed in a pale blue Chinese kimono and a little black cap, setting off his snow-white beard. He always wears Chinese dress, although his wife and children had all adopted European style clothing. His young Chinese secretary, attractive Miss E. G. Keat, also wore Chinese dress, as did his nurses.

For all his wealth, Sir Robert Ho Tung is not a man to be envied for he has been dyspeptic for the past 60 years. By the time he was 52, three prominent Chinese doctors gave him up as hopeless, saying he would soon die of undernourishment. Determined, Sir Robert set out to discover the secret of his own life, and now at 86 he has outlived two of his doctors. His diet is not very appetizing but it keeps him alive and happy. Sir Robert's formula: a glass of sour milk containing two teaspoonful of glucose and two teaspoonful of plain sugar taken in bed at 6 a.m. A second glass at 8 a.m.

Work consists of reading, writing letters, meeting people, and visiting persons and places until 1 p.m., when he has half a glass of bouillon soup. A back vibrator (one of those machines which thumps up and down the back bone) is then applied to make him relax.

At 1:30 p.m. his only solid meal of the day is taken while resting in bed. This is usually rice or mashed potatoes flavored with marmite and butter, and some finely ground spinach. When available, calf brains boiled with onions or minced chicken is also taken. An afternoon sleep follows this meal, then work again from 4:30 to 6 p.m. The sour milk is repeated in the evening. This diet has been increased from the four egg yolks and eight glasses of sour milk taken in 1938 when Sir Robert could eat no solid foods whatever.

About 10:30 p.m., Sir Robert takes a bath which lasts between an hour and an hour and a half. Here again he relaxes. Bedtime is between one and two a.m.

Despite this handicap, Sir Robert thoroughly enjoys life. Last week he visited one of his old friends of whom he is a great admirer—George Bernard Shaw. The latter, with his wife, was the guest of Sir Robert at his Hong Kong home in 1933. On this present visit, a photograph of Sir Robert and "G.B.S.," both wearing kimonos, was taken and an oil painting of the same has been commissioned for Sir Robert to take back to China with him.

[Sir Robert Ho Tung was the first Chinese person allowed to live on Victoria Peak in Hong Kong, an area previously open only to Europeans. He died in Hong Kong in April of 1956 at the age of 93.]

Saturday, Aug. 27, 1949, morning

Mum, I'm at it again—losing interest in all males around me. I'm dreading David's return, enjoy the others, but still no burning flame lit anywhere—not that I'm looking, understand. Gee! Maybe I ain't human, suppose???

Love, Ouida

"IF YOU HAD A BRAIN YOU'D BE DANGEROUS"
September–November 1949

Sunday, Sept 11, 1949 [in Scotland on holiday]

Dear Mum,

Will start this now as I sit on top of a hill overlooking Balmoral Castle. Which reminds me, afraid my morals have slipped on this trip, as I've missed mass two Sundays and ate meat on Friday. The first Sunday, at Loch Lomond, there was no church. This morning we had planned on seeing the Royal Family going to church, so I missed again. Friday, the tourist house lady gave us meat when we got in about 9 p.m. and as I was starving I ate!! Guess confession comes next although I explained in my prayers last night that I needed the story today.

It was quite a sight, seeing them all so close—we were in the front line and the cars passed almost on our toes. I tried a picture but doubt if it will turn out, as the lighting was quite poor. Princess Elizabeth was wearing a lovely lemon-coloured frock with matching hat. She and Philip came in their own car with Philip driving, while Margaret, the King and Queen were chauffeur driven. The Marquis of Blandford was also around as were several others I didn't recognize. Evidently Philip and the young Duke of Kent are always wandering about here so I may meet one of them yet!!

Monday, Sept. 12, 1949, evening [written on stationery from the Invercauld Arms Hotel, Braemar, Aberdeenshire]

Was talking to Prince Philip's chauffeur for a while this morning. Came out of the post office in Ballater and there was the car standing across the street. The chauffeur had driven Philip up hunting, then came into town to meet a train. I even had my picture taken beside the car—a terrific thing which goes over 100 mph and often does.

Monday, Sept. 19, 1949

Met Chris and Sally Cochran at Waterloo—nearly froze Chris when I didn't recognize him in uniform (Lieut. And did he look handsome!!!) and mistook him for a fresh American I had seen a few seconds before . . .

The [Odiham] air show was quite terrific, and the cocktail party in the evening most amusing, although I'm getting rather tired of that sort of do . . . The women start out looking beautiful and end up quite high and looking a wreck. Good study of life, though, I guess.

Guess I'm also in the soup with Chris. You see, when I first started seeing him, we were both emphatic about how much fun can be had when two people get along well . . . Sally first put things into words Saturday night when she said it may be friends with me, but it sure wasn't with Chris. He's let a few remarks drop that had started me wondering and is so darned attentive it's a wonder people don't think we're engaged anyway. Now what the devil do I do?

Mrs. Bennett is very keen on Chris—but then that's natural, as he is so easy to get on with and such pleasant company. I haven't the foggiest idea of how I feel and don't want to hurt the guy and yet here we are again, nothing has been said and Chris certainly isn't in the financial position to be serious or anything so I can't see what harm is being done. Also there is always the day coming when I'm supposed to be going home, so-o—Aw, heck!!

Saturday, Sept. 24, 1949

Wednesday night we all went to the dance (formal) at Sheen [an affluent suburb near Richmond], a party of about 30 altogether, and had a riotous time. Mike Castles [tennis club friend] and I won a dancing competition by holding an apple between our cheeks the longest and changing steps to suit the tempo of the tunes. We looked a wreck and my jaw was terribly sore from being pressed against the apple but it was fun. Had the last dance with David, and he's simmered down some, so maybe we can get along alright together after all. He's trying to be quite indifferent and casual but still asks me for the important dances . . . which is rather cute.

Thursday, Sally Cochran and I had lunch with Chris then took in a movie and had tea at the Wayfarers. Sally is good company, and it rather looks as though we might be having the same problems soon, as Mike Smart seems to be going as serious on Sally as Chris is on me. Chris is no fool, however, and from what I can gather, he's trying to pull out of this dive quickly. He's extremely practical, and since there would be little or no future, for the time being anyway, I imagine he realizes he had better not get too involved. Ah well, we shall see!

Monday, Sept. 26, 1949, 10:30 a.m.

Saturday at the office wasn't too bad. I had to chase around after a wedding of some society dame and guy—nothing much to it—but it kept me occupied most of the day and kept me out-of-doors. Had lunch with the boys—two Johns and Max—and afterward we drove down by the Tower of London and over Tower Bridge in John Junor's new Morris convertible. It's a lovely car, and although we went on a one-way street, it was fun.

Sunday, Oct. 2, 1949

Well, I don't know how things stand now. I had to wait half an hour for Chris Friday night, and although I had rather expected a bit of a wait, as he had to attend a meeting, I was in a foul temper when he arrived and treated him like dirt all evening. Also, instead of going to a movie or something, we picked up Mike Smart, and someday Chris is going to learn that when Mike is around I always end up talking to him. Anyway, Chris seemed pretty worried by the end of the evening and apologized for everything, then came crawling down to my desk at the office yesterday to ask if I were in better humour and could he phone me Monday. So it seems as though the whip is back in my hand—too bad, because that means I lose all fear of losing anything and become bored and difficult. What a mean character I must be!!!

Both Johns have advised me to write Beaverbrook a note gently reminding him of his promise of more work and asking if it would be possible to go on one of the dailies. Don't think it would do any harm, as the Beaver is leaving this country for Bermuda or someplace on October 16 and if I don't get something by then, my goose will be cooked. Have a couple of other ideas I want to try out also, but think I shall probably write him.

Wednesday, Oct. 5, 1949

Well, I guess the saying "If you had a brain you'd be dangerous" could apply to me right now. Have been wondering all morning what to say in writing Lord Beaverbrook so instead just phoned his secretary Mrs. Ince and asked her to see if Lord Beaverbrook could see me before he leaves for Bermuda. Shouldn't be surprised if he says yes, so then we'll see what we can see. It's much easier to talk things over with a person rather than try to word it right in a letter; besides, it's time he was reminded of me again anyway!

Friday, Oct. 7, 1949, night

Dear Mum,
Well, I've had another couple of those crazy days when you're up one minute, then down the next and just plain confused generally. Tonight I feel lousy and don't know whether things are looking better or worse.

It all started Thursday morning when I went up to town for the perfectly harmless job of doing the hotels. While talking to the Dorchester press officer, Mr. Thomas, Walter Pidgeon walked by, and before I thought, I tore out behind him and called after him. Told him who I was and where from, and he was sweet saying, "God Bless my soul, how are you." We stopped on the street corner chatting like old friends while other guests at the hotel simply stared. He asked what I was doing over here, if you people were over and how you managed to allow a young thing like me so far away. Joked about the way I said "house"—you know that "ou" sound—and ended up by asking me to come to tea. As I—naturally—was without a calling card, he asked me to phone him at the hotel and come. Sounded as if he meant it, too, and I have no intention of passing the chance by. [The actor Walter Pidgeon was born in Saint John, New Brunswick.]

After that, I was in the clouds, which went even higher when the press officer at Grosvenor House asked me to attend a special fashion show that afternoon with her . . . such beautiful gowns. Not only that, but Margaret Lockwood was there too (there were only about 10 of us present), and I also saw two dresses Jane Russell has ordered. There was one evening dress in particular, a darkish-green velvet which I was crazy about but didn't dare ask the price.

Next stop was the Scala Theatre to audition for Mr. Lloyd, the producer of their amateur productions. Seemed very impressed and certain that he will have me placed in both a musical and a straight drama very shortly, which will give me something to occupy my free time (and more, I suppose), and something I love to do. Felt good again by that time.

Mollie washed my hair this morning, then I tied it up and we went shopping in Richmond. Just arrived back when Beaverbrook's secretary phoned for me to be at the flat near St. James Park at 3 p.m. Travelled up to town with my hair in curlers and it was still wet when I arrived at his front door. A lovely flat, and the old boy was going through some 200 books with some female that he afterward told me were for UNB [University of New Brunswick]. After waiting half an hour for him to finish, he talked to me about 10 minutes then said he had to go to the dentist but that he'll speak to Mr. Robertson about my working every day, and Robertson would contact me. Also he'll want to see me when he returns—what a hope, spring!!

He asked me how the column was getting on, said I must persevere and never get discouraged, that he had enjoyed them and I must never put any stock in the comments about them made by others to my relatives.

Felt rather deflated when I left, for somehow I'd been expecting to at least talk to him more, or something. Also suppose my hair looking rather wild had a rather dampening effect.

So there you have it, I'm all mixed up again, sore with myself and the whole world.

Saturday, Oct. 8 [added]

Feel more settled this morning, so suppose I shall survive all right. Oh, yes, had a note from the CBC saying they were unable to arrange anything for me with the Canadian radio. But suppose that's just as well as I probably won't have the time in the end. Also I'd like to carve my niche over here, not over there at present. Time to get ready for the office,

Love, Ouida

Wednesday, Oct. 12, 1949, morning

Dear Mum,

Just got a phone call saying Mr. Robertson, general manager of the Daily Express, wants to see me tomorrow when I go in so shall know then what my future is liable to be. Am more anxious to get onto the Daily Express rather than the Evening Standard, as I think there is more chance for originality there. Keep your fingers crossed!

Sunday, Oct. 16, 1949 (Pay day for Dad and rain here for us!)

Dear Mum,

Well, I'm sort of half way in between again. Saw Mr. Robertson on Friday, but he wasn't very encouraging, as they are already overstaffed on the Daily Express, but he said he would make inquiries and of course with the Beaver out of the country now (he left on Friday) my ace in the hole is gone. However, after thinking it over, perhaps it is better to work only a couple of days a week and get nothing in the paper than work every day and still get nothing in, as Mr. Robertson says most of the daily staff do. Also it gives me more time to attend all the things I want to, such as fashion shows, cocktail parties, teas, etc. which I would probably never be assigned to otherwise.

The Dorchester and the Grosvenor House press officers have gotten so they ask me for just about everything that goes, and I love it. Heather MacConnell (Grosvenor House) asked me for a cocktail party on November 18, and Geraldine Lee (Dorchester) mentioned a hat fashion show with Princess Margaret soon and a dance with the same young lady on November 1. If I can keep getting to these things on my own, it will be worth not working, since no one ever seems to get anything in—yet, there are printed words in the papers! Strange, isn't it!!!

While I think of it, when writing other papers or firms regarding my column, don't you think it might be wise to use another name or present yourself as my secretary or friend or something rather than my mother? . . . You could even write the letter in my name signing it per/me or something—but no, better not, for I have an idea of what kind of letters you can write!!! Possibly—wait a sec, write them as my agent in Canada using a fictitious name . . . Really, I feel that if an agent wrote instead of a member of my family, especially a mother, who they would expect to try to push her kid anyway, it would be a lot more successful.

Nothing very exciting going on at the office yesterday, and honestly, there's going to be a blow one day, for John Prebble again came down and worked crossword puzzles with me. Nothing seems to phiz John and I seem to learn an amazing amount of things from him. He has his fourth book being published in April and has promised a copy. He is quite a brilliant writer in his own way and already Hollywood's MGM have asked for a manuscript for possible film rights to the book. Rather looks as though I'm travelling in high-class company and didn't know it, for John Junor is a Liberal candidate for the next election and will be running against the present Food Minister, Mr. Strachey, in the constituency of Dundee.

Friday night Isabel Greene and I went to the monthly social in the church hall and I met a new male who is quite interesting. He's a production manager, late of a nylon company in Wales, and now with the Hercules bicycle people by name of Jim Drury . . . He's tall, well dressed, 26, was in the Indian Army, and since he was stationed with Americans, has quite a good sense of humor. He brought me home from the social . . . and although he didn't mention another meeting, expect I shall see him again.

Also dancing attention on me was my friend Joe Foley, who was quite sweet this trip and couldn't have been nicer. He beat Jim Drury in buying my tea during intermission and I felt quite queenly having the two most decent lookers in the crowd both trying to feed me! For some reason, I was in good form Friday night and thoroughly enjoyed the social.

Chris phoned to say he would be coming out between 6:30 and 7 p.m. tonight, so I'll have company for the evening. Chris is coming out to supper, as Mrs. Bennett said he might, and I said I'd make him some fudge if he brings some walnuts with him. Otherwise I won't!

Crazy as it may sound, I've had a sort of simmering down feeling about Chris. Possibly it was after realizing I'm still capable of interesting new males on Friday night, but I don't think he's going to worry me in future as he has been doing the last week or two. May know better after tonight, but guess I can still control the feelings and that's what counts.

Love, Ouida

Tuesday, Oct. 18, 1949, morning

As for my own affairs, I'm away again. Quite free of worry and interested in all new males which happen to approach within eyeing distance. As I told you, Chris came over Sunday night and we had a pleasant evening, a girl must keep her technique in practice you know, but he doesn't worry me anymore, and although I still think he's quite nice and enjoy his company, my stomach is back to normal and my eye roving once again. The funny part is, he doesn't know it yet, and I'm quite certain he left with the idea he's calling the tunes and that possibly I've fallen for him quite hard. However, I don't think it will do him any real harm when he learns the truth—maybe he's even saying the same about me, so the future promises to be interesting—maybe even interesting enough for the plot of a short story which I could write and make for myself some extra money. Have given up the hope of ever winning any money dishonestly in the raffles!

Sally Cochran phoned me yesterday and I'm meeting her tonight after work for a Turkish bath. We both discovered the other night that it was something we have both wanted to have for ages, so here goes—we think! If we manage to have one all right, it should be good column material and shall be written Wednesday (tomorrow) and mailed off. Otherwise I shall have to think up something else in a rush, as copy seems a bit low at this minute.

[The column that Ouida promised on October 18 about her visit to a Turkish bath with her friend Sally Cochran appeared in the Moncton newspaper on November 19, 1949.]

IN BRITAIN TODAY by Ouida MacLellan

A long-standing ambition was fulfilled this week. I had a Turkish bath . . . Sound advice to choose a place with a good reputation led us to The Ladies Turkish Baths at the Dorchester Hotel in Park Lane.

The "pay-as-you-enter" system is employed at the baths, thus enabling the customer to stay as long as desirable. Neat little cubicles are complete with bed, hangers, and a bedside cabinet-cum-table affair in which to put valuables. A large white towel which went round me twice and stretched from neck to knee, along with a flimsy pair of canvas slippers, were produced by the attendant. Plastic caps are provided for those not wishing to have a hair-do later . . .

First of all you relax in a sundeck-style chair in a medium-warm room, where the body becomes accustomed to the slight heat. Next comes the steam room, where you sit on a hard wooden bench with feet on a little footstool and try not to mind the drip off the end of your nose. The steam gushes forth from beneath the bench and, as the visibility drops to zero, you are aware of a tight, rather suffocating feeling in your throat. The fascination of watching the perspiration ooze from the pores, however, makes life bearable and interesting.

Next stop is the hot room where the perspiration is supposed to continue on its own without the aid of steam. Wrapped in towels, you are again designated to a deck chair and with eyes on a sign which reads "Silence," you listen to the prattle of the surrounding women: this could be considered the most interesting part of the bath.

The morning of my first trip, there were five women in this "hot room" and each one had something to offer to the melting pot of personalities. To the right of the door was a suntanned woman of about thirty with her dark hair falling loosely about her shoulders. She gave the impression of being tired and worn out—while she sat wrapped in towels an ice cap sat on her head. This customer described her recently completed home just outside London. In detail, the garden and the house, including sun porch and kitchen, were described as "lovely" and going to be "lovely" to live in after being in a flat.

There was a middle-aged woman from Leicester, who seemed to be having trouble with her towel; she would forget to hang on to the corners and appeared half the time as Lady Godiva except that her hair was much too short. This lady had a five-minute reply ready for every question asked.

Then, there were two women who must have had a lease on the baths for they talked as if they were there continually, and close observation showed they had their own rubber suits to help the process. They also had brought along their own lemons for the hot drinks. Their conversation ranged from "I know a better spot than you do in Italy . . ." to a Baker Street doctor who could remove excess fat easily with sand bags and electricity.

The fifth lady in the room spoke with a broad, foreign accent and was more interested in taking her bath properly than in the morning's gossip. She kept rubbing herself and inspecting various portions of the anatomy to make sure all was proceeding as planned.

When the masseuse arrived to say it was my turn, I looked at her with a bit of surprise, as all her efforts in slapping the weight off others had made not one iota of difference to her own portly figure. However, I proved to be a bad "sweater" and was banished to the steam room again for another five minutes before I could be "taken."

Being taken means entering a canvas-enclosed cubicle wherein is a large padded table covered with a rough towel. At first one is massaged lightly. A good going-over with a large, rough, rubbery mitt comes next, followed by a thorough washing down with sweet-smelling soap. Between each operation one is rinsed by being squirted with tepid water from a hose. Then comes the pushing and the pulling on the flabbier portions ("You certainly haven't much to lose!" remarked the masseuse to your reporter.) The finishing touch, and it was getting quite close to that for me, is given while standing over a draining system and enclosed on three sides by canvas—the masseuse stands about five feet distant and thoroughly washes one down with a hose that closely resembles a fireman's hose. The stream of water is gauged according to where it is hitting, with a narrow, stinging spray for those "flabbier" parts again.

The customer is returned to the original cubicle, wrapped in towels as well as warm blankets and left on the bed, either to pass out or just sleep . . . When one feels her strength has sufficiently returned, tips are distributed and leave taken.

Tuesday, Oct. 25, 1949, morning

Dear Mum

Tonight I attend a Chopin concert at the Albert Hall and sit in the top-price 21 shilling seats. Yesterday I met Mrs. Vera Biggs, a professional organizer who must have taken a liking to me, for she not only arranged for complimentary tickets for the big Halloween Ball at The Dorchester which Princess Margaret is attending, but also handed me the tickets for tonight and told me to book December 16 for the Cresta Ball at Claridge's.

Yesterday after meeting Mrs. Biggs, she had me go around to see the Arthur Banks fashion salon, and I met the co-partner, Lewis Aaronson, who told me Eaton's buy from them. In fact most of the expensive creations shown in the fashion shows come from them. Gave me some material for a short column bit now and promised to invite me to the show when the Eaton buyers arrive, which should be good.

Friday, Oct. 28, 1949, 2 p.m.

Things are going so well I can hardly believe it! My datebook for next week is almost filled already, and such goings-on! Monday I meet the Canadian actor Bernard Braden at the CBC studios at 10 a.m. for an interview. Saw the play "A Streetcar Named Desire" in which he is one of the stars with Vivien Leigh [he played the role of Mitch], and want to build a story around him. He sounded very nice on the phone, and it will also be a chance to see the CBC over here and maybe meet some of the big shots. Wednesday I turn up at Grosvenor House for my first glimpse of the famous Winston Churchill, who is being presented a prize at the Sunday Times book exhibition. Oh, yes, sometime between Tuesday afternoon and Thursday morning I'm to phone a dress designer friend of Heather MacConnell's to see what my chances would be for a few odd modelling jobs. It will probably never come to anything, but should be fun anyway.

Saturday, Nov. 12, 1949, morning

Suppose Chris is around quite a bit, but the funny thing is he's one of the few fellows (one of two to be exact) that I enjoy as much when he's with me as I do when he's not. Other than that I can't say much. We have lunch every Thursday together and right now we're rather excited, for it looks as though he'll be taking over the Crossbencher column much sooner than expected. Usually see him sometime during the weekend and he always comes down to say "Hello" on Saturdays at the office . . . At the start, in June, we both expressed opinions on how silly people are to become serious and spoil things, so you should see us now both terrified the other will think we might be getting serious. I for one don't know how I feel, so we just go on having fun together . . . Told Chris last Saturday I was going up to Cambridge for a dance with David and he looked a bit funny for a minute then said it should be fun, so I don't know his view either.

Wednesday, Nov. 16, 1949, morning

Oh, while I think of it, do you suppose it would be possible to send us a ham for Christmas? Suppose it's asking a lot but ham is just out of the question over here and a nice cooked one would be so wonderful to have. Also candy is still rationed—a pound per month—which makes it hard on the kids. The twins have never seen barley toys (you know, the figures), so I think if you could manage a bit of fancy Christmas candy it would be greatly appreciated. The reason I mention this is, since we're all spending Christmas at the house here, everyone is sort of chipping in to do their bit and I'd like to help out, too—not that I haven't already. The parcels you've been sending have been wonderful.

Sunday, Nov. 20, 1949

Mum, I don't see how a "nip" of a cocktail, as you described it, that Frances has at parties can affect her any. At the cocktail party Friday night I took a glass of whatever was passed around, tasted it and found it all right, rather like a grapefruit juice. After I had finished it I discovered it had been a white wine—quite diluted though, I think—but had no bad effects, for I went on to a church social. Have had a long gin and lime a couple of times, which means little gin and lots of lime, but don't like anything else. If I am at a party where there is nothing else or it will cause a fuss, I take whatever it is, sip it once or twice and either trade it off for an empty glass or hold onto it until I can put it down somewhere.

Friday, Nov. 25, 1949, morning

Had to go help Chris buy a new pair of sox after lunch yesterday as he had torn a hole in the heel of the ones he had on. I wanted either a bright yellow or a diamond pair but he chose a conservative grey. There were really rather pretty ones but I would never admit that. Told him I thought he should wear a yellow sleeveless sweater and yellow sox, so he said he would if I'd knit them for him. To that I assured the man my mother would certainly take the first plane over and confine me to the nuthouse if she ever heard I had started knitting for a male being . . . We had an almighty row last Saturday with me biting Chris's head off, so he just walked off and left it, until yesterday morning at 9:30 to ask about lunch at noon. I commented that it was rather late in the week and he said I was not to start that again so decided I'd better behave. Was very sweet and acted as though nothing had happened when I met him. It's the only thing to do, he's got a mind of his own. Don't know when I've ever backtracked so many times for a man. Oh well, maybe it will teach me patience or forgiveness or give and take or something, surely!!!!

Love, Ouida

Monday, Nov. 28, 1949

Dear Mum,

Well, by now you must have last Saturday's Evening Standard and I'm dying to know what you think of the picture.

It was taken at the Kinsman Scholarship Trust cocktail party although it isn't mentioned at all. It was really quite funny, for whenever one of the reporters asked to meet one of the students, the Rileys always led him to someone else, but they eventually found their way to me. I had on that green satin job again and funnily enough, I decided just at the last minute to wear the £5 black hat instead of a new green effort as I previously had planned. What luck, for it was the dress and the hat combination that pulled me through again! Guess I'll have to stick by that hat till I die for I've never had any outfit bring me so much luck.

Was very afraid when the photographer found out I worked for the Express he would stop, but the picture was taken—after the photographer had asked publisher Hamish Hamilton to step out of the way, please! Numerous other pictures were taken, including several of Mr. Riley with other trustees and students, but mine was the only one that appeared.

The boys got quite a kick out of it Saturday, although John Prebble and Chris both said they didn't think the picture flattered me—I'm not nuts, it did flatter me!

Saturday wasn't too exciting a day at the office, and at noon, as we finished lunch a little early, Max, John Prebble, and I went into a pub and played the pinball machine a while. After work, we all drifted over to The Bell—another pub—and sat around talking while the boys had a beer for a while. It was quite fun, as the whole staff eventually drifted over and we almost took over the whole place.

Love, Ouida

"I'VE JUST GOT TO GET THIS JOB"
December 1949

Friday, Dec. 2, 1949, 5:50 p.m.

On Sunday evening I'm going over to Ann Swinton–Lee's for cocktails. She's one of the top writers on the Evening Standard whom I met at the Kinsman cocktail party. She seemed interested in me and when she phoned just now I was rather tickled, as she's a great contact to have. Tall, quite heavy, blonde, and very nice.

Took some of my columns in to Mr. Gordon to read today, suggesting the Express might like them. He said they'd like a lot of things but just haven't got the space, and word has just come through that they won't be getting any more paper. That rather hinders any chances there. Anyway, I asked him to read them over and tell me how he likes them.

Sunday, Dec. 4, 1949, 3:05 p.m.

The dance Friday night went off very well, and we had a grand evening, although I was a bit tired. Chris got along great with the kids of the gang but then I knew he would, as he's an easy mixer. I was away off all evening and usually forgot to finish half my sentences and left people wondering just slightly what on earth I was talking about. Did have one grand dance with John Delanghe, which was in true creative style and wonderful.

Chris's dancing could easily stand some improvements, and I had to smile when I caught him concentrating like mad and counting, one, two, three, one, two, three during a waltz. He irritated me a bit during the evening by showing me too much attention. Oh, I know it sounds crazy, but none of the other girls are waited on so carefully, and he'd catch me by the hand every now and then or tease me by blowing on the back of my neck. It embarrasses me, and I suppose it's the same old story of "What will people think?" Don't know whether it was just an annoying minute, or whether it's the start of an interest-losing campaign again.

Suppose this is going to sound rather hard, but I'd hate to be forced to return to Canada in February. Every time I think of returning to the Transcript office, I go cold and am quite certain I'd even wash dishes to stay over here longer, and I realize once I leave this country, I shall never return.

You know, Mum, it's rather a terrifying feeling to have not a single plan for the future. If someone asked me today what I want, I couldn't answer, for I really don't know. I think I'd like to be famous one day, but I'm sure I don't know in which field. I do know that I don't want to lose my independence but whether that means to a man or to an employer, I don't quite know.

Have been almost seriously thinking of just knocking around Europe every way possible next summer to gather enough material for a book. It would be on the "Our Hearts Were Young and Gay" style, and somehow I seem to have enough things happen to me to make my experiences readable. Possibly I could manage the job of hotel clerk or something similar in some of the summer resorts, or perhaps even get something with a travel agency to guide parties around, etc. Would be worth a try to see the country.

Monday, Dec. 5, 1949, 10:20 p.m.

Last night at the cocktail party at Ann Swinton–Lee's, she and a colleague got together and decided they would recommend me for a job on the night reporting staff of the Evening Standard. I have been thinking about it ever since and although there are some disadvantages, the advantages definitely outweigh them.

The work is from about 4 p.m. until midnight or perhaps later, but so long as I am able to get back to Richmond afterwards, that wouldn't make any difference. It would entail visiting all types of places, and while avoiding the obvious stories, one would have to make up unusual stories out of just about nothing. That would probably hit me hard for a few weeks until I got into the swing, but I'm used to asking people embarrassing questions, so that would be all right. Also it would mean being capable of condensing every story into almost nothing, but that would be good experience.

It pays very well—at least £13 per week, which is usually brought up to about £17 with expenses. At the old rate of $4 to the pound, you can figure that out for yourself. Also, as I would have only Saturday and Sunday evenings free, I should be able to save most of the money, which I badly need. Then again, the hours stated would also allow me to still do the work I'm now doing for the Sunday Express, which would mean a few more shekels, which would be appreciated. I could still keep the present friends I have on the Sunday and get the experience I haven't had besides.

Of course I realize I'll have to cut out many of the things I'm doing now, like my Caledonian dancing, weekly theatres, and even the amateur production which I accepted a role in only yesterday, and probably the modelling, which I wasn't going to get anyway. I could get used to that easily for the amount of money and experience which I so badly need.

Now note this carefully! I must have references! The fact that I have six years' experience is my big card, and the references must stress the general reporting, which covered every imaginable phase. The column work will help some, but the beat work I did and the on-spot-coverage are what count.

What do you think of talking it over with Ed Larracy? As my news editor [on the Moncton paper], he should be able to give me a good reference and that would count, as it's the news editor over here that I will be meeting. Also the news editor is the one who can really speak of a person's work. Grainger [the managing editor] should also give me a good reference regarding the column work, and make one of them mention the daily stories from the towns while I was travelling.

You do realize how important it is, Mum, don't you and besides, the Standard is also a Beaverbrook paper and it is one of the ones Mr. Robertson said couldn't use me, and I must make it to prove I have the stuff without their help. Please hurry with this, as every day counts so very much.

Love, Ouida

Sunday, Dec. 11, 1949, 3 p.m.

Friday, did my work and met Chris for lunch. Was rather hoping he'd be in an aggravating mood, but the darned skunk was a perfect pet. (Had he been in a mood, I would have had a good reason to enjoy myself on my date with John Shannon [friend from the Richmond "gang"] that night.) Did some checking for a story in the afternoon then went to see the movie "Pinky" with Jeanne Crain, which is excellent. You must see it, as the critics have been very high in its praise and I can easily see why. It's the story of a mulatto and is very well told.

Met John Shannon at Charing Cross station at 7 p.m. and we went to the Scala Theatre to see the Stock Exchange amateur production "Three Men on a Horse." It was quite good and we enjoyed it fine. Don't get your hopes up though for I'm far from being gone on John. He's pleasant but too anxious and instead of offering me his arm, he grabs mine and I don't like it.

It struck me funny, for when I got home I found your letter saying you were getting jittery again—about Chris, I gather—when along comes a new one. Well, I hate to disappoint you but Chris still holds the lead and since I don't seem to feel like shopping around anymore, they're turning up thick and fast. John Osborne asked me to the next church social this morning and another chap phoned to ask me to go ice skating.

Wednesday, Dec. 14, 1949, morning

Dear Mum,

Miracles continue to happen and sometimes I think I'm the luckiest girl alive but can judge that better after this afternoon. Last week I composed a short snappy letter to Mr. Gunn, the editor of the Evening Standard, stating what I wanted and my experience briefly, in fact so briefly it took only one page and not all of that.

By gosh, Monday came a letter saying I had been granted an interview with the news editor, Ronald Hyde, who is in charge of the London late night staff, for this afternoon at 3:30 p.m. Now, this morning in the 8 a.m. mail come both your references, Grainger's and Larracy's. How's that for timing? . . . So I shall trot off to see the said Mr. Hyde this afternoon, put on my brightest smile, dig out the old personality (have been told he's very susceptible to charming females), and try to give the impression of efficiency and brains. Will write you again tonight to let you know how I make out. Oh, I've just got to get this job, for despite all the inconveniences, it would be marvellous experience for me and a terrific recommendation for any other papers, AND it's still in the Beaverbrook outfit, which is what I want, for despite the fact the old man has done nothing for me yet—he will, just you wait and see, he'll come across with the earth, even if I have to burn down London to make him take more notice.

Well! Last night I had a perfectly wonderful time at the Caledonian Ball! John Osborne came to call for me—although we both had our own tickets—and we went on the bus to economize. Didn't mind really, then I didn't see John again until we left to come home together . . . We seem to have a good understanding again as John has asked me to attend the local church social with him this Friday night. Anyway, the fun was between David Ross and John Shannon. Oh boy!!!! Neither had evidently been aware of the other's existence and I was barely aware of either of them. Anyway, David (looking very handsome in his new dress kilt) arrived evidently intent on not paying me any attention, so he could more or less make me suffer, I guess, silly boy! I couldn't have cared less, but as soon as he noticed John Shannon around a lot, David pulled up his sox and moved in, cabbaging everything, including the last dance, and asking if I'm going to the regular Caledonian dance class tonight, then decided he'll come too. I was still very casual and friendly etc. but not too much, so he even went to the lengths of singing ever so softly to me during the last dance. I was tickled pink—especially as David ranks second among the best Scottish dancers of the younger set and his ballroom dancing is excellent.

John Shannon, on the other hand, was a bit bewildered when he saw someone else around—David's first appearance since leaving for Cambridge in October. I had the first dance with John and a couple of others much later on, still being very sweet, nice and friendly, and the next dance he apologized for neglecting me, saying he has been talking shop—he knew darned well that I had been booked for every dance. It really shook him when he realized David had grabbed the last dance, so he tore up afterward to ask if I was coming to the class tonight. Boy, am I enjoying this, so long as it lasts!! This will be proof of my powers as a female if I can keep them both on the go!

Friday, Dec. 16, 1949

I find it becoming more difficult daily to get at my work. I just don't have the peace, and although Mrs. Bennett has been grand to me, I guess it's a little difficult for people to understand the whims and feelings of a writer . . . Without central heating, the rooms, besides the kitchen, are ice cold, and in the kitchen, pans are rattling or someone is always talking to you. I have to make the most of every time they all go out, but that is not always the most suitable time for me to write. I suppose I should live on my own, but then I'd never eat, so that would be worse.

There is a mix-up about New Year's. Heather MacConnell asked me yesterday to spend New Year's Eve at Grosvenor House, on the house with a special press party she entertains every year. As Chris is also press, he could have come with me, but Luke White has invited him down to his father's estate for the weekend and Chris said he'd go . . . Heather still wants me to go anyway, as she has asked a couple of single pressmen and was only including Chris because I rather wanted him. That would be fine if I wasn't a non-drinker, but being the kind of person I am makes it difficult. Press people drink like fishes, and had Chris come along, he buys what I want, thinks nothing of it himself, in fact he prefers that I don't drink, then no one else thinks anything of it. However, with perfect strangers, they wouldn't understand and especially on New Year's Eve would only think I was a prude or spoilsport. Also I hate not having some definite person to turn to, and if I didn't like the stray men—even though they'd probably be good contacts—I'd probably shut up like a clam.

Now on top of everything else David Ross has asked me to go to the Richmond Club with him, but it will have to be Dutch, he said. The kids in the crowd usually go Dutch, I know, so that wouldn't be too bad, except that I'd be afraid of hurting David. He's nice and all, but when it comes to midnight and people get amorous, I'd probably freeze and be embarrassing . . . Drat that Chris, he's the only one I'd like to spend the evening with and I feel like chucking everything and going to bed, but that would cause trouble, too, I suppose. Guess I'm just not the party girl type.

Sunday, Dec. 18, 1 p.m.

John Junor drove me home last night and en route said he thought I should give up journalism and get married and settle down. He claims no nice woman has ever become a successful journalist, but I've known that for ages, and that's why I'm so keen on features and column work. The regular hard reporter is always a terrific trollop. Got a kick out of John's advice, for he seems to think it's so easy to return to Canada and marry—especially when I tell him there's no one there to marry!! . . . Also I don't know how to cook and it's perfectly all right to starve myself but one couldn't starve a husband now, could one?? Maybe I'll find a rich count or earl over here who can afford a maid. I'd never manage otherwise, I'm sure!

Friday, Dec. 23, 1949, afternoon

Chris and I went shopping for something for Peter, his kid brother, and he got an "Old Boy's" tie for their school. All the men wear them over here if they have a school to belong to. At the same time, Chris pointed out his regimental tie in the window—among other things . . . Later I stopped in at Canada House to say "hello" to Ted Ritchie . . . He was enquiring about friends made here and I jokingly said I had just been presented a gift by a "MALE" friend and handed him the parcel Chris had given me earlier. He thumbed it and said, "Books." Well, at first I nearly flipped, for I had never thought of books, and you know my reading capacity. I fumed all the way home and then wondered if Chris had been trying to be funny and given me some weird gift. By the time I got home I had practically decided not to give him the photo as promised, when curiosity got the better of me. I had to know what it was so I'd know what to give in return. Imagine my face when on opening the thing in Mrs. Bennett's presence I found two of the most beautifully red leather-bound little books you ever did see. Inside is "Chris Xmas 1949" and they are each in little red box things. One is modern poetry from 1900–1940, and the other a copy of "Wuthering Heights" by Charlotte Bronte. You see, the Englishman reads a great deal, and books are considered a very nice gift indeed. Stopping to figure it out, I realize Chris chose very wisely, and the editions are really lovely. The more I think, the more tickled I am . . . Anyway I'm giving Chris his gift tomorrow, the photo he asked for ages ago, and his regimental scarf. Was a bit doubtful about the latter but it is something I know he'll be very thrilled with and I rather wanted to give him something he's very keen on having . . . You're probably muttering about me giving anything the first Christmas after meeting him, etc. but I've thought it over very carefully and talked it over with Mrs. Bennett, and it's not as though we've just met or are like strangers. We're good friends and felt like exchanging things.

Sunday, Dec. 25, 1949, Christmas Day

Dear Mum,

Well, I've just listened to the King—and very well he did, too—so now I know what you people are doing. But I didn't really need the King's help, for I've been able to picture what you've been doing all day. It is now 3:15 p.m. here and we're just in the middle of our Christmas dinner and it is good. It's 11 a.m. over there and you have just finished opening up all your gifts and are probably cleaning away the paper which is cluttering up the floor. The breakfast dishes have still to be done and the turkey is all ready for the oven, or maybe—nope, it won't be in yet.

Our Christmas dinner, by the way, consisted of tomato soup for a start, then turkey, dressing, peas, potatoes, ham, and gravy. Then came the plum pudding with a sprig of holly on top and burning with a blue flame. The lights were turned out for its entrance. Around the table are Mrs. Bennett, Teddie, Denise, Mollie, Norman, the three children, and me. The house has been in a complete turmoil since Friday and it's been rather fun . . .

Saturday at the office I got one of the biggest thrills of the whole weekend. The three boys (Johns and Max) were there per usual. John Prebble kept walking around with a white paper package in his hand, which I thought was a pudding or something he was going to take home. When we got into Junor's car to go for lunch, John Prebble cleared his throat a couple of times then said, "I think this is the right time, ahem, on behalf of all of us, we give you this," and presented me with the poorly wrapped parcel. It was a lovely big box of Richard Hudnut dusting powder, and I didn't know whether to laugh or cry. Honestly, they are the sweetest things that ever happened to me, so big and yet so small and considerate in so many ways. They always look after me as though I were a little breakable doll and I love it. I don't know when anything has every moved me so much.

Love, Ouida

"TICKLED PINK . . . I HAVE MY FIRST STORY"
January–March 1950

Wednesday, Jan. 4, 1950

Dear Mum,

First of all, you will probably want to know how my second meeting with Mr. Hyde went yesterday. I should say it was satisfactory, although I still don't start to work. He does seem very keen on having me on the staff and I'm to contact him again on February 1st. In the meantime, he asked if I would like to do space work—that is, feature articles for space rates, which would provide me with some extra cash. That will be most satisfactory as it will give me yet another month of freedom—which I love—and still a chance of more money if I work. I really think he will put me on just as soon as he can, and that's quite soon enough for me. It will still give me a chance to scout around a bit more and get a lot of things cleaned up that were quite impossible during the Christmas season.

Monday, Jan. 9, 1950

Shall do my best for the National Home Monthly [a proposed article on foodstuffs from Canada shipped to England to relieve shortages]—you're probably screaming because it hasn't been sent yet—but as I've already told you, I can't quote Harrods or any other stores, as they don't know what is or isn't Canadian when they get it. The stuff is still rationed, pooled when it gets here, and people take what they can get and ask no questions.

As for your comments on the Chelsea story [about a visit to a nightclub], I am now looking it over and think it is very good. Don't know what more you could ask in the way of description and I don't know whether you wanted it about Chelsea itself or the night club I went to. Chelsea is the Greenwich Village of London, the section where all the "artistic-type" persons desire to hang their hats. There are any number of little mews—back alleys where people live, to you—where painters, etc. have their so-called "studios." Of course, many are famous, like Olivier and Leigh, but on the whole when walking down the main drag you see young men in beards and tweeds, highly made-up women in slacks and bright-coloured hair bands and sloppy sweaters, and I'm sure some of them never even wear matching sox. To be eccentric seems to be the style and they all try very hard. As for the club, there are dozens like it, little smoke-filled back rooms where be-pop predominates, and it's the mood that counts. Sometimes these places can be like a Basin Street club in New Orleans, others are more dignified and quiet, but not much. Sort of an "eat-drink-and-be-merry-for-tomorrow-we-may-die" attitude by all present.

Chris and I are going to the Bertram Mills Circus on Thursday night, John Shannon is taking me to a movie tonight, Gay Delanghe wants to see a stage play either tomorrow or Wednesday night, a formal dance on Friday at the Richmond Club, Saturday night is the Kinsmen Dinner and dance as well as Chris's birthday, so the week is pretty well gone. Oh yes, I have a tea tomorrow, too, and dinner at Chris's house Thursday before the circus.

[The column Ouida's mother complained about described an evening spent with Chris Dobson and twelve friends at a club in Chelsea where she encountered for the first time the more Bohemian side of London. It was in the Moncton paper on Jan. 7, 1950.]

IN BRITAIN TODAY by Ouida MacLellan

The entire week between Christmas and New Year's seemed like one long party . . . I found the evening of Boxing Day the most unusual. Our party—fourteen people—met at a pub known as Holybush in Hampstead. From here we set off for the Connoisseur Club in the depths of Chelsea, the heart of the "arty" set of London where artists, actors, and musicians, both known and unknown, live in weird little out-of-the-way flats and rooms . . .

The Connoisseur Club is in a small side street, and the entrance is by means of a dark, narrow doorway which looks as though it was the back door of a large building. There was no sign whatever for this club: instead a small painted notice about a barber shop upstairs somewhere. On entering the door we turned sharp right, went down a narrow stairway into the club. To a stranger, this alone was some experience, and when we entered the room, we realized this was to be a different evening for us.

The place was dimly lit, quite smoky, and gaily decorated with streamers. There was a brightly lighted Christmas tree in one corner partly hiding a grand piano being played by a man in shirt sleeves. On a raised platform, just behind the pianist, was another chap, also coatless, and completely surrounded by many types of drums and noisemakers.

We found two tables in a corner right beside the drummer, which made conversation a bit difficult but a grand place from which to watch the drummer at work. The chap's hands and feet moved continuously and at times keeping two quite different beats, yet still in proper tempo . . . As the evening proceeded, we discovered that the tall, over-plump owner of the Connoisseur Club was also versatile and could spell both the drummer and the pianist. At other times he would croon a fine tune and his huge frame would quiver when the tempo was "hot."

Before leaving home for the evening I had asked my escort what the form of dress was to be and his answer of "anything" was most appropriate. While a glamorous blonde with hair piled high and wearing a very off-the-shoulder sweater, rope pearls, slinky skirt, and spike-heeled shoes, danced under the chin of her partner, right behind came a dark-haired Hawaiian girl in a rusty sloppy-joe sweater, baggy brown slacks, and moccasins, cutting a rug with a blond, bow-tied chap. On the edge of the dance floor (a hard polished surface about ten feet square) sat a sweet-looking girl, in a lovely brown taffeta dress, watching the scene in utter amazement and fascination.

I would have liked very much to chat and discuss with her this very obvious new experience for both of us, but there is a fixed custom that one party does not intermingle with any other. Each couple on the dance floor seemed quite oblivious of anyone else, even though there was barely breathing room among the dancers. The "atmosphere" was gay and happy, and as the evening wore on the excitement of the season caught hold of us all. Not until we emerged into the fresh air several hours later, did one realize how heavy and smoky the inside had been, but that did not matter. Chelsea is well worth visiting.

Tuesday, Jan. 10, 1950, 12:10 a.m.

Dear Mum
What do you mean I wasn't steady with any of my boyfriends? I thought Bryce Coyle plus the boil on his neck was wonderful from grade eight through to grade eleven, with a few others thrown in for variety, of course . . . Now this remark about Chris. Not sure of what you're looking for—either a contradiction from me or assurance that he really doesn't count. You do make me laugh with all this beating about the bush when I know darned well you're wetting your pants 'cause you're afraid I might have met a real man and you're not close enough to look him over. Well, when I've decided which it is, I'll let you know; in the meantime I thoroughly enjoy teasing, just to see what kind of replies you'll send . . . I quite enjoy it when Chris takes me by the arm or pays me little attentions . . . Another thing I like is Chris's ability of making me proud to be with him in public, being able to hold his own with anyone and not make me keep looking over the fence for something better . . . He has Daddy's pig-headedness and stubbornness, and when he makes up his mind to a thing I always lose—or pretend to lose, just as you do—he also has Daddy's knowledge of my expensive taste and likes to buy me things but can't afford very much. That what you expected?

Tuesday, Jan 10, 1950, evening

Dear Mum,

Have just come back from the actresses' tea party, an annual affair sponsored by former actresses. It was really a wonderful affair, attended by many of the old Gaiety Girls who are now in their 70s and 80s. It was quite worth a story, and that will be sent off tomorrow along with some other column material.

Am enclosing a real gift for you. Three of these hankies arrived at Grosvenor House today by registered post airmail from Hong Kong. My good friend Sir Robert Ho Tung also enclosed his best wishes for a happy and prosperous new year and said he hoped my paper would soon send me to Hong Kong to cover the China affair,[7] and he would be waiting with a most hearty welcome for me . . . rather thought you might get a kick out having one of these hankies to sport around Moncton. I still don't use handkerchiefs but may one day so will hang onto a couple.

I got a lovely yellow sleeveless sweater today at the Jaeger shop for Chris's birthday, which is Saturday. He did ask me to knit one but that was asking a little too much—sew?—anything—but knit?—sorry!

[The column about the Gaiety Girls luncheon was published in Moncton on January 28: in the same piece, Ouida described her first encounter with television. It would be another two years before television stations opened in Montreal and Toronto.]

IN BRITAIN TODAY by Ouida MacLellan

Never shall I tire of this most fascinating city of London with its history, relics of days of glory, and its atmosphere; the latter perhaps the most important of all, for in addition to its history London has some very up-to-date items, too. Now there is television, which about half the population are able to enjoy. An upright bar supporting what looks like an "H" is getting to be a common sight on rooftops which indicates a television set inside.

All the important events are televised as well as a great many of the new shows. Last Sunday the children in our house watched a full-length performance of the Bertram Mills circus from Olympia. Every Wednesday night the older members of the family catch up on the latest plays. The other day we watched the ice show and it was splendid. Of course the television screen shows only black and white but when Technicolor does come, and the beauty of costumes and scenery can be seen, it will

---

[7] The "China affair" arose from the problem of mass emigration from mainland China by nationals into Hong Kong after the founding of the People's Republic of China in 1949.

be still more wonderful. All one has to do is to be careful the screen is properly adjusted, then the watcher has a front-row seat and a marvellous view of everything.

I made my debut on television this week. Not so anyone would notice particularly, but still I made it quite unexpectedly at that. I was dashing down Kingsway when a sign, "Do you televise easily? Come in and see," caught my eye. Having often fancied myself a movie star, I decided to take a few minutes to find out what my chances would be, so in I went. Next came another sign placed near the floor, "You are now being televised, look at the screen above." Halfway up, about level with my chest, was a strange-looking affair, resembling a streamlined toy cannon, but was evidently a camera. Above was a television screen, and sure enough there was my face—a rude shock indeed! A quick glance around assured me there was no one very near, so I tried my best smile—not much improvement—then I tried various funny faces—some of these were not too bad.

I was deciding it must be the lack of proper makeup that made me look as though I had not slept for a week when a giggle reached me from around the corner. There, lo and behold, was another similar screen, and while I had been watching myself on the first screen, some ten complete strangers were enjoying my antics on the second screen. I am sure that the colour that came then would be too much for even television.

Friday, Jan. 13, 1950, afternoon

Dear Mum,
Well, here it is, Friday the thirteenth, so really anything is bound to happen, but I'm quite certain nothing more could. After yesterday I don't think I could stand anything more. In fact, I must be really going to pot, for this morning I actually cried, something I haven't done in years and the worst thing is I can't say why. A lot of little things sort of all piled up and this morning I broke down and had a darned good howl. Mrs. Bennett was very sweet and said she was rather glad to see me cry as it proved I was still human and had some feelings after all.

Not sure I can explain all the things that happened but I'll try. To start with, I've been worried about work a bit and had a lot of things I wanted to get rounded off but never had the time. Then Monday, just when I thought I was better, a second cold hit me almost harder than the first and I've been feeling rather rotten for a couple of days . . . At lunch at noon I gave Chris the tickets for the circus and he was wild when he saw the price, then I spent 7 shillings on some new chocolates I wanted to try and that shocked him too. He didn't say much but after the circus—which I think he quite enjoyed—he seemed hardly able to say anything, and I felt rather rotten to think that I had spent so much on the tickets. He claimed it wasn't the form at all, as when a fellow takes a girl out he wants to pay. I fixed that a bit by saying I had insisted we go, and after all, I'd been eating dinner off him weekly for months. That seemed to help a bit, but the tickets, the chocolates, and then some silhouettes for which we paid 9 shillings between us rather got to him, I guess. Thursday, of course, is the day before payday for Chris and he was pretty flat and felt it. I asked him if he were really angry over me buying the tickets and he said No, but that it made him realize his own broke-ness. He said it in an almost choking voice and seemed terribly downhearted, yet I didn't know what on earth I could say or do. Now I'm terrified he thinks my tastes are much too expensive for him altogether and will just haul out—especially when he gets my birthday gift which I mailed yesterday morning, and of course there is nothing I can do about that now . . . Of all the crazy things—but then I can almost hear you say, "I told her she'd do that one day, being so impulsive and independent, etc." Never mind, I know—now!

Monday Jan. 16, 1950, 2:40 p.m.

Yes, I know my copy has been pretty lousy lately . . . I hope I get that job with the Evening Standard soon, as I'm mighty low on material! Just phoned the Montreal Standard people and will see their Howard Clegg on Thursday afternoon at 3 p.m.

Oh, before I forget, I had to cash my last traveller's cheque the other day. Could you possibly ask the bank for a couple of cheques and send them to me, but for heaven's sake, get them in dollars, not pounds!!!! I was extremely stupid to bring money over in pounds, as I lost a lot on that deal. I hung onto that other cheque until I was desperate—had a bill for £3:2:9 while shopping at Dickins and Jones and only £3 in my purse!—so had to cash it. I always like to have something tucked away for emergencies, so please send a couple as soon as possible. A couple of $10 or $15 ones would do fine, I think—dollars are so much more valuable.

Friday, Jan. 20, 1950, morning

Dear Mum,
After a full day in town yesterday I returned to find your first letter this week and really, Mum, I do think you're disgusting!! Do you honestly expect me to tell you what kind of "Smackers" I get ??? Besides, who ever said I got any?

Felt really down on reading the first part of your letter, then when at the end you said not to mind, I decided not to. You see, I had just come in from meeting Howard Clegg of the Montreal Standard and he seems quite interested in me. I believe I could even get a job with them to tide me over until I got what I wanted, if needs be. He told me what the work would be like, not all editorial but some executive etc. too, and that wouldn't be too bad. He did say the Standard is a great outfit to work for and getting better all the time. He also said they might be interested in feature articles, and judging from the pay he mentioned it sounds wonderful. Do you remember that series they carried on Scotland Yard cases? Well, E.V. Tullett, who wrote them, is on our Sunday Express staff and I know him very well. Yesterday Clegg mentioned they paid $1,000 for that series. He said that is a bit high for regular Standard prices but they usually pay $100 for a short series or couple of articles and, when they get used to one writer, will sometimes give him assignments on commission. He isn't even down on women but thinks they get terrific breaks, so that's the outfit I'd like to hook up with . . . I left some of my columns and a couple of short stories with him to look over, and he'll phone me.

Nope, I wasn't homesick at all when I cried, just muddled up per usual and afraid I had loused up too many things at the same time. However, the sun is more bright now . . . Ages ago Chris promised to take me to Cornwall when he goes to visit friends there. Yesterday he said he couldn't take me unless he married me, for the people are very narrow-minded down there and he knows so many of them there he can't take me. Too bad!

Tuesday, Jan. 24, 1950, evening

Nope, definitely no pictures ever with my column. I want to sell it on its own merit, not for the pictures. You never find any of the really big columnists using pictures, and besides, "getting a plate," as you call it, is next door to an impossibility over here, for you'd have to get permission of every kind and description and probably have to pay for it too. Nope, no pictures.

On Saturday I was ready to really blow a fuse! Here I've been yelling about my column for months now to the two Johns and Max, when suddenly Max says, "Have you ever thought of trying to syndicate it?" What does he think I've been screaming about, anyway????? Then he casually mentions that the Daily Express has its own worldwide syndicate service and they're always looking for new material and perhaps they might be interested. After I'd gotten over my first shock at his thick-headedness I said I certainly did want it so he's going to see if he can arrange an interview for me with the man in charge. You know the Daily Express world syndicate might even be a decent outfit to work for, for a while. It wouldn't get me too much notice here in London, but then what I'm doing right now is getting me even less, but would be a great opportunity for straight feature writing, which is what I really prefer in the long run. Anyway it will be worth trying and although I'm not counting on much, you never can tell where the bough is going to bend first.

Have an interview at 11 a.m. tomorrow morning with Phil Grune of the Evening Standard feature section and let's hope that brings results. Gwyn Lewis told me Grune is a sucker for females, and as he sounded pleasant but businesslike and rather gruff on the phone, I should be able to manage him OK. Then there is always Howard Clegg to hit up again, as he told Tom Tullett he was very taken with me, but Tom's advice is to keep after him and I'll probably do all right.

Friday, Jan. 27, 1950, evening

Am still waiting to hear from Max regarding anything with the Daily Express syndication department over here and shall probably have to keep after him . . . As I said before, nothing may develop but it's worth a try . . . Of course you realize that if I had a name it would be quite different and sometimes I'm tempted to try the stage or modelling or something like that to establish a quick name then thrust the column down their throats. Of course there are millions trying already for the stage and modelling and I have no experience to speak of, but that never enters my head. Somehow this personality I seem to be endowed with has kept my head above water thus far and I'm going to keep right on playing it to the hilt while I'm still young enough. If I have to use face, etc., to establish brains (which I sometimes wonder if I really DO possess), that's exactly what I shall do. Watch me!

Now, I've got a problem for you. I've been invited out to the theatre, dinner, and dancing by the son of the personal surgeon to King Farouk of Egypt and I'm trying to decide what to do. I met the son—one of the handsomest and most charming men I've yet encountered—when I went to interview the father, who is an absolute pet. The son was very pleasant and at the conclusion walked me to the elevator and very humbly asked if he might phone me the following week and perhaps we could have dinner together. Taken by surprise, I said all right and forgot about it. Then on Wednesday afternoon he phoned, having first called the office for my number, which he declared he had great difficulty in getting. He suggested this Friday (tonight) but I, wanting some time to think, said I was busy . . . He then asked if I was free either Thursday or Friday evenings? I consulted my diary and both are as blank as my head, so I was stuck for an answer and said yes . . . Since then I've been sweating and have decided it's really quite ridiculous.

This chap Nakeeb (his last name) is a medical student at St. Thomas Hospital, tall, very white skin, with contrasting beautiful dark eyes and dark hair. So help me, his eyes are the most beautiful things I've ever seen, deep blue with the longest and curliest lashes possible! In fact, when he opened the door of his father's suite, I actually gasped at the sight of him. He seemed to be just as taken with what he saw under my green hat and since I have no intention of marrying anyone and it isn't every guy who can manage a theatre, dinner, and dancing all in the same evening—most of them spread it out over three months!—I think I'll go. He could prove a good contact, good company, and maybe even a story. Also I'm quite capable of looking after myself—at least if I'm not, I shouldn't be here—and if I don't like the evening I needn't go again. I remember the first night Chris asked me out, I fretted just about as badly, as I thought he was going to be a terribly fast wolf and look how he turned out!! I told him about this chap yesterday and although he wouldn't say much he didn't seem to think anything of it. Suppose you are all het up by now!!!

Wednesday, Feb 1, 1950, night

Dear Mum,
Today has been a funny day but I think a profitable one. To begin with, there is still no vacancy on the Evening Standard but one of the stories I sent in is to be used shortly, Mr. Grune said, and I'm to keep submitting them. That's a few shekels. Then I've made an appointment with the Daily Express syndicate people for tomorrow which may produce something, you never can tell.

Best of all, however, was Howard Clegg of the Montreal Standard, for although he gave me nothing monetary, he did give me advice and it's good. He even said he would be willing to give me time to show me exactly what he means. He claims I have stopped learning too soon, stopped before I became a perfectionist, and there is still a lot for me to learn about the actual mechanism of writing. (Can see you nodding your head now.) Anyway, he said he believed I definitely have talent but it is not fully developed by any means and the reason there are so few good writers in Canada is not the lack of talent but the lack of guidance and training. He claims the newspaper and writing standards in Canada are terribly low and too many people, when they qualify for these low standards, just stop and are satisfied.

I asked his opinion of my columns and he said to be truthful he enjoyed them but they are very provincial—all right for people who know me but no good in trying to introduce a new person. That is just what I felt all along, which means that until I establish my name through sheer writing ability, my column will not go. You keep comparing me to Eleanor Roosevelt, Billy Rose, etc.; well, they had the name to start with. In Moncton I also had the name to start with but I haven't anywhere else—yet! Anyway, if Mr. Clegg is willing to help me, I'm willing to stick to features until I find a way to stick my name under the noses of the people; then they'll swallow anything. You should see what some of the columnists here produce, absolute drivel, but they have the name!

I attend Caledonian dance classes with the Richmond "gang" here. We go every Wednesday night and before the big class, there is a class for beginners to learn the basic steps. Miss Buchanan is the instructress and we now know about 15 different Scottish reels and sets. You would like them—at least Daddy would—because it's all solo dancing although you do have a partner . . . but none of this close-up dancing like in a waltz. There are always eight or ten people in a set and you dance with them all during the one dance.

Friday, Feb. 3, 1950

It is raining today for the fourth day and much like spring. Yesterday I went up to town per usual, got caught without my umbrella in the rain, got completely soaked, almost ruined my black velvet hat, my red coat is still wet and looks rather woebegone, my shoes were soaking, my temper none too good, my hair straight as a ruler, and I was in a mood fit to bite anyone. However, despite everything I think I came out on top. I have a subject for a series of articles for the Montreal Standard, possibly a £5 story for our own Sunday Express gossip column, and a contact with the Daily Express syndication department that could really pay off.

Howard Clegg of the Montreal Standard gave me the press release material, pictures, etc. for a story that is to be done some time between now and 1951. There is a possibility there for a series of four or five articles to be spread over a period of time. Nothing has been promised but if I can turn in a series within the next couple of months or more worth printing, I may have a few hundred dollars paid into my pocket . . . Next I saw David Roberts of the syndication department, and they may accept a position as London bureau for a new Canadian weekly—to be run on similar lines to TIME magazine but more Canadian and British news—called Newsmirror. For goodness sake grab a copy when the first edition appears, which should be this or next week and let me see one. If this comes through, they will want a couple of feature writers to work on a commission and not to be tied into the office on full time, which would suit me to a tee . . . Then also this department handles London work for dozens of newspapers all throughout the Middle East, Far East, Australia, etc., and any stories I come across about people from those sectors would do fine. Then, of course, there is still the feature work with the Evening Standard (they have one story to be published already) and I'm first on the list for the London late night staff. Haven't heard anything more about that except that John Prebble isn't very keen on me accepting it, as he heard they work their staff like slaves with three or four assignments per night and they are usually tight. A darned hard life, but just the same, if I could stick it for a few months the experience and money would be worth it.

Sunday, Feb. 5, 1950, 2:05 p.m.

Still haven't a settled income over here but think I'm half safe for a while. Was talking to Mrs. Ince yesterday (Beaverbrook's London secretary) and she was asking how I liked it. Told her I wasn't being worked hard enough, and she quite agreed, then said, "You're staying on with us aren't you?" so that may be some help. Anyway the old boy returns from Bermuda next week and I'm not above yelling if I'm really stuck. Have yet to find out just how much the Evening Standard feature section will pay, and the syndication department, but that will take a lot of hard thinking to rake up stories, which may do me good.

Yesterday I was talking to John Prebble about furthering my writing knowledge and he has given me several books to read and suggestions to follow which should be of help. Believe he is my safest bet for help at the present time, and since he seems to be extremely interested in my well-being I'm going to take advantage of the chance. Certainly I know of no other person with the command of knowledge and the English language that John has.

By the way, I saw Michael Redgrave in "Hamlet" with my Egyptian friend Friday night, and afterward we had dinner at a fashionable Soho restaurant and arrived there at the same time as the Earl and Countess of Harewood with the Earl's brother Hon. Gerald Lascelles. The evening will make a rather good column along with the Egyptian's story too. After all, people must realize that journalists mix with all types of people in order to get the best experience and stories. He was very pleasant company but nothing spectacular—just the eyelashes.

Friday, Feb. 10, 1950, afternoon

Dear Mum,
Am tickled pink today for I have my first story—a feature on a woman named Jean Brown-Sanders—in the Evening Standard. Shall send a copy along to you. Now I've got to really plug and see how many more I can manage. Still don't know how much an article will bring me in, but Mr. Grune said they pay very well, so I've high hopes. If I could manage at least one a week and get about £5 for it and still keep my present job on the Sunday Express I'd be able to manage fine. Am just keeping my fingers crossed about the Sunday Express position, but there has been nothing about it stopping, and now that the Beaver is back in the country, I feel a little easier about it. He did ask to see me when he got back from America but I shan't be seeing him for quite some time yet—until after the election at least! [British general election on Feb. 23.]

You know, try as I might, I'm not very economical. Yesterday Chris had to look up some sheet music in Charing Cross Road, so we got that first, then looked for a place for lunch.

Came to Freddie Mills' Chinese restaurant and I stated I loved Chinese food. There was a sign that said lunch 3/6 (about 60 cents), so we decided to try it. I suggested we let the waiter bring us something and Chris agreed but he didn't mention the price. You can guess what happened! We had four lovely Chinese dishes and decided to wait and have coffee somewhere else and no sweet and it came to 10/9 ($2.00). We discovered each dish had been about 3/6 instead of that amount for the whole thing. We laughed our heads off when we got out and Chris said goodbye to the trousers he had been looking at in the window next door! It seems as though every time we get together we spend money without meaning to!

Must dash and get shoes from shoemaker—soles and heels again!

Love, Ouida

Wednesday, Feb 15, 1950, 6:45 p.m.

Dear Mum

Have been on the go all week. Monday I went out to meet Lady (Kenneth) Clark in Hampstead. Sir Kenneth is head of the National Gallery (art) and a director of Covent Garden. They have one of the most beautiful homes in Hampstead—a real museum filled with beautiful paintings and antiques.

Then saw the Evening Standard chap and gave him another feature I had cooked up. Was rather disappointed at the amount Grune said he'd pay for the Jean Brown–Sanders article but can't kick until I get a few more in, then watch me!!! Today I attended the Dickins and Jones fashion show. It was lovely but the suit I liked cost 72 guineas—about $300!!! Inquired at a shoemakers re having a last made—£20 per pair of shoes—about $80, so I'm starting doing the football pools in the hopes of winning money fast!!

[The British general election of 1950 was held on Feb. 23. In her column for the Moncton paper on Feb. 18, Ouida wrote about the issues of the election, even though politics were not often a subject of her columns and articles.]

IN BRITAIN TODAY by Ouida MacLellan

The British must be among the most politically conscious nations of the world—the subject dominates every conversation . . . My friends include several members of the three main parties, Socialist, Conservative, and Liberal—I don't think I know any Communists, but these days one never can be sure. I have listened to the arguments of each party, then used those arguments against others and found it fun.

Suddenly, my attitude changed. While I am not a politically minded person, chiefly I suppose because I was not old enough to vote before leaving Canada, when notification came that I have a vote in next Thursday's elections, I at once began to seriously consider the problems facing all voters.

My problem is that I see good and bad in every party and it is going to be difficult to choose. From the Socialists I get free dental and medical care; then someone will tell you that the Conservatives first thought of this national health scheme. A third person tells you the Conservatives had plenty of time to bring it in between 1932 and 1939. Then another vote-seeker tells about the French, who get free teeth in England and sell them in France, or of the Canadians who spend only $89.00 on their boat fare and then receive $250 operations free in Britain.

There is much discussion of the Socialists' plan of nationalization [of industries], which the Conservatives claim is being carried out at the expense of another country—America. On the other hand, the Conservatives are holding out a bribe in a promise of lower taxes.

Political columnists are having a free-for-all with the demerits of all parties coming to light. Mr. Churchill is making his usual flowery, yet pungent speeches. Anyone listening to this great wartime leader would be convinced that Winston Churchill is not only concerned with getting the Conservatives back to power, but that he again has a great job to do, that of bringing Britain back to a happier state. There is a Brighton candidate who is making a house-to-house canvass with the help of his actress wife. And J. B. Priestley, the noted author, while claiming, "I am not a politician at all, I don't even belong to any party," goes on to say, "I have a very clear recollection of Britain in the twenties and thirties and I beg my young listeners not to believe fairy tales about it. The country we have now is worth ten of it."

One important question is the state school versus the public school. In the state schools, children, chiefly of the working class families, are in together and educated free. At the public schools, the parents pay for their children's education and feel the child receives more personal attention . . . Many of these public schools are boarding schools where sports are prominent, fair play emphasized, and the child's life carefully disciplined. Somehow you can always tell a public school boy, no matter what his form of dress: it is his manner that shows.

This school question brings out the class distinction in England. The people may be slow to admit this, but that is the reason the middle and upper classes are fighting to keep their public schools and their traditions. What father has had, the son will have at any cost, for at these schools the boys meet boys of their own class. One can readily see it will take ages before all classes will be able to mix comfortably, if ever.

The newspapers are running every conceivable type of contest, such as matching present-day pictures of prominent politicians with a set of baby pictures; questionnaires asking readers to fill in their choice of cabinet members, and prizes for the best slogans for parties. This last week should be most interesting, exciting and packed full of history-making events.

[The election resulted in Labour's receiving a slim majority of just five seats over all other parties. Clement Attlee, the Labour prime minister, called another general election eighteen months later, in 1951. Despite losing the popular vote, the Conservatives won the most seats and they, along with the National Liberal party, formed a government under Winston Churchill.]

[There are no more letters until April. Ouida got the job on the *Evening Standard* working from 4 p.m. to 2 a.m. for a daily column called "In London Last Night."]

"URGENTLY WANTED AT THE SAVOY BY THE BEAVER"
April–July 1950

Thursday, April 13, 1950

Dear Mum,

Yesterday was one of those hectic days which nearly drive one out of mind before the finish. It started off with a friend and me having a Turkish bath at the Dorchester. That was fine (next we have a straight massage, which should make a column). Had a bite to eat, then off to my first assignment, which was a cocktail party for models and agents. I felt like a tramp in a room full of beautiful women until a chap came over and asked me what page of the new model directory I was on!

Met three very interesting people. No. 1 was a photographer named Robert Greene, who used to be with Vogue and is now a big shot over here. He insists we've met before and has invited me to his studio (in the afternoon, don't worry) to let me watch him working, which should make a good yarn. No. 2 was Peter Duncan, who is a pretty big shot in the BBC and best noted for his "In Town Tonight" programs on Saturday evenings. He asked if I would be interested in going on the program but am sure he must have been kidding, so we'll let that pass. Nice guy, however. No. 3 was Hollywood's famous Ava Gardner, whom I found to be very, very nice as well as a beautiful woman. Her North Carolinian accent was quite sweet and she very pleasant. Met slews of others, but those were the pick of the cocktail party.

Assignment No. 2 was a hunt ball at the 21 Room—one of Princess Margaret's favourite nightclubs. When I went there I found I HAD to be formal and since I was without a dress, that fixed that. Had been warned that the manager was a bit tough to handle and had been complaining to the Standard, but believe it or not, he even hired a car to bring me to Kew and back to change and insisted I be made an honorary member of the club. The evening was pretty grim, however, for without an escort it's not fun, and with one, work would be difficult. Started off by having actor Peter Lawford buy me a Coke—he was the sweetest guy I met all evening. After that came Sharman Douglas [socialite daughter of the American ambassador] who was quite curt, the Duke of Marlborough, who was very pleasant, and more lords, ladies, dukes, etc. etc. than one could ever find space to mention. It was fun seeing them all, but I still don't particularly care for that type of person.

Didn't get home until after four and as a result slept until 12 then had to cancel lunch with Chris.

Friday, April 21, 1950

Dear Mum,
Sorry about the slow letters. Dad said he thought you were getting a bit jumpy about them but said he understands that I must be more occupied. Really, he was quite sweet in the way he put it. Oh, yes, about the box of Easter gifts, I found a perfectly darling little frock I want for Joanie the other day and ordered one in a red rather than the yellow. It's so very dainty and sweet and summery that she should look adorable in it. Hope you think so too when it arrives, which will be a little while yet as it won't be ready until about a fortnight. Anyway, what I mean is that, if you don't mind, I'd rather like to just pick up things I like and send them as presents when I feel like it rather than have to get any old thing for an appointed time, like Easter. What do you think? By the way there are dozens of sweet little frocks over here with smocking bodices and puffed sleeves. Can Joanie wear those? About Marion, I'm quite undecided. [Joanie and Marion were her sisters, aged eight and sixteen.] Would like to send her something big like a dress, but don't know what she prefers. Is there anything you can suggest that she'd like? Also Daddy, what does he want? English shirts with stiff detached collars?? Ha!

Jobs this week have included another Paris fashion show at Ciro's, where I spent some time chatting with Bonar Colleano, an American actor who is playing the lead in "Streetcar Named Desire" [The Marlon Brando role of Stanley]. Tuesday I had a mayor's party in Hackney, a Philippine party at the Dorchester, Wednesday a dowsers' meeting (water diviners), and two dinner dances—one with the Anglo-American Friendship, where I had a meal. Then last night I had a party at the Savoy and another at the Grosvenor House and dropped into one at the Dorchester. Tonight is the last for this week, thank goodness, and I'm supposed to be going to a concert at the Albert Hall with the gang here in Richmond but may try to get out of it. Have to dash up to town now and see an Egyptian parliamentary delegation.

Love, Ouida

Wednesday, April 26, 1950, evening

Dear Mum,
Your Sunday letter came this morning—or at least I grabbed it from the postman as I dashed to the station. Where, may I ask, did this silly idea that I am leaving the Express come from? I'm doing both jobs, working 6 days per week. As the Evening Standard hours are 4 p.m. to midnight or later, I can still do the hotels on Thursday and work during the

day on Saturday at the Express. After all, I wasn't going to throw away the 7 guineas per week ($21) from the Express for nothing. And Chris is not the main attraction for me on the Sunday paper; John Prebble is, and I wouldn't pass up seeing him for anything, I learn too much from him.

Friday, April 28, 1950, morning

Tuesday night while I was waiting for the train home, a young, dark-haired, nice-looking chap grinned at me and said, "Boy, this is sure red flannel underwear weather isn't it!" I couldn't help but laugh and agree. He turned sharply and asked if I was a Canadian, and it turned out he is an Australian, trained in Edmonton in the RAAF during the war and now works for the Australian news agency next door to the Canadian Press office here.

When my train came in I headed for the nearest coach, when he suddenly said "Do you smoke?" I answered no, so he suggested we take a non-smoker, as he hates smoke—which we did. He travelled to Turnham Green station and I learned that his folks are still in Australia, his sister in South Africa, and he wants to go to New York. He has a flat in Chiswick and said he's the world's worst cook, has a car—he was on the train that night because it was in the garage . . . As he got out he said he'd like to see me again and maybe he could give me a lift home next night if I was around. I said maybe and that was that.

Last night as I returned to the office about 10 p.m. there was a message for me to phone Mr. Foley of Australian Associated Newspapers . . . A voice on the other end said he had a story for me. "A young man had been walking along the station platform two nights previous when he was suddenly smitten. He suddenly laid eyes on a very lovely young girl in a red flannel nightshirt. Police are not investigating but it was rumoured that a naked little boy carrying bow and arrow was seen in the vicinity and the young man was wounded by the arrow in the heart."

Well, I must admit it is a most original approach and I couldn't help but howl with laughter . . . I could use a new male right now too, as Chris and I seem to be heading for the rocks. Several things he's said and done lately have annoyed me; he says I'm sensitive, and I claim it's crudeness on his part or something. Probably it's just me making mountains out of molehills again, I don't know, or maybe I'm just tired of it all. They always say a change is as good as a rest, don't they?

Tuesday, May 2, 1950, 1.15 p.m.

Dear Mum,
Have just come in from a shopping excursion in Richmond with Mrs. Bennett and got a great kick out of your Saturday letter mentioning Marion's demands, as I had just fulfilled them. For goodness sake don't scold her, as that's what I want her to do . . . She's dead right about me making some money and since I'm not permitted to send any out of the

country, getting things you want is the best I can do. Want very much to get you something for summer, either a new coat or a dress, but will have to know what you'd like first, please. As for Daddy, I'm stumped, so for heaven's sake make some suggestions. Don't worry about my banking, because I'm doing that too, but this is the first time I've ever been well enough off to be able to get you what you'd like, so help me out . . . This afternoon I'm going to Bond street to get the little summer frock I ordered a fortnight ago for Joanie. It's a sweet thing and should look very good. You can either tell them about these things or leave them as a surprise—maybe the latter would be more fun.

You can't imagine the thrill I get out of being able to get something for Marion. Have been worried for some time now, as we're both at the age when I should be a help rather than thousands of miles away. A big sister is supposed to be a useful creature in the way of extra pocket money and the loan of clothes, and here I am quite useless.

Another thing I have been thinking of, what would you say about Marion coming over for her holidays, probably next summer. Don't know if I can pay the passage both ways from here or not but if I can't, you could pay her way over out of my earnings on that side. Don't think I could manage this summer, but thought she might like it before going to college or before her last year in high school.

Tuesday, May 16, 1950, morning

Last Thursday I found out at the Sunday Express office that the staff were being entertained at tea by the Beaver. Thought that might be a good way of seeing him again. Then thought it over so just phoned Mrs. Ince his secretary and said, "He said he wanted see me again when he came back this spring; is he still interested?" She said he was terribly busy but she would mention it and let me know.

Yesterday I got into the office about four per usual and just as they were about to hand out the assignments, the phone rang for me and she said the Beaver wanted me at Arlington House at 5 p.m. I had to run without my assignments and got there in time. He was sitting out on his roof verandah, which overlooks Green Park. He asked me how I was getting on. I told him about Robertson having nothing to offer so I got my own job, and he thought that was great and laughed like mad. Then he asked how much I was getting and if I minded it being known, so I said "NO." At which he picks up his phone and dictates a letter to someone for the editor of the St. John's Telegraph Journal—Truman I think the name was. Anyway, he said here was a success story for him but the source was to remain anonymous and gave the details including the $5 per week from the Moncton Times. He also told them to get a picture, as he thought I was quite beautiful and if St. John's hadn't got one then get one from Moncton. I nearly passed out and bet Grainger will too if it goes in. At first I thought it might be a dirty trick, but then I've been told over and over again that I'm a darned fool to write for only $5 a week so maybe it will do some good, and besides, I'm not the one sending in the story.

I was with him about an hour and a half and he had me go through some Evening Standards and show him what stories I had written. Oh yes, I told him you were trying mental telepathy on him to bring me home for a visit—just so he'd know what it was in case your sending apparatus is weak. He howled with laughter and thought that was a really good one. Just before I left he gave me a piece to rewrite in my own hand and submit it to the Diary. He's just like a kid and loves to fox his own papers every so often. Anyway, he still remembers me, so that's something.

Friday, May 19, 1950

Seem to be getting into some terrible stews right now. Wednesday was terrific. Beaverbrook gave a cocktail party for the Sunday Express and the Evening Standard to which I was not invited, just the big guns. Think I told you that on Monday he had given me a story to write out in my own handwriting and hand in to the Standard Diary, which I did. I was not to reveal the source of my information.

Anyway, shortly after the guests arrived at the party, the Beaver asked Gunn where I was and where my story was. Gunn had never heard of the story of course because I had given it direct to the Diary editor. While I was thoroughly enjoying a meal with the kids in a little restaurant, about four people were frantically phoning all over London for me. When I reached Claridge's at 6 p.m. to meet Irene Dunne for an interview, the reception clerk sounded as though a murder had been committed and told me I was urgently wanted at the Savoy Hotel by the Beaver.

Off I dashed in a taxi and on arrival discovered most of the people standing over by the food table while in the window sat the Beaver with Gunn, and most of the editors. I was rushed to the window group. Gunn nearly fell on the floor jumping up to offer me his seat and the Old Man chuckled and asked how I was. He then asked about the story and I told him it wasn't new enough, as the Diary editor had told me the previous day—but they were glad to have the statistics and would keep them for further reference. He smiled and looked at the Diary guy and said "That's a good story" to which Jenkins answered "Yes Sir" and it was in the next day. The Beaver then told Gunn to get me a drink, asked me what I liked, and then shouted "Get her a lime juice" after Gunn. I followed him to the table and he was all honey and cream then rushed me over to talk to Max Aitken and Bill, the son and nephew. Bill was born in Antigonish [Nova Scotia], by the way. I talked to them a bit—Gunn had excused himself—and spoke to John Prebble and a couple of the

Sunday boys, then returned to the Beaver—everyone else was standing around waiting for him to call them over—said I had to dash, he gave me a message for Irene Dunne, and I left, Gunn shaking hands with me as I went, and I said goodbye to Max and Bill. Prebble was laughing when he came over to me saying that a movie star couldn't have made a better entrance. Anyway, the whole affair will either do me a lot of good or a lot of harm, and I'm hoping for the former.

Had lunch with Bob Greene [photographer] yesterday instead of Chris and he has invited me up to his place one evening for a feed of Aunt Jemima pancakes and Log Cabin corn syrup. Don't know if I'll ever get the chance to go but it sounds good . . . He has mentioned a photo of me but I'm not pressing, as I'd hate the guy to think that was why I gave him a write-up. He's rather interesting, has studied ballet and speaks perfect French.

Monday, May 23, 1950, 11:10 p.m.

By the way, Chris and I have come to a parting of the ways and the only feeling I seem to have is one of relief, so guess it's good. We're still good friends of course, but doubt if I shall be seeing much of him from now on. Have a couple of new prospects in the offing, so it won't be dull—not that working six days a week could be anyway.

Friday, May 26, 1950

Don't worry about Bob Greene. I'm quite aware of how men can behave and would never take any chance. Give me a bit of credit for some sense. Larry Foley [the Australian] took me up to his flat that Sunday we were out. We had tea there and after the concert he cooked scrambled eggs on toast for me and couldn't have been sweeter. Claims he's going to feed me up and put some flesh on me, but haven't seen him since, so guess I'll have to stay thin.

Tuesday, June 6, 1950

Dear Mum,
That crazy old MacLellan luck is still hanging on and somehow it scares me skinny. Last night, the night before the big heavyweight championship, every morning and evening paper in London was looking for Bruce Woodcock and Lee Savold [English and American fighters in a championship match]. I was given the Woodcock story and went tripping off to the theatre he was supposed to attend, like all the others. He didn't turn up, so with the Evening News chap (we travel together a lot as our assignments usually coincide)

we went to his hotel. No dice there either, so I sauntered out a side door near the stairs to chat to the doorman, and darned if I didn't run smack into Woodcock. He slipped in the door and up the stairs before a soul noticed him so I dashed up after, caught up with his younger brother, found out where they'd been, etc. and got my story. Bruce himself wasn't in a talking mood, but by watching his movement you could easily sense his feeling of tenseness. He stopped only once on his way to his room and that was to look at me and wonder who the devil I was. Now, have just finished reading the morning papers and none of them say where he went, so here's hoping I'm sitting pretty. The News chap—he tried to follow me when I dashed up the stairs but took a wrong turning—bribed the elevator man, got the room number, and spoke to one of the brothers, but no one else actually saw Woodcock or could describe his movements as I did. It took a couple of seconds to sink in who he was, as I've only seen pictures, but no other human in the vicinity would have such a powerful frame and battered face. [He was virtually blind in his left eye.]

Beaverbrook has taken a terrific interest in Chris, says he is the most promising young man he's had for ages. He's working him hard but it should pay off big dividends eventually.

Rather startled the office gang on Friday by going to a party at the Gargoyle Club [haunt of artists such as Francis Bacon and Lucien Freud] and coming back with Bonar Colleano—male lead opposite Vivien Leigh in "Streetcar." He's tall, dark with a Latin-American mug although he's Irish, is 26 and good fun as well as a good dancer. He has a beautiful pre-war Buick and is good company . . . When he asked if I'd phone him this week, I replied "no, it's unethical." Bonar complained that we were both in rather unethical businesses but could he call me then? I don't expect to hear from him, but it might be fun if I did—I love good dancers.

Friday, June 9, 1950, afternoon

Well, my luck can't always last so I've had some let-downs this week. First of all, my scoop of Bruce Woodcock didn't make the grade. Despite the fact I was the only reporter to find him on the night before his fight, the sub-editor on our column spiked it. Next day when I inquired, Mr. Hyde was slightly angry and asked for an explanation, then went out and forgot about it, and a second editor handed me the morning Express saying "No, he (Woodcock) wasn't out, the Express said he stayed in his room." In other words, I was a liar and the Express is written by God despite the fact that careful reading of the Express story showed they had not seen Woodcock. Anyway, he lost Tuesday—I saw the fight, by the way—so that's that, although it's pretty disheartening. [The fight was stopped because of Woodcock's cut eye after the fourth round.]

Wednesday night I got another scoop when I accidently walked into Grosvenor House and met the King and Queen slipping in for a quiet pre-opening look at the Antique Dealers Fair. This did make the paper—no other paper had it, and from what I've heard, the morning papers were pretty sore—but all I got was a "Lucky break" comment from one reporter and not a word from Hyde or anyone else.

Poor Chris is having a terrible life. The Beaver is working him madly and driving him just as mad. Yesterday he wrote five articles on his own, three under the direction of Max (B's son). The Old Man said the ones Chris had written on his own were great, but that the others (written under Max's direction) stunk. Max sat there not saying a word in his defence, so Chris is pretty wild. The Beaver leaves for Canada next week, so what will happen to Chris then no one knows. Anyway, we've taken turns pouring our troubles out to each other and when one phones the other it's just sort of a case of who starts yelling first—we take it in turns with no preference for sex. When Chris isn't around, John Prebble bears the brunt of my attacks and does it beautifully—only trouble is I think Chris also shoots off at John, who therefore is nursing us both.

Today is very nice—have been sweltering for a week now—and maybe tonight I'll meet a handsome prince on a white horse who will carry me off to the Never Never land—I hope. If I don't, then I shall continue to keep an eye open for him tomorrow and the next day, you never can tell when the guy is liable to turn up. And if he doesn't turn up? Then I shall probably enter a convent and shock all the good sisters by telling them the facts about the hard cruel world.

Love,

Ima Nut

Monday, June 12, 1950

When the Beaver hits Fredericton he will have in his company a young man named Dobson who would like very much to spend a weekend or a few days enjoying true MacLellan hospitality, about which I've bragged. Chris phoned me as soon as he got back from Leatherhead yesterday and he's terrifically excited. The Beaver only asked him yesterday and they sail on Friday, which is pretty quick. They'll be away about two months and if Chris doesn't muff this—and I'm pretty sure he won't—he's made. He'll probably try for a weekend with you and you'll love him, I'm sure. He's heard a lot about you and he's the type Daddy will really enjoy. There is just one thing, he isn't mine. Another girl, Kate, seems to be ahead in the running at the present minute, but I don't think his mind is made up yet and although mine isn't either, I don't think I'd mind in the least having him around for a long time, so do your best.

Friday, June 16, 1950, 2 p.m.

Well, the ball at Cambridge with David Ross has been and gone, Chris has gone, and I don't know whether I'm coming or going . . . The ball was wonderful and despite the fact I didn't see a bed until 8:30 a.m., I felt quite all right and was rather pleased about my durability. It rained torrents from about 3 a.m. onwards, which rather dampened things a bit but the event was most enjoyable. We spent most of the time with Mac Hayward, secretary of the Cambridge ski club, and his partner Sheena MacIntosh, who is Britain's No. 1 girl skier . . . David was a good escort and I've gotten to know quite a few of the kids up there now.

Caught the 11:05 down from Cambridge yesterday and had lunch with Chris then went with him to the bank for his currency . . . I don't imagine this trip is going to be any picnic, as the Beaver will probably work him like a slave. By the time he's reached you he ought to know pretty well whether he is being successful or not. It's a make or break proposition I should say, and John Prebble—who usually looks on the gloomier side—says his chances are about 50/50. If he stands up to it all right, he'll be a pretty big guy when he gets back. That's another thing: John says that I can say goodbye to Chris, as he'll have no time for the companionship we've enjoyed this past year, no Thursday lunches, etc., so I might as well get used to it. See what you think: if John is right you can tell me and I shall plan on buying my own lunch on Thursday hereafter.

Monday, June 19, 1950, 1:20 p.m.

Just one thing—don't ask Chris if his intentions are honorable because I'm quite sure he hasn't any at all, and if he has, isn't aware of it or maybe wouldn't even know what honorable intentions are. He's a true male and may try to give the impression that we're very thick, but don't let him fool you, as he's seeing Kate very regularly indeed and possibly getting rather serious with her—although he yells like a steer when I mention it. He bullies me terribly and acts as though he is the lord almighty as far as I'm concerned, but I rather enjoy being bullied and it probably does me good so I never let on that if I don't want to listen I just don't!

He has often joked about marriage with me and laughing said, "Well, a chance to work on the parents first," the day he left, but he's never serious . . .

Am going this afternoon to see what the Plan Travel people have to offer for the first two weeks of my holiday in August . . . Will plan on Paris for my third week sometime in the fall I think—unless Chris insists on Cornwall, but then he says we must be married if we go and I couldn't afford a wedding gown right now. Besides, every time I agree, he gets scared, and another thing, he may snore and I couldn't stand a man who snores. He claims he doesn't but I have no proof.

Monday, June 26, 1950, morning

One chap at the tennis club that I have had my eye on turned up at the club dance for the first time this year. His name is Tony Cheatham—ask Chris if he knows him, as I think they are in the same regiment. Tony was a POW for five years, is a teacher at St. Paul's School (very famous old public school in London) and is tall, blond, and interesting looking. Although we have never been formally introduced he is now at the stage of saying "Hello" when he comes down, and his pals—one of them anyway—have started chatting to me. Never can tell what comes next!!

Wednesday, June 28, 1950

Tomorrow is Thursday again—used to be my regular lunch with Chris—but I'm not stuck for dates while Chris is away. Last week I dined with the photographer friend of mine Bob Greene. Am supposed to be going to a cocktail party and photographic display of his tonight, and meeting the Australian Larry Foley also, as well as my regular assignment, so shall be rather busy.

Larry is just back after a couple of weeks in Sweden, so should have some good pointers to pass on for when I go there on holiday—not the kind my mother would give me—as he puts it. He's a terrific tease and is always riding me about being a character with "virginal airs" but I couldn't care less and he's good company and has a car and lives out my way, which is useful when he's on nights too. Besides his bark is much worse than his bite and he's never so much as laid a finger on me so far—hasn't even tried to hold my hand, just feeds me on scrambled eggs and complains about my slimness, which Chris will probably do too as he claims I'm getting too slim, but don't worry, I'm just getting in shape for the fall fashion season in case they want a new wasp-waisted mannequin for the Paris collections.

Monday, July 10, 1950, morning

A letter arrived from Chris in the second post Saturday along with your Wednesday letter and it was really funny noting the things each of you remembered . . . Chris seemed a little upset to think I was taking my holidays as he said he has two weeks coming and would have come to Sweden with me, as Sweden has not the same ties as Cornwall has. He's dead right; the Swedes are noted for having no morals at all!! . . . I've already had an offer of a guide in Tony Cheatham, a fellow officer in Chris's regiment whom I really got to know last Saturday night.

At the tennis club dance on Saturday my timing was superb, couldn't have done better had I worked at it! All three irons in the fire burned freely. First was David Ross, whom I hadn't seen for a fortnight and had the first and last dance with him, which kept him quite contented. Another guy, Gordon Porteous, asked me, just after his arrival at the dance, to go to the gliding club with him yesterday, which meant he was secure, then in walked Tony Cheatam or maybe it's Cheatham, I don't know. He was more difficult, but a friend who was with Tony asked me for a dance, then offered me a drink after, which took us to the bar where Tony was standing. Conversation opened when a dancing couple bumped me and I stumbled backwards into some very ready arms which happened to belong to Tony. Then the fact that he is a fellow officer of Chris's started things nicely. Discovered he already knew my name, and correctly at that, so from then off things ran smoothly. He is an Oxford grad, majored in languages, teaches languages at St. Paul's School, his father is a bigwig in the Ministry of Transport, and Tony usually spends his summer meandering around the continent, often on freight boats (says stoking is the only thing he really does well). Anyway he speaks perfect French, has offered to show me Paris if I can make it by mid-September. He is tall, blond, rather good-looking, slightly nervous in habits, nice voice, and strangely enough was almost a Beaverbrook protégé, only he turned the offer of a job down in preference to teaching.

Anyway, if I can't make it, Bob Greene is going again to Paris in November for the collections and he is also good company. Am having lunch again with Bob again this Thursday and he is a perfect sweetie.

The gliding club with Gordon Porteous—we had a grand day out, made the trip down by motorcycle, will make a good column.

Wednesday, July 26, 1950

Life seems to be just a little crazy these days. Seeing rather a lot of Tony—every day, to be exact, and he's at the stage now where he picks me up right from work. At first I was rather indifferent but am completely puzzled now. Never planned this and I usually plan everything myself . . . I'm frantically trying to keep my head above water . . . Tony talks sort of in long-range terms and I find myself wanting to swallow it hook, line, and sinker.

Thursday [added the next day]

In a different mood today after a swift kick in the stern last night from a pal of Tony's, so disregard the above. Will keep it strictly for laughs, so don't fret about me going overboard again.

Chris is due to dock tonight.

Friday [added]

Met Tony and we had a bit of tea then met John Prebble. He stayed an hour and a half with us. It was a great feeling hearing them discuss so many things, books, authors, views, personalities, etc., on such common grounds. They seem to share many views.

Then we walked a bit along the embankment and home. Tony shined my shoes and I ironed, then we made coffee, listened to the radio, and made tea when Mrs. Bennett came in, and Tony left about 11 p.m.

Saturday, July 29, 1950, morning

The very last thing I wanted to happen did—the office sent me to meet the QE boat train and of course I bumped into Chris first thing. He planted one on me to the amusement of the other reporter with me, and me too. He's all hot and bothered about something. I don't know what, but right off the bat he wanted to know how Tony was, then asked if I was getting seriously entangled with anyone over here. It seems he's in love with Canada and could be with a certain Canadian too. What the devil did you do to him??

Love, Ouida

"I WANT TO SAY YES"
August–December 1950

Early August [undated, on stationery of Hotel Cosmopolite, Copenhagen]

I'm no woman of the world, Mum, and there's no problem about all the men. Larry's out, (neither of us very keen), David's off to Italy (I hope) and never did count anyway, Tony's a pet and "rambunctious," as you call it, at the moment but he'll probably cool off, and I've known Chris too long for you to worry. Tony and Chris are the only eminent prospects and I don't feel I want anyone for keeps so it's up to one of them to convince me I do. This ought to be fun!

Early August [undated, from the Hotel Cosmopolite, Copenhagen]

Tony will be away for 8 weeks on a boat jaunt and I'm so fickle and forget so easily. Had a short note from Chris on Saturday, he has been transferred from the Sunday to the Daily Express so don't know how much I shall see of him now. He has the one day off—Saturday—and I'm going back on nights. By the way, you might like to know John Prebble said he thought Tony's a very fine chap but an unhappy one who I couldn't pin down. I'm not worried about pinning anyone, it would have to be vice-versa to work. John's a bit jealous of anyone else around anyway (not sure that's the word); he just has a protective brother air.

August 5 [from Copenhagen]

Had my second letter from Tony today. He sounds as though he were really keen, but it's still going in one ear and out the other—giving me a kick en route, I might add. It's not every day I have handsome young men of 30—he's still the rage at the tennis club, nice legs, I hear—writing to say he misses me a lot when I've only been away a week.

[After her return from holiday, Ouida had bad news from home. She had two sisters, Marion, seven years younger, and Joanie, only seven years old when Ouida went to England. Joanie was born with Down syndrome. She was doted on by her parents. They had found a place for her in a special school in New York. The night before she was due to go there, she died in her sleep in her parents' bed. Ouida was told by telegram and phoned by her father. She wrote the following letters to them.]

Saturday, August 20, 1950, afternoon

Dear Mum,

Am about three days late with this as I promised to write on Wednesday, but, silly as it may sound, I couldn't think of what to say. Just can't believe that Joanie is gone somehow. Here I am miles away without seeing her for 18 months and the fact that there is a hole in the family on that side just doesn't seem to register.

Have tried to be very practical about it all and guess in the long run the Lord has been pretty good to us. He let us have her for eight long years while she was both healthy and happy, then took her suddenly without suffering. He prevented you from losing her while she was alone at school miles away or on a train en route and, being a bit callous I guess, before you undertook an expense that might have meant hardships for the rest of your life. Yes, Mum, we've been mighty lucky, for we might never have had her at all.

So well I remember the night she was ill when just a baby. I came out of my room to find Daddy sitting in the rocker with Joanie who was vomiting every few minutes, and you were running back and forth and calling the doctor in between. I only remember one thing you said but have never forgotten it. You told me that night, Mum, that you were afraid we were not going to be allowed to keep Joanie.

Well, we did, and for eight long, wonderful years, so maybe we've come out on the long end of the bargain, which was put into words so early on that trip to the special doctors in Montreal. We've always wondered how and when it would come, and whether she would be healthy until the end or gradually grow weaker until she became a complete invalid. God's been good to Joanie and us, Mum.

Only wish I could have seen her again or have been with you when it happened. She must have figured I was a pretty poor godmother walking off for such a long time like that, but I hope not. I wondered when I left if I would ever see Joanie again and somehow had a feeling that perhaps I wouldn't. Maybe that's why I wasn't too surprised when I saw the telegram, for I knew what it was before I opened it. It's like Beth in "Little Women," there's a great empty space left here, but there's no doubt about where Joanie is and she's bound to be happy because they're bound to love her as much up there as we did down here. They just couldn't help it. Ouida

Thursday, August 25, 1950, evening

Dear Daddy,
Your Sunday letter came today and I have just finished reading it after coming in from work . . .

It left me in tears for about the sixth time inside of a week. Every letter I've had about Joanie has done the same as did the original telegram before then. So you see, Dad, I really do have a heart somewhere.

What hurt most though was being told of our lack of affection. You must realize how terribly fond I am of both you and Mum. Sorry if I've never shown it, but somehow I never thought you'd like us to be gooey in public. Although I don't know if the knowledge would have improved me any, for I don't seem to be the affectionate type. Sorry.

I fully realize what you mean about Joanie, though, for I, too, loved that sweet, gentle, affectionate manner she possessed. I quite agree, it does make one feel good to know you are loved—only wish I had realized it sooner.

How well I understand your loss, Daddy, for you've devoted every minute to making her life a happy one—and you succeeded. She lived a normal, healthy, happy life the whole eight years, then left us while in that state and quickly without pain. God was good to you, Daddy, he let you be with her at home when she went. I wish he had done the same for me.

To not see her again is one reality I find hard to face, and selfish as it may sound, I'm rather glad I'm not returning home right yet. Guess I'm a coward but I'll need the time to steel me for the day when I must face the gap . . .

Do keep your Sunday letters coming, as I so look forward to them.

All my love

Ouida

Monday, August 28, 1950, evening

Dear Mum. Believe it or not, this is the first time I have used the typewriter since returning from holiday. Just haven't felt in the mood, I guess, and really don't much tonight, as I've had a dull, thudding headache all day long . . .

Funny you should think the picture of Tony makes him look bitter, guess it is his mouth and the way his chin juts out. John Prebble got the same impression, that Tony is an unhappy man but I rather think it is because he is still not completely settled and is very restless in his movements . . . He's often fidgeting and is rather nervous-appearing and quick-spoken when he first meets people, but as time wears on, he calms down and stops his ranting about.

It's his age that worries me too. I quite realize I can't play around if he's going to get serious intentions but so far I haven't taken anything he says seriously at all . . . He struck me at first as the Errol Flynn or playboy type . . . Now after seeing a fair amount of him and hearing him talk in long-term policies—says he's become very fond of me etc.—I still can't bring myself to believe him, for after all, when a guy has as much to offer as Tony has, why on earth should he pick on a cluck like me?

As for me, I haven't a clue as to how I feel. Am seeing a lot of Chris but don't get the same thrill out of having him around as I used to and I'm terribly afraid I'm hurting him by it . . . Tony's letters haven't been as frequent as I thought they might have been—only two and a card since he left a fortnight ago now . . . Anyway, I've still got three weeks before he returns so I'll probably be completely browned off by then and more than likely so will he . . . I'm still not anywhere near the settling down stage, and yet here is 23 staring me in the face this Friday.

Chris is taking a pretty bad beating. He jumps to my every request, goes out of his way to do and get things for me, tries very hard to act the boss, yet he knows I don't pay a particle of attention, and he's pretty afraid of Tony . . . I don't want to hurt him but somehow I just seem to keep right on saying the wrong things. Every now and then I catch one of those "scolded dog" looks in his eyes and I feel like a heel, but it doesn't stop me from kicking a guy when he's down. Ain't I a stinker!!! Chris is young, he'll get over it, or maybe I'll change my mind again in his favour, you never can tell with me—even I can't.

Sunday, Sept. 3, 1950, evening

Felt rather funny this evening, as I've been with Chris all day and we got onto some pretty heavy nattering this afternoon. Both tired out, we just sat and talked about anything and everything and ended up on the subject of marriage. Chris laughingly decided that Ouida Dobson sounded quite all right but I had no remarks to make and let his comment slide by without notice. Still hope he is just joking but don't know.

Funnier still are my own feelings tonight. I seem rather resigned to Chris. We get on well, I like him, and I almost feel as though I had been playing for too big stakes with Tony anyway and was perhaps over my depth. Maybe it's just because I'm tired but seeing or talking to Chris every day is bound to have some effect sometime I guess . . . I seem to keep meeting all his relatives and find I'm already known about anyway. But baldness runs in Chris's family, and I hate baldness. Life, bah! Oh for an assignment in Korea.

Thursday, Sept. 14, 1950, evening

Chris has asked me to marry him and despite my talking about it, I couldn't be more stunned. Never really thought he would, I guess, and since I'm still not ready to settle down, it's a bit of a jolt. He's being terribly sweet, quite realizes my quandary etc. and is perfectly willing to wait until I do decide to settle down and make up my mind. His being so patient almost makes it even harder.

Then to top everything off, Tony arrived back today, a day earlier than I expected him, and came to find me before even going home. He seemed terribly glad to see me and despite my reserved welcome, it's nice to see him again too. Now I don't know where I stand . . . I can't go on playing with both if they are playing for keeps. Guess I'm a coward, for I sure hate to admit that I'm grown up and must face the future sooner or later.

Somehow I rather thought love was something that came in a rush, and suddenly big lights go on . . . I'm very aware that Chris is an exceptionally nice guy, one I get on with so well, he'd make a wonderful husband and good father but still I keep hoping that somehow a decision will be made for me and I'll just wake up to the result. Am so afraid I'm going to hurt someone—probably me.

Saturday, Sept, 16, 1950, 5 p.m.

Suppose you're flapping like mad after my last letter and I was too at first, but now find that I'm calming down and honestly think everything will work itself out. Thought at first I'd feel self-conscious with Chris around and would hate him for admitting his feelings, but I've suddenly discovered I'm rather pleased, very flattered, and feel sort of good all over. He's so terribly sweet, not pushy in the least but just sort of patient and understanding . . . Not that you need to be told, Mum, but it's rather a grand feeling to know someone really cares and that someone is a person I too care for. You are probably wondering about Tony—so was I for a while, but now he is back I have found I'm not as interested as I thought I was. Somehow, although he's very nice, I don't feel so at home and that first excitable attraction I felt has worn off and I'd rather he didn't take my hand or touch me or anything now . . . It's pleasant just to hear Chris's voice on the phone and now that I know how he feels I don't have to worry about whether I'm beginning to care and whether or not I'll show it by saying or doing such and such. It's a grand feeling. I can say just what I like and know Chris won't be shocked or annoyed or take it the wrong way, and if he does, he'll ask me what I mean.

Tuesday, Sept. 19, 1950, morning

Don't you start any of that "Chris should do something for you in your work" line. The Old Man is rather tricky and now that he is getting older must be handled with care. We're going to be very lucky if Chris gets a solid future settled for himself before the Old Man loses interest or dies. Right now Chris is nothing, just being trained as a sub on the Express and doing the political column as a fill-in. BUT if the Old Man's interest is maintained until he is thoroughly trained he could easily end up in one of the big executive positions with a mighty golden outlook. It's sort of touch and go now as to who is going to get fed up first, Chris or the Old Man, as the latter can be a pretty exasperating person to associate with and pretty "I Like Me" in his views and ideas.

Friday, Sept. 22, 1950, evening

I've told Chris that I'm just not ready to think about anyone and he might ask me again in two years if he's still interested—he says he will be—and he also insists that Tony is in the same state. He'll get the same answer if he's silly enough to try to tab me now . . . I don't want to flit around from guy to guy, but I also don't want to be pinned down to anyone just now, although I do admit that having Chris around and sort of secure is a pretty nice feeling.

Monday, Sept. 25, 1950, evening

Chris came out last evening. We worked a jigsaw puzzle for a while then had some supper. All I made was the tea (Mrs. Bennett had left the rest ready), but Chris fooled around and teased me about that anyway. He's great fun to have around, Mum, and so relaxing. When I talk to Tony on the phone I have to think of things to say; with Chris I just natter on about everything I think and do.

One thing that amazed me in the advice you offered. You said you became engaged to another even after meeting Daddy. I didn't know you were puzzled at first too. Guess I always figured it was love at first sight . . . Chris sort of grows on you; I can't help liking him when he's around although he sometimes makes me cross but then I annoy him too I'm sure. Oh nuts! Almost feel like jumping in quick and hoping for the best—like I used to when jumping into water off a high pier although I was scared skinny.

Thursday, Sept. 28, 1950

Got a load off my chest last night by talking a few things over with Tony and he was so darned casual about putting things on a "good fun no strings" basis I almost got mad, and you know how I am—now more unsettled than ever with a higher opinion than ever of Tony . . . I see Tony again tomorrow night and as Chris will probably be going back on night duty next week, I'll have all my evenings free. As soon as I got the load off my chest to Tony and he was so darned sweet, I felt right at home with him and quite relaxed, as he'll not lay a finger on me at all now—and I do so like holding hands in the movies—unless we get around to a warmer stage at some later date. Aw nuts! Men drive me mad and much as I hate to keep Chris dangling, I'm not making up my mind for a while yet.

You know, I think I'll have to have a guy ride down the street on a white horse, carrying a sign which reads "I is him" and hit me over the head with it then sweep me off before I really know it's it!

Monday, Oct. 2, 1950, afternoon

I went to the Standard, saw Hyde, told him I had a week of holidays still coming. He said take it and come back to work on the 16th—that gave me a fortnight. Chris saw Christensen, editor of the daily, got his two weeks, so we started to plan. Cornwall was out, as his aunt is a bit niggly right now. John Prebble suggested Ireland at the little hotel where he spent his holiday, which is nice and quiet with good food, and we both need a rest. Wired the hotel, they said yes, got bookings, Beaverbrook called Chris, had him down to lunch yesterday but didn't mention taking him to America this fall and told him to have a nice holiday, so we're off tonight.

A little crazy, isn't it—especially since I had lunch with Tony on Saturday, find I like him more than I bargained for, and although he only jokes with me now, his thoughts are running along the same lines as Chris's and I rather like that . . . He knows I'm going to Ireland, but not that Chris is going too.

Have thought about it a lot since we arranged it and realize in some ways it isn't right, but as far as I'm concerned I'm going on a holiday with a good friend whose holidays happen to coincide with mine. I know me and I know Chris, so there's no worries—except that the weather looks like being lousy . . . The address is Royal Hotel, Glendalough, Co. Wicklow.

Thursday, Oct 5, 1950 [from the Royal Hotel, Glendalough]

Dear Mum,
Have been here now since Tuesday noon and it's really lovely. As I sit writing, a brook is rushing by the window at my elbow and its gentle roar lulls me to sleep at night . . . Chris is a good companion and behaving like a lamb, even when I'm in ugly moods.

Sunday, Oct. 8, 1950 [from the Royal Hotel, Glendalough]

Dear Mum,
Am forced to write letters today, as the sun and rain are taking turns and a whole hour without a downpour is rare. Am hoping there will be a direct letter from you either tomorrow or Tuesday, as I'm curious as to your opinion of this trip. I told Chris you'd probably go straight to the phone and tell Dad at the office—did you?

This first week has been very pleasant—Chris says I'm getting the roses back in my cheeks. This morning we both had breakfast in bed, and what a grand feeling!!

Tuesday, Oct. 10, 1950 [from the Royal Hotel, Glendalough]

Dear Mum,

Well, of all the rotten letters to try to spoil a grand holiday, yours that came this morning takes the cake. At first I was terribly hurt, then worried, then shocked and angry in turn. Now, after several hours of thinking it over, I'm just plain disappointed and ashamed—but of you, not of me. It doesn't say much for your faith in your method of bringing up children, Mum, for you to put into words ideas that had never entered into Chris's head or mine. Somehow I never for a minute thought you would take such a view. Chris is more sensible, I guess, for he claims your attitude is most normal for a mother, and he had been pretty terrified of the first letter that would come. Dad's opinion of Chris was better, Mum: he is a very fine guy and would no more think of bamboozling than the man in the moon. He was dealt quite a blow by your attitude, perhaps even more than I was, for you see, he is very much in love with me—much more than I am with him right now—and everything that hits me seems to hit him even harder. As for our having a "casual marriage," there has never been such a thought. Despite all my ramblings, it will have to be all or nothing for me, and Chris feels exactly the same way.

By the way, it was John Prebble who suggested this trip, and he possibly knows us both better than anyone else. I talked it all over with Mrs. Bennett, and she had no worries whatsoever. Just the same, we have told no one outside just in case there were any low minds lurking around. At the hotel here, we join in everything, rarely go on even walks alone, never go into one another's rooms and are particularly careful to give absolutely no cause for talk. We seem extremely popular and even one woman we considered an old battleaxe has now latched onto us like mad. The other guests seem to consider us bright and cheerful, and always join in after-dinner games we organize. Chris has been wonderful company, so much like Dad in doing little things, and looking after me and treats me with the utmost respect.

As for not telling Dad, I wrote him myself and somehow I don't think he'll let me down or adopt the attitude you have. He liked Chris and was quite right in doing so,

Please be reasonable Mum: this holiday has meant so much to me. The colour is back in my cheeks, I've been happier that I have in ages and feel great again, no longer tired and fretful. It's done a world of good, for Chris too has lost his tired strained look. For heaven sake don't you lose faith in me, for so many people over here live such rotten lives and look down on me for not doing so. My mainstay has been the fact that my mother and father have had wonderful happy lives and still been good—I can too. Please write and tell me you've thought again.

Monday, Oct. 16, 1950

It was good to hear you on the telephone today and took a great load off my mind. I quite agree I have been stupid I guess, but you can explain to Dad that my bringing up has been such that so complete is my confidence in my own inability to do wrong that I forget that "society" as you call it is not so confident. You know I'd never let any man lay a finger on me for love nor money, but I see now that is not enough and the rest of the world must understand that too. Should the "rest of the world" or "society" meet me, they would! Anyway I'm sorry for any worry I've caused and let's end it there.

Saturday, Oct. 24, 1950, 6.20 p.m.

Dear Mum,
Well, here I am in the Sunday Express office after a full day on with the Evening Standard work. Luckily though the remainder of the evening does not promise to be too difficult—I hope. Today has been fairly full, with most of it spent outside Clarence House waiting for Princess Elizabeth and Prince Philip to leave for the christening of Princess Anne at Buckingham Palace. But I did get my story on the front page, so it's not too bad. Also made friends with about five policemen, two photographers, and got taken into the back door of Clarence House to meet Philip's equerry, Michael Parker, by the court photographer Barron. But it was still darn cold, and tiring waiting and standing around.

Tuesday, Oct. 25, 1950, morning

Have just come back from a full-day session at London Airport waiting for Irene Dunne to arrive for the Royal Command performance. Particularly wanted to get her impressions of Al Jolson of course; did his obit this morning before leaving the office and darned if I didn't get a lump in my throat doing so! Poor old guy, he sure pleased a lot of people in a short while.

Sunday, Oct. 29, 1950, afternoon

My dear mother, I'm not a complete fool yet! Have handed in at least 4 stories of my own ideas the last week or so and got a compliment from Mr. Hyde on one scoop. I seem to be getting good assignments with Hyde and am keeping my fingers crossed that they won't look my way when cutting down on staff. Not terribly worried, just a bit prepared!

Seem to be seeing a good deal of Tony, although Chris is around too but working nights keeps him busy. Spent Friday with Chris (my day off) and am having tea with him tomorrow. Right now I seem to like Tony better.

Saturday, Nov. 5, 1950, afternoon

Dear Mum,
Here I am at the Sunday Express again after a rather shaking week. So many things have happened that I hardly know where to begin. Fleet Street is quaking with the numbers being fired from their jobs for "economic reasons." My biggest blow was Wednesday when John Prebble was fired—not because he isn't one of the smartest guys around, but he's been a long-standing hate on the part of editor John Gordon, and this "economy" stuff was a good excuse. John is hurt, naturally, but we have hopes of him getting something better so it may turn out all right, as he was never very happy here. As for me, I'll probably follow, as Mr. Head has said he can't keep me on the evening shift of the Express and I can't get every Saturday off from the Standard, so-o-o. The loss of 7 guineas per week would be quite a blow but not so much as the loss of the whole 20! Have been getting some very good stories in the Standard lately with no big boners so there's hope—sort of! Had two good stories in today, one a page lead and the other smaller but my own idea. Only thing is to sit tight, hope for the best, and keep my ears open for other jobs. I'm not particularly worried, so don't you get in a flap!!

Thursday, Nov. 9, 1950, evening

Dear Mum,
"Oh what a beautiful morning, oh what a beautiful day . . . la de da . . . " Am in an excellent mood today, nothing could be better and I don't even have to write you a column because I suddenly came across the ones I thought I sent you ages ago on the Festival of Britain and they will do fine. You can use what you like and maybe make it do for two or three columns.

Funny how a day can start out black and end up rosy. Was terrified of losing the Sunday Express job but today's interview with Mr. Head—I had four suggestions ready for him—finds me working the Saturday evening shift after all with only a 1 1/2-guinea dock in pay and no dock on the days I can be in all day, still my 3 guineas for the hotel work, extra pay for good hotel stories I get in the paper—so that's a big help, as last week he said he was firing some off the night shift.

Then I'm to remain free-lance on the Standard—they can't fire a person who isn't on staff anyway—and that allows me to pick my working shift hours as well as my days off; a word with the editor's secretary told me the cut isn't liable to hit the Standard too hard, so I'm not worried there anymore.

Tony is off tomorrow evening for a weekend scheme with the army, and didn't Larry Foley phone out of the blue and ask me to the Thames Rowing Club dance! (Haven't been dancing for ages as Tony doesn't dance and do I miss it!) Then a letter just now from David Ross asked me out for Saturday night. Whether he'll want to wait until 9 p.m. when I get off work, I don't know, that we'll have to see about. So I'm not on the shelf yet and may still get some fun in.

Last night Tony was talking about Majorca and thinks we ought to try living there for a while—married, of course! He was just joking I'm sure, but when I said I didn't consider him the marryin' type and that he'd quite hate married life I was sure, he said I was dead wrong, he'd like to be married and was sure he'd be most faithful, etc. It rather tickled me.

Saturday, Nov. 12, 1950, morning

Yesterday was a crazy day, pouring rain, stringy hair, sopping feet, lunch at Chris's house, dance in the evening with Larry Foley, and in the midst, over a lousy cup of tea, learn that Tony's intentions are fairly serious. Like everyone else, he's evidently waiting until I make up my mind and doesn't want to rush me. Suppose I've thought about the idea more in connection with Tony than anyone else . . . Now don't get me wrong. Tony hasn't actually asked me, but I don't think I'm wrong in understanding his intentions, should I decide the feeling is mutual . . . Yesterday he as good as put it into words only the words weren't all in the same sentence. Almost looks as if it will be a teacher, doesn't it? . . . Somehow it's a life I'd like, always a few changes and still the meeting of people that this newspaper racket has. Also long holidays in which to live a bit.

But don't start fretting for fear I'll go rushing off. Remember you always said I'd have to return home for a couple of months before a wedding to learn cooking and housekeeping—well, I still have that in mind. Besides, I'd quite like a couple of months hanging around the house attempting to look busy.

Tony has an offer of a professorship at a new university in Stoke in the offing (he goes up to see about it in a couple of weeks) which would allow 6 months' holiday per year—plenty of time to wander back and forth on freight boats, which his father can arrange free of charge. But there's plenty of time to think about all that.

Monday, Nov. 14, 1950

I seem to be running completely out of ideas for columns these days—you got any? Have seen quite a few plays lately, and with a couple more this week, will do a column on the winter theatre offerings. Am also attending (if Tony gets the tickets) a play at St. Paul's on Friday night, with the boys taking all the parts, including those of the girls. It should be quite cute and fun, too.

Tony is being so sweet it tickles me pink. The other day he said, "You wouldn't want to marry any fellow your people hadn't met, would you?" When I said not really, he said he entirely agreed with me.

Sunday we sat in, listened to the radio, and just generally did nothing, yet it was fun. Oh yes, he did say his intentions are of the very best and although it sounded terribly unromantic in a way, I nearly fainted when he said he intends to just stick around until I do feel like getting married, then he'd see if I feel like marrying him and he feels like marrying me, but this was not a proposal. Laughing, he said he'd sure be taken aback if I replied I felt like getting married now and when I asked what he would do if I did, he said he'd probably say he had to catch a train and leave. But I do notice he talks finances, homes, etc. to me every now and then and quite evidently has a few pretty sound ideas about his future. He wouldn't even mind teaching in Canada for a couple of years, he thinks.

Haven't a clue as to what to get him for Christmas: have you any suggestions?

Saturday, Nov. 18, 1950, 1 p.m.

Had a queer session on Thursday. Have seen the last of Chris, I guess, although we shall remain good friends, I hope. But he knows there is nothing doing as far as a future goes. I didn't even have to tell him, he said he could tell just by looking at me—crazy, isn't it! Felt pretty lousy the rest of the day as I've known him so long and am really very fond of him—even bawled when I got into bed and wished like mad that you were here. But Friday evening with Tony assured me that I'm not making a mistake—I hope, and it would have been rotten to keep Chris dangling any longer.

Last night was such fun, Mum. I was proud as punch of Tony—we went to the boys' play at St. Paul's where he teaches. All the boys call him "Sir," yet you can tell they like him a lot. As I waited in the front hall afterward while he got his coat I kept watching the mass of nondescript faces passing. Then Tony suddenly appeared among them and I almost shuddered as I realized how handsome he is and that out of all the girls he knows he's picked me. One little chap was terribly cute: he waited until we were leaving and Tony had his hand under my elbow, then he came up, cap in hand, and said "Please, Sir would it be all right if I miss rowing tomorrow?" What else could Tony say but "Yes"?

Friday, Nov. 25, 1950, morning

You know, Mum, I must be getting on fairly well over here—as far as being pleasant to people, that is. Tony has had about 3 "hard-boiled" reporters tell him to be nice and treat me well or they would do him in. It seems I'm still a little different from the mob in my ways and manners, etc. Rather nice to hear, isn't it? Last night I heard Alan Hoby, the sports reporter, tell Tony he didn't know of any other girl who had as many men friends in Fleet Street who all treated her with respect, felt like big brothers, and intended to look after her. It tickled me pink 'cause some of these old critters are pretty hard-hearted. As for Tony, he treats me like something that might break and every so often asks if he is treating me all right. There are times when he reminds me of a kid with a precious gift— and I do love it.

P.S. See you on the 23rd at 8:50 p.m. at Moncton Airport!

Saturday, Nov. 27, 1950, afternoon

I try not to think about getting home for fear I'll go all screwy inside and not keep my mind on my work. It's going to be wonderful seeing you all again, even though it is to be only for a short while. Tony seems a little worried that I might not return, but have already booked a return flight, so he's fairly safe. That's about the best way of making sure I do come back, I guess.

Thursday, Nov. 30, 1950

What would you say if I arrived for Christmas with a ring on my finger? Now don't get excited, I'm just sounding. Tony sort of officially asked me last night and the more I think about it, the more I want to say yes, but am still sitting tight in order to make dead sure and let you think it over too. Do so wish he was coming with me, for I want you to meet him, and 3 weeks without him is going to be a very long time. But he's rather planning on meeting you on his own at Easter if everything goes all right and he gets a cargo ship as soon as his holidays start. Know you'll love him Mum, 'cause I'm pretty sure I do, and we always did have similar tastes. As for religion, Tony seems perfectly willing to become a Catholic and I'm in hopes he'd find it easy, as the clever ones, although they are sometimes harder to convert, usually make the best Catholics. I find myself becoming more thrilled at the prospect each day so it looks really bad, I guess. My big problem now is when and where. Know you want a wedding in Canada but it would mean a second trip for me. Also, all our mutual friends are over here, but Tony is willing to come to Canada. As for the date, I just can't think and he hasn't mentioned anything. But with another war looming up, as it seems to be, and Tony a No. 1 on the reserve list, I don't want to chance losing him that way. Funny, I didn't think I'd ever be capable of seriously facing the future and now it all seems so wonderful and easy and simple. I seem to go around all day with a swelling pride inside and feeling as though I'd like to burst.

Friday, Dec 1, 1950, night

I phoned Chris today, first time I've spoken to him for several weeks, just to tell him I'm going and I was rather amazed at how little pleasure I got out of talking to him. Right away almost I noticed the silly little remarks etc. that annoy me. Still, mustn't be mean and must have tea with him or something before I go.

Monday, Dec. 4, 1950

Dear Mum,
It is now 6:50 p.m. and I'm sitting here half frozen waiting for Tony to call. Boy, will I be glad to live in a centrally heated house again, have registers to stand over and take baths in a full tub in a heated room instead of a half-full tub in an ice-cold room! Those are a few of the things I'm looking forward to most, along with the meals and plenty of sleep. For gosh sake don't mention cabbage to me or Brussels sprouts or I'll go raving mad! My kingdom for a squash!

Brrr-rr. Tony just called and I'm nearly perished! The phone is down in the front hall by the door and this drat house is always like an iceberg except for a couple of rooms. There is never any heat in the bedrooms or bathroom, and in the front room only when in use. I've got the fire (a miserable little coal fireplace) started in there now in hopes of having it warm when Tony comes about 8:30 p.m.
19 more days!

Lots of love Ouida

Wednesday, Dec. 10, 1950, afternoon

Dear Mum,
Will start this now and finish it after I hear from Tony. He is in Stoke this weekend seeing Lord Lindsay, as the latter is head of the new university up there and has, we think, something in the way of a job to offer him. From what I could gather before his leaving, it may be a wardenship of one of the colleges, part administrative and part lecturing, which

would be very good indeed, as the university seems to have all the earmarks of something big. It is staffed mostly by Oxford men and its degrees are recognized by both Oxford and Cambridge, and it is government sponsored. Also they are making reasonably good provisions for staff. Such as a house with cook and maid on the grounds as well as a pretty good salary and 6 months' holidays a year.

Sounds like a fairly decent set-up and I'm expecting Tony to phone me any time now to say what time he will be back and how it went. The only disadvantage is Stoke, although the university is located outside the main city, still it isn't London but with such long holidays, London can be pretty accessible.

The reason I mention all this – as if you didn't already know – is that Tony wants me to be able to go with him in October if he accepts this Stoke job.

Monday evening [the next day]

Got a bit delayed in this as you can see . . . Anyway, the Stoke job is there, on a beautiful big estate outside the city, and Tony was very pleased with both job prospects and location. But it isn't available until the fall of 1952, so he will probably remain where he is at St. Paul's until then . . . Now he's just gone and I'm sitting here wondering what the future holds.

We were talking plans tonight, as to when and where, etc.—forgot to mention I've made up my mind quite definitely but we'll keep it quiet for a time, at least until I return from home after Christmas. Tony is easy about everything and is leaving it up to me to make all the arrangements and decisions. Wretched men, they seem to think they are being helpful by just turning up at the appointed time and place—suppose they are, in a way. Don't worry, I'm going to leave the planning to you—easiest way out!

He's a little worried about taking me away from London if he accepts this Stoke job—silly goof, I shan't mind in the least as long as he's around. How will you feel being a grandma one day?

Shall get the column for December 23 off in a day or two, have all the ideas down, just have to put 'em on paper. Yes, I do want to keep the column on—might be pretty difficult from Stoke, but if we have a year in London first, that'll be OK.

Well, Christmas is just a fortnight away. Hardly seems possible that today fortnight I will have been home two whole days! . . .

Lots of love Ouida

"I'LL DO AS I PLEASE WHEN I PLEASE"
January–March 1951

Saturday, Jan. 20, 1951, 7:50 p.m.

Dear Mum,

Got my pay packet tonight to find £30:7:0 (91 dollars), as the Sunday Express paid me all the time I was away, so I'll be pretty well square with Mrs. Bennett. Then my feature money—providing I get some—will go directly into my account as I had originally hoped it would. A nest egg shouldn't be too long in forming.

Tony asked me last night if I wanted him to turn into a Catholic for the wedding. I said definitely "no."

Tuesday, Jan. 23, 1951, 8 p.m.

Well, last night I was about the most dumbfounded female on earth. I know I probably gave the impression while home that the idea of marriage at some future date was in my mind, but it won't be within the next ten minutes, and I hate being rushed!!! Yesterday I had a letter (loaded with stamps, special delivery and air mail) from Edmonton, Alberta, from some female who signs herself May Bingham and said a friend of yours named Allie Crandall in Fredericton had told her to write me. She was polite about it but what she said was that she had heard I was leaving this profession for the all-important one, she wished me the best of luck and could she have my job! Suppose nerve is all anyone really needs these days, but Holy Cow! Who does she think I am, the managing editor who can just hand over my job at random to any old person? And besides I never heard of Allie Crandall in my life and who the heck ever told her I was being married. Honest to Pete I was boiling when I read that!

The chances I have of getting her a job are about as good as those of a snowball in Hades! As for my job, I have no intentions whatever of leaving just yet, and if I did, there are about a dozen vultures sitting outside the door waiting to pounce on it. On the subject of marriage, there's nothing settled, don't forget, and as you should know, I am quite capable of changing my mind. If there's anything I loathe, it's people telling me what I'm going to do! I'll do as I please and when I please!⁸

Oh, yes, I got 9 guineas or 28 dollars out of Howard Clegg of the Montreal Standard yesterday. He originally offered me 6 guineas and said they had really lost my articles. I quickly told him I had seen a short piece on the Festival of Britain in the Standard and several of the phrases had smelt more than familiar. He said he was quite sure they didn't use any of my material. Then when he said 6 guineas I hummed and said those articles had taken a lot of time and legwork and they had been so slow publishing them it was hopeless for me to market the stuff anywhere else now, and he said 9 guineas right off. The skunk, of course I didn't tell him I had sold the same articles ages ago to the Express syndication bureau. Still, 9 guineas isn't too bad, but could have been much better. I've heard before of the Standard staff using other people's material, then returning or losing it.

Thursday, Jan. 25 1951, 4:00 p.m.

Sorry to hear you are a bit upset about Tony, for since arriving back I find I missed him even more than I thought I had and he's mighty wonderful to have around again. About his staying up late, those are strictly male parties, don't forget, for he's very particular about me and always keeps an eye on the clock to make sure I don't get too tired. He's had me in bed by 10 o'clock every night this week so far. And as for the drinking, there again it is only on stag parties for it did bother me at first until I realized he knows exactly how much he can take, always takes less and never, never has much when he's with me for he knows I don't care for it. Don't worry, we've hashed that all out and I'm no longer worried. Last night at the squash club he had one glass of beer and a ginger ale. When Tony says "a drink" he means just that—a glass of wine with dinner, a highball afterward—but then as you say, you can decide for yourself, for I think he'll probably get over there this summer.

Just before I got back, he had a letter from Lord Lindsay saying he wanted a warden sooner than he thought and for Tony to forward his application. The job must be advertised also, of course, but we expect to hear within the next week, and that may mean this September at Stoke. Anyway time will tell.

---

⁸ Ouida's boss kept a number job applications on a spike on his desk, knowing that the staff would sneak a look—and be alarmed at seeing how highly qualified most of them were.

Friday, Jan. 26, 1951

Dear Mum,
Don't know what's got into me but I've got that browned-off, itchy-feet feeling again—same as before I returned to Xavier [University] in '48 and before I came over here. Sort of feel the need of a big change and don't quite know what it should be. It's a horrible feeling, for I'm restless, unsettled and I know I'm liable to hurt people again. Afraid I thoroughly annoyed Tony last night but all I seem capable of is complete indifference.

Saturday afternoon [added the next day]

Well, you see the kind of mood I started off in yesterday, but funnily enough I ended up feeling perfectly ashamed and crawling on all fours.

Maybe for the first time in my life I'm getting some sense—if so, it's about time; anyway, I suddenly realized that by pulling such stupid tantrums I was liable to lose some of the love and respect Tony now has. It didn't seem worth it.

Anyway, Sally and I went to see "Cinderella"—the movie—last night and it was sweet, then on to the squash club to meet Tony and his partner Tony Bell. My Tony was a bit cool at first but got over it as I was as sweet as humanly possible. He finally ended up—after I had apologized for behaving so stinkingly—saying I could get away with murder as far as he was concerned, but that's something I really don't want, ever. I remembered you telling me "no matter how mad you get, never let it get the better of you, as you'll lose something you can never regain." So I'm OK now.

Tuesday, Jan. 30, 1951, evening

Tony and I had quite a chat on Sunday evening. He seems a bit worried about whether or not I'll miss my newspaper work—little does he know I'll be tickled pink to be away from offices but that it won't prevent me from doing some stories on my own at home anyway. Also, he's terrified he won't be able to make me happy and he claims it would make him miserable if such should be the case—and our different interests, him not dancing, and me being rather "gay" at times, etc. Rather sweet to know he is concerned, but I don't think there is anything to get really worked up over.

The only other thing is kids—they rather scare me and I shouldn't want any for a few years yet. Tony agrees that it should be a couple of years at least—sort of until we get used to one another—and until we are able to afford them comfortably.

Still there is no news from Lord Lindsay, and the future rather rests with him for the minute.

Sunday, Feb. 4, 1951

I'm not planning on Tony rushing into the Catholic religion. He's a scholar, but I'm not so sure he wants to think about religion. He's not anti-Catholic, thank heavens, but he doesn't want to have any religion as far as I can see, and I'm not harping. When the right moment presents itself, I shall ask him to see someone about it, not to convert him, but so he will better understand me. In that way, his curiosity may be invoked a bit. He has some queer ideas about it, I'm afraid, but he's not yet ready to air them and have the answers supplied. After all, accepting a religion like Catholicism is no easy job, as you probably know [Ouida's mother was a converted Catholic], and in some countries, England included, it can cause difficulty in jobs etc. . . . Possibly you could get him on the subject if he gets over for Easter, but I'm terrified of Dad with his set views annoying Tony. He's at a precarious stage, for it is only on my account that he is even thinking about religion and when all it seems to do is make our getting together more difficult, the stage is not very well set . . . I believe his parents are just as worried as you are about the difference, although they think that we would make a good match—at least Tony said he had been given that impression.

Tuesday, Feb. 13, 1951

Dear Mum,
Once again am posted outside Clarence House—that drat woman Elizabeth [Princess Elizabeth] returned from Malta yesterday. It is horribly cold, raining, and thoroughly miserable, and no one hopes more than I do that she will return to Malta in March. Boy, what a lousy job this one is!

Now it's 1:50 p.m. and on phoning the office have been told to stick around in case Liz decides on a car ride. S'help me, I wouldn't go out unnecessarily on a day like this, especially if I hadn't seen my kids for 11 weeks, so I'm not anticipating a big scoop. Feet are frozen so I've come into a tiny restaurant to eat while Bill Alden the photographer paces up and down for a while.

See today where those blasted Yanks have crossed the 38th parallel [in Korea] again. Tony calmly tells me the military heads here are expecting a flare-up in Europe between March and May. Comforting, isn't it!

Tuesday, Feb. 20, 1951, morning

You called me a coward about settling down—I couldn't agree more but what do you suggest I do about it? I like the money I'm making and the freedom I have, yet I often feel, or rather wish, I didn't have to turn Tony out at 11 every night or keep arranging to meet him and waste half of the evening waiting until we have both eaten at home to cut expenses. Oh well, Stoke isn't settled yet, so there's time to fret later.

Have discovered his mother makes most of his shirts, but he's not sure I could do so well! The nerve of the guy!!

Mum, Tony keeps asking when I will marry him. You know I'm completely incapable of planning anything for myself; couldn't you sort of think about coming over sometime within the next year and do it for me? I simply cannot imagine getting married without you and Daddy with me, and I'm afraid the prospect of us both going over there is pretty expensive right now. Besides you have never seen England and could stand the trip, whereas it would just mean adding to wedding expenses for us. I'm quite sure that if you don't do something about all this business you'll have me on your hands forever. How miserable to be so incompetent as me! As for all our differences, I'm just hoping they will work themselves out.

Lots of love from a muddly girl.

Ouida Ann

Thursday, Feb. 22, 1951, afternoon

Dear Mum,
Here I am again, today is my day off—no more of these, either, since I'm going back on the night shift and will be working six days a week again. Have been trying very hard to convince myself that the change will do me good—the only good it will do is prevent me from seeing much of Tony or Tony much of me—if that can be considered good! Weekends will be my only free time and then he is usually busy with army schemes. It ought to be fun! I'll be like Barbara Stanwyck when she got her divorce yesterday—a telephone wife who just shook hands with her husband when they passed at the door—except that I'm not a wife, of course.

Tony has an offer of a 2 to 3 month cruise with a cargo ship to Vera Cruz, Mexico, and back to Tangier starting just after Easter. He's terribly tempted to take it, and I wouldn't mind going too. Think that is worth getting married for?

Friday, Feb. 23, 1951, night

Dear Mum,
Well, you wanted me to keep an eye on the Canadian Fashion show to be given in Eastbourne, but I've gone one better—I'm going to be a model in it. Caught on to the fact they are having all amateur models, Canadian girls living in London, and volunteered and have just come back from being accepted—I think.

Also saw photographs of the clothes they are sending today, but OH? OH? OH? they don't add up to that big boast of mine about Canadians being so well dressed! Some of the combinations are terrible, two tweeds, chiffon scarf, and veiled hat all in one outfit. The Harper's Bazaar woman had to suggest that some of the pix be dropped from those to be used for publicity as they were so bad. As for the clothes, the bridesmaid's dress is shocking, all frills and a flowered hat set on straight that looks like a cake. Some of the styles are not at all new, and the only thing cute or even eye-catching is the teenage play clothes.

[The show of Canadian fashions took place in Eastbourne on Saturday, March 3. The show was organized by Kate Aitken, a well-known radio and television broadcaster in Canada. Ouida's column describing the event appeared in the Moncton paper on March 10, 1951. During her years in London, Ouida showed an interest in fashion modelling, both for shows and pictures, and even, at times, performed as a model.]

IN BRITAIN TODAY by Ouida MacLellan

Three big cheers for Kate Aitken—Canada's "flying grandmother"—who has more "V's" (vim, vigour and vitality) than ten ordinary mortals put together. Any woman who can carry off a show as she did at Eastbourne last Saturday deserves a medal for devotion to duty. Following fashion shows in Toronto on February 22 and Montreal the 23rd, and a session with the dry cleaners for the first part of last week, Mrs. Aitken took off from Montreal on Thursday, Mar. 1, for England. Then the trouble began!

Some over-excited customs man in Montreal hauled her $10,000 worth of fashions off the plane because she was not there one hour beforehand to declare them. Mrs. Aitken arrived in England to find them missing and the trans-Atlantic calls started. The clothes left on the next plane, only to be detained again in Prestwick, Scotland—customs men there didn't have the authority to clear them, they had to go to London. Then, the good old reliable British fog closed in. The planes were grounded at Prestwick and two men were hired to drive the clothes by road to London . . .

Fifteen models—all Canadians living in London—caught the 4:45 p.m. train from London's Victoria Station . . . A bus met us at Eastbourne and we were taken to the Grand Hotel. There, in the ballroom, stood Mrs. Aitken, calmly explaining the type of music she wanted to a slick black-haired pianist. He assured her he knew exactly the melodies desired, then played a waltz when she mentioned her jazzy "Coke Bar" scene! Still quite calm, Mrs. Aitken explained to us the different sets of clothing [for the various "scenes"]. There were to be play clothes, junior miss, business girl, afternoon frocks, evening wear, and a bridal scene. She showed us how to make our entrance, where and how to turn on the runway, and above all to keep smiling. Fittings? She hoped they would take place later in the day, or the next morning, or sometime!

Following the short rehearsal we went off to the Burlington Hotel (where we were to sleep) to freshen up a bit, as we were expected at a dinner at the Albion Hotel. This turned out to be a great success—small wonder. The porterhouse steaks (flown over by Mrs. Aitken) were grown in Alberta, processed in Winnipeg, frozen in Montreal, and cooked in Eastbourne. Mrs. Aitken, still calm and serene, arrived in a smoky grey chiffon gown, was in the chair, and handled it beautifully.

Saturday morning call was for 6:45! Breakfast, checking out, a taxi dash and we were again at the Grand Hotel Ballroom—the clothes were still missing! At 9:30 a.m. the show was due to start, the ballroom filled with people, the pianist and violinist were attempting to start their scores for the third time, the models, in underslips, were standing in an improvised dressing room, the five baby models (all under five years) were getting fussy, but still there were no clothes.

At 10:00 a.m. the first model walked onto the stage in a dress she had never before laid eyes on and almost a packet of pins, which she fervently hoped would not start pricking her. Can you imagine the confusion behind the scenes? As the clothes were unpacked and brought in, we quickly chose the first thing that looked close to our size, got inside it, then raced to locate gloves, umbrella, hat, and scarf to match. It seemed confusion, chaos and disaster—yet the show went amazingly well: we were told the models walked on the stage looking quite composed and professional.

The show ended at 11:30 a.m., then the movie cameramen and the press photographers took over. They wanted pictures from this angle and that of this girl with that—well, it was quite fun being on the answering instead of the asking end of the game for a change!

As for Mrs. Aitken, when we left she had most of the clothes already packed, a car ordered, and a plane seat booked. She was due back in Toronto at 3:30 p.m. on Sunday and was going to make a gallant effort to keep that date. My hat off to you, Mrs. Aitken!

Friday, March 2, 1951, morning

Had to keep tabs on Princess Margaret again yesterday when she visited the Sadler's Wells [Ballet] School for lunch and a look around. Here is what I do: I arrive at least half an hour before her, try to sneak inside to find out what she will be doing, who she will be meeting, and what they will have for lunch, then get promptly shown the door when I'm discovered on the inside. I return to the pavement, take up my position in front of a bunch of ill-mannered old curiosities who spend the time making rude remarks about my size, shape, etc. (my red coat is a big one), and then start on either the meat ration, the weather, or the government (pro or con) and attempt at the same time to push you into the notice of a sturdy policeman who will push you back again or try to banish you completely. Next to you stand by some really hardbitten photographers from the news agencies. No other paper except yours has a reporter there—it isn't important enough really but it gives your paper a chance to get rid of you for a while and see if they can't browbeat you into quitting. Finally she arrives, probably a few minutes late, greets the director (Arnold Haskell with his grey goatee) in tones so low you can't possibly hear, smiles once, and walks directly inside (two minutes is stretching the time that takes).

Then you've only got to phone in a story to your more than grateful news editor who genially says, "Well, better stick around until she comes out, the roof might fall in on her." So you stick around for two hours while absolutely nothing happens, no one goes in, no one comes out, then you queue up again with the second lot of curiosities to watch her come out, which she again manages inside one minute, looks straight at you as if to say "you're very faithful," and you glare back as if to reply, "it's not by choice," and she gets into a big plush car, has a warm rug put over her knees (she's already walked from the door to the car on a thick red carpet), smiles sweetly, and drives off in comfort. You bring your almost numb legs into action, dash up and ask the director what happened. He shuts down the conversation with "Everything went very smoothly, she was very knowledgeable, nothing happened," and goes in. You try to imagine a story, phone the paper again, they will of course use nothing more than a slight caption under the picture (you really knew that before you left the office) and you're expected to go on, in perfectly good humour, to interview a man who studies roads and who is bound to talk both to and at you for at least two hours—that means being late for a third appointment. Yesterday, I was fortunate. I saw an excellent stage play in the evening that didn't make it all seem too bad and I sat right next to that same old stiff-lipped director from the Sadler's Wells school—in the third row of the stalls. I do think he was rather annoyed at seeing me again and in the same position as he was.

Sunday, March 4, 1951, afternoon

Dear Mum,
Looks like this is going to be one long explanatory note as there seem to be quite a few things that need clearing up.

Life in Britain today is vastly different from life in Moncton. You can say, "Rubbish, the principles are still the same," but that really doesn't quite apply. Marriage is also a different matter. Very rarely does a girl marry and give up her job at the same time, firstly because the chances are they will only have one or two rooms at the most to live in, and secondly, salaries today are such that most young couples just can't manage on the man's pay alone.

You seem to forget that Moncton is still a growing community, lots are plentiful, housing restrictions none, builders available, and building material available. None of that applies over here. London is no longer growing and during the war half the housing space was knocked out by bombs so that the population is crowded into half the space. The prices of houses for sale are fantastic, beyond all normal pockets and even then you can't be assured of getting the present residents out. Building lots just aren't available—or if they are, the prices are much too steep. Then comes the actual house. Building restrictions are completely crippling. First one needs a permit and they are granted only in cases of dire necessity such as to a farmer (agriculture is a good profession now) or to people erecting blocks of flats. I know people who have already been waiting five years for a building permit and there is still no hope. Then, if you get the permit, the cost of your house is restricted, as is the size of the rooms and the number of them. You can't possibly build what you'd like in England today. You even have to have special permits to redecorate a place. So you see how difficult life is.

On the other hand, if a newly married couple can locate a two or three room self-contained flat for up to $10 or $15 per week, they are mighty fortunate.

Tony is saving, but he is only paid 4 times per year and then he banks his cheque immediately and draws out only what he needs when he needs it. He has somewhere in the vicinity of $1,000 put aside now. Actually we are extremely fortunate. At Stoke, a furnished house is thrown in with the job. Granted we probably won't like all the furniture but it will allow us to shop around and pick out what we really want rather than trying to furnish a place inside of a few weeks with all the modern junk, which has no character at all.

On the other hand, if the Stoke job is not for this year, then St. Paul's have offered Tony another £125 ($375) per year to stay on there, so we would probably live in London. That means a small flat somewhere and there is no use starting a building fund for that!

Then again, Tony quite honestly doesn't like England and prefers to get away to the continent as often as possible. He can live over there cheaper than he can live here so that seems a sensible thing to do. And don't forget, he teaches modern languages and likes every opportunity to get to France and keep his French up to the mark, and it is never a lazy holiday for him for he is continually reading and studying (he took 8 books back to the library yesterday after having them only a fortnight—I don't read 8 books a year!)

Tuesday, March 6, 1951, afternoon

I'm not married to Tony—yet—so you still have time to change my mind if you work really hard . . . I don't mean to be stinking about it Mum, I know you worry a lot about my light-headedness etc., but everyone can't pattern their lives on the Moncton standards. Do you honestly think I'd be content to live in a nice modern house, belong to the IODE [Imperial Order of the Daughters of the Empire] and learn to play bridge, have a party with "the girls" once a week, have a husband who goes out in the morning and back at night in deadly monotony, who takes me for our fortnight's holiday over to the Point [New Brunswick seaside vacation area] once a year, who never really wants to travel, to continue to learn by experience, etc.? Maybe I would, I don't really know, but somehow I have a feeling I'd either give up my zest and sink into the rut or become so discontented I'd go traipsing off on my own.

You mentioned Tony saving: he doesn't get out at all unless it's with me, he eats rotten school lunches to save going out and spending more, he signs on for wearing and tiresome army schemes to earn more money so he won't have to dip into his savings, and—this I think you have forgotten—he passed up a good job with the Oxford University Press because he thought the one at Stoke a better offer for a married man, particularly because it includes a house.

My life here is no picnic either, Mum, as you may have already guessed. Mrs. Bennett, nice as she is, makes it very difficult, for I have nowhere to take the guy and I'm quite sure she isn't terribly keen on Tony. Not for any particular reason, but every so often she'll warn me to be careful, that he's quite serious, etc. and she always ends up with the fact that SHE liked Chris very much.

Honestly, Mum, there are times when I could weep, I feel so rotten. I usually ask her if I can bring him in on a certain evening, but she never is gushing in her replies and has never suggested he come for tea or supper like she used to for Chris. And if she does put out a supper for us, she'll never eat with us—which again she always used to with Chris.

It's no fun to keep a guy out walking along the street late at night or sitting in a cinema or some other place just because you can't take him home . . . When we come in for a cup of tea after an evening out, I always have to bring him into the kitchen, and here we sit—like servants. Tony's terribly sweet and doesn't seem to mind, but I do.

What I wouldn't give to have a place of my own, for there are also several girls I would like to have in but never can and it makes me feel sort of mean to be always going to their homes and never able to invite them back in return.

Thursday, March 15, 1951, afternoon

As you probably already guessed, Tony's holidays now last until the last week in April and he is planning on the south of France and I could join him—oh, don't worry—it wouldn't be another Ireland. He would fix for us both to stay with friends of his or he will book me at a hotel in the same place where he is staying. Quite honestly, I feel we almost need the chance to really get to know one another, for the only chances we have nowadays seem to be a few minutes on underground trains or while walking along a street or sitting in a film. Sometimes I almost feel the guy is a stranger.

Sunday, March 18, 1951

Was told yesterday that my work has come ahead by leaps and bounds in the last few months, and from the careful way the assistant news editor asked my name, I may land a by-line, but don't hope. It was mighty encouraging anyway.

Thursday, March 22, 1951, afternoon

Still no word from you on your opinion about my south of France suggestion. Hope something comes before Wednesday, as I think Tony may be leaving for Portugal then and he'd rather like to know. Hope you see it my way, but then I can only hope. I realize how it must seem to you for me to even put forward the idea but I feel I must have a break of some kind (even got on the wrong train the other night and travelled about three stations) for a bit and it would also serve as a good opportunity to see how we do get on in big doses.

David Ross just phoned me and wants me to go out to some club with him next Friday evening. If Tony gets away to Portugal on Wednesday, I'll be able to go—they have dancing and I'm longing to dance again . . . Suppose Tony would be cross if he knew I was planning on going out with someone else—and suppose, too, that I shouldn't, but there is no fear of me ever falling for David (I did that once and came out of it quick), and he is a good dancer, and Tony did promise I could go to the Cambridge May ball if David asks me and how am I to get an invite if I'm not pleasant in between??? But then men never figure the same way as women do and I'm so used to having good men "friends" with no strings or thought of strings, but a guy never believes that! Ah, men, bah!

Friday, March 23, 1951, afternoon

Tony came over last night and we sat with Mrs. Bennett and had the best evening for quite some time—as far as cordial relations go, that is. Tony is going to Spain and Portugal and she knows that section of the country, so they had plenty to talk about.

Now he's gone off on a four-day army scheme until Monday afternoon and then will leave Monday night to join this Estonian ship up north somewhere. You know I think I've got these weeks Tony is away remarkably well managed. Tony Parkinson, a sub-editor at the office, is away for next week but has invited me to a theatre when he gets back, which should be fun, then David is home for just a few weeks, and Pat Ashton is coming to stay at the house here for a couple of weeks and he has a motorbike, so I intend to accept any rides I can wangle him into offering. Guess it doesn't sound much like a girl thinking of marriage does it—but gee, Mum, sometimes a girl has to cut loose and kick up her heels, and when Tony isn't the type to go dancing then I have to seek that fun elsewhere, and so long as I don't hurt him, what's the difference? Sometimes I think I'm too selfish ever to be able to love someone else enough to make the necessary sacrifices. I don't like dogs or cats much and am never over keen on small kids, which they claim is a very bad sign. Maybe I'd be much wiser and save a few broken dreams if I did make up my mind to remain the hard-bitten career type—providing they let me travel around a bit and I don't have to work so hard I get too tired, as I sometimes do now.

Friday, March 30, 1951, morning

You asked me if I really love Tony—I don't know. Sometimes I think I'll never know. You know how inconsistent I am. I do know I've never been more fond of any guy and I've never wanted to marry a guy before like I often do Tony, but then there are days when I don't want to do anything except stick to myself. But Tony knows I'm temperamental and moody and seems to be able to cope or just leave me alone, as is required. Some days I sit and think about life in Stoke with Tony and I get quite excited. Like this morning I was looking at tweed samples for suits suitable to the country and yesterday I was wondering if it's possible to get pastel shaded linen wide enough to make sheets—I think coloured sheets would be rather attractive. I'd quite like to be let loose in a house and fix it up as I liked and of course I'd have to have a sewing machine for making bright and gay curtains. And flowers. I don't want too many but I'd like to be able to pick some for the house all the time and I'd want my own vegetables too. It could be quite fun.

Love, Ouida

"FIRED BY THE SUNDAY EXPRESS"
April–July 1951

Sunday, April 1, 1951

Got a rather good front page story yesterday on the wife of the Czech ambassador who has been recalled to Prague. All the papers had tried and we had an exclusive. It was impossible to see Madame Bystricky herself, but didn't I find her little girl out playing in the park opposite the house and talked to her a few minutes before her nurse came and whipped her inside! Anyway, it made a good yarn with front page in all editions, and no other paper had anything.

Saturday, April 7, 1951

Saw Chris yesterday, first time in six months, and he's looking very well. I was very glad to see him as I'm still very fond of the guy and he feels the same towards me. Wish I could still see him sometimes, but Tony wouldn't stand for that—which is supposed to be quite natural for a guy. Something happened yesterday that I think may prove to you how innocent the Ireland trip was. Chris thinks he may be going to Canada with the Beaver in May and the first thing he asked was whether it would be all right to visit you again. He really wants to as he likes me and likes you, so you see how little he dreamt that you would be so angry. Actually, it was one of the best holidays I've ever had and except for the worry it caused you, I'm glad I had it.

Thursday, April 19, 1951, evening

Dear Mum,
Well it's amazing. No one could possibly be in a better mood than I've been these past few days—I've been on top of the world, humming or singing most of the time (much to the annoyance of some), have thoroughly enjoyed everything I've attended, seem to put those around me in a fairly decent mood as well—and cut my hair into a tiny kiss curl or bangy thing in front which eliminates the bobby pin and makes my appearance much softer and brighter. Yesterday and Tuesday I had three people I haven't seen for quite some time tell me how wonderful I am looking—rather a bad recommendation for Tony, who has been

away all this while. Had a card from him today and it seems he has picked up some kind of present for me in Casablanca and will be back next Tuesday. Alan Hoby (Sunday Express sports columnist and a very good friend of mine) asked me today when old "push face" (he will insist on calling Tony that) will be back and whether or not there was time for us to work in one date before he arrived . . .

I am awaiting Tony's return with trepidation—or some other such big word. I have a feeling that I haven't been getting the "most out of life" as it were and I'm not sure whether it has been my fault, both our faults, or Tony's. Anyway, weather permitting, my present mood should last (I'm at my very best on sunshiny days) and I should soon discover where the blame lies. I have a feeling that Tony's seemingly set ideas and ways possibly rob me of that extra joy I usually get out of things—on the other hand I also have a strong feeling that mingled with my sunny moods, his can become the same, and it just requires a bit of clever angling and greater sharing of feelings on my side.

You know, his family are amazingly reserved. One would never dream of butting into the other's business, and then there were those shut-away POW [Prisoner of War] years during the war for Tony, which have made him pretty much of a closed shop. I have a sneaking suspicion that patience and the gaining of his complete confidence on my part will bring him out very much more, and that he would, deep down underneath, love to be brought out. Maybe I'm wrong, but it's worth a try.

Had a phone call from Bill Aitken today—Old Man's nephew or brother, I'm not sure which. He wanted to know if I would be interested in augmenting my income by joining him and David Roberts in a special service to The Fredericton Gleaner paper . . . I said I sure would . . . it should start about May 15th, but everything is very hush, hush right now, so not a word to anyone or I'll be done in. It sounds like a good thing and I've certainly got the contacts over here now to handle a pretty fair coverage of all New Brunswick angles. As for the "augmented income," I'd like nothing better . . . What do you think of this scheme? It wouldn't interfere with my column.

Wednesday, April 25, 1951

Tony got back Monday night and I went over to his home—or rather he met me halfway and took me there. He brought me a lovely light tan handbag which he got from an Arab in a marketplace in Casablanca. It's a beauty, with some lovely handwork designs. He couldn't have chosen better, as my poor old black one is about finished.

He looks terrific, very tanned and makes me look anemic although I was mighty glad to see him. Already today I've been swimming in the Richmond baths and feel great after that.

Sunday, April 29, 1951

You asked about General MacArthur—Tony regarded him as the biggest single menace to peace in the world today, and naturally was delighted when he was fired [by President Harry Truman]. Afraid much of Britain thinks the same and although most of his speech was broadcast over here he is regarded as a bit of a showman and he sure made it a dramatic epistle! The papers gave him great play at first but it died quickly, although the new Chinese offensive [in the Korean War] does make you wonder a bit. One thing is certain: no matter how hard they kick, it is going to remain as much America's war as it is now and you can't really blame Britain. America left them pretty alone during the last war but the minute they get a fair sized battle on their hands they yell like stuck pigs! Only the future can tell where we'll all end up, however.

There is a dance at the tennis club tonight and Tony is meeting me at Richmond station about 9:40 p.m., so we'll probably go along and have a look at least.

Thursday, May 3, 1951, 1 p.m.

Tony washed my hair the other evening and just like Daddy he nearly took the scalp off me, then commented that he thought it all looked rather matty. I started to do it myself, but he seemed rather disappointed so I had to let him go ahead.

Tuesday, May 8, 1951, morning

Stoke is definitely out now, as Tony had word the job has been given to someone else under a rather queer set-up. Believe he is quite disappointed as well as annoyed as he turned down a rather good job with Oxford University Press, which would have meant going to New York in about 4 years' time, as he thought living accommodations would be better for me in Stoke. I don't really think I would have liked it, too far from London. I want him to take a year off and tramp around the world, then get a university job in the U.S., although he wants New Zealand. He doesn't like cold climate.

Wednesday, May 16, 1951, evening

Saturday I have to catch a train about 6:15 into Richmond, a second into Waterloo, and a third to Hook in Hampshire where I will be met by Flying Officer Alan Marshall of the RCAF (he's been a good friend of mine ever since the jet pilot gang arrived over here) and am to spend the day with the No. 426 Red Indian Squadron at Odiham and have a flight in a jet plane with them. It seems Al has laid on a photographer, and I shouldn't be surprised if pictures are sent to most Maritime newspapers.

I called Roberts of Syndication [the London Express Press Service] and he has suggested that I do a by-line story on the squadron and my day, etc., and with pix we can send it to the Gleaner as an introduction of me to the paper. Sounds good to me. Thought I'd do a very personal story on my impressions of the jet for the column, then for the Gleaner make it more a story of the squadron, bringing in as many NB boys as possible. That should make it quite different and still allow me to pass off the same job on both papers. Might even manage a little publicity over here with an "NB-trained squadron entertains NB girl" angle. Could be fun! Anyway, I'm thrilled to bits with the prospect of the trip and only hope my tummy doesn't go woosh as it did on the return flight on TCA[9] at Christmas.

Al asked me to bring slacks, as it seems I have to get into all kinds of harnesses, parachutes, etc. Then I'll come back to London and work the usual evening shift for the Sunday Express.

I'm so darn unsettled these days. Sometimes Tony makes me so darned mad I could yell—that's probably why I stick around for more, I suppose, it would be too smooth sailing if he didn't. I've never known anyone who can jump me from the depths of depression to the clouds and back down again so quickly. Golly, I'm moody enough on my own without his help! And he's rather moody himself, so the combination is sensational, I'm sure . . . On Thursday eve we went to a play and he had a rotten cold so his mood wasn't top form, then he went off last weekend to North Wales with the army and when I saw him again last night I got a welcome about as warm as you'd give the morning newspaper boy on the corner. Yet only last week he said he didn't see half enough of me. One of us is quite mad and I sure hope it isn't me! Suppose it serves me right to meet someone who shows his feelings even less than I do for a change, but it's a bit hard to take at times.

As for this summer, he won't know until almost time to go if there is a merchant ship going to Canada but I shouldn't be in the least surprised if he doesn't make it.

Sometimes I almost feel I've dilly-dallied so long about making up my mind he's getting fed up and I've probably lost him, yet he still seems to consider me his property—sort of. If only something would happen to force me to decide my future and quickly, but as nothing is at present pressing, then I remain evasive and content with each day as it comes. I just can't bring myself to face a decision to settle down.

---

[9] Trans Canada Airlines, forerunner of Air Canada.

Wednesday, May 23, 1951

Dear Mum,

Well, I've had my first trip in a jet and what a ride! Boy, it was one I shan't forget in a hurry and never before have I been so darned sick and embarrassed at the same time! Wow!

One hundred men around and I have to turn violently ill and end up in the station hospital for the afternoon! Embarrassed, I'll say I was!!!

The most pleased person was Jim McElroy the squadron doctor—said he hadn't had as nice a patient in ages, but that wasn't much comfort, nor were the loud acclamations of all the officers who said they were all ill when they started. But they weren't ill on Monday, and that was what mattered to me.

Johnny Rainville, the Second in Command of the squadron, took me up in a 2-seater Meteor—it seems I am the first civilian woman to fly in a jet fighter. It's a beautiful craft and rides like a well-sprung car. He went straight up to 20,000 feet in 4 minutes and next thing I knew we were over Southampton and the Isle of Wight. We did a slight dive meant to black me out—just give me the feeling of a blackout—but bright-eyes here didn't black out through grim determination—but my stomach!

Had only a cup of tea and piece of toast for breakfast on purpose as I didn't want to have a full stomach just in case I was ill. As a result I think the whole lining came out—into my oxygen mask and down the tube. It wasn't much but enough to make me angry, so I fought all the harder to stay fit and made it worse, I suppose. A couple of steep turns—got to turn steeply at that speed—600 mph—just about did me in, so when we landed I stretched out on the grass for a bit, then took it gently into the medic's room but finally had to cave in and go to bed. I kept insisting I was really quite all right but had I seen my dirty face which was chalk white with a few blotches I would have known better. Was reasonably fit by evening and came back with Al Marshall, who was nearly crazy with worry, and stayed home from work Tuesday and today . . . feeling groggy.

By the way, I intend going up again first chance I get. No silly little aeroplane is going to get me down. But it sure can drain you on the turns, you feel all face muscles sag and your whole body feels like going thru the seat.

[Ouida's feature article about her jet flight was not finished until early July, when it was distributed by the London Express Overseas Press Service to various Canadian newspapers.]

"I'D GO AGAIN," OUIDA DECLARES by Ouida MacLellan

I hope they never form a jet fighter wing in the Women's division of the RCAF—unless they first discover a race of stomach-less women! Why?

I should know, for I have just become the first Canadian civilian woman ever to fly in a jet fighter airplane. And it was an experience I am unlikely to forget.

For speed, grace, handling, manoeuvring, and thrills, jets are miles ahead of anything else. But they certainly are designed for strong, healthy men; not weak-kneed women. The truth of this was painfully brought home in my flight, which came to me, as a journalist, through the courtesy of the RCAF's famous 421 Squadron (the Red Indians). After two years' training in Chatham, N.B., the Squadron is in Britain for operational training with the Royal Air Force.

It was a lovely sunny day when I arrived at their British home, Odiham in Hampshire . . . I signed in at the gate in high spirits—then had my courage shot down in flames . . . The second-in-command of the station told me flying a jet was like driving a car—a cinch. Then the commanding officer chatted about the improbability of getting out of these planes alive. At the speed they travel, the chances of not hitting the tail would be slight and there are no ejector seats in Vampires or Meteors. We drove across the aerodrome to a dispersal hut on the far side where it was suggested I go up immediately so that I wouldn't miss dinner. In the end, I didn't care if I missed dinner, supper and breakfast for a week.

It was decided I should fly with Flt.-Lt. John Rainville of Hamilton, Ont.—tall, dark, and handsome type. The other pilots collected around to watch me bundled into a blue nylon flying suit with zips here and there to hold it together—unbelievably my head was considered "small." We walked to the waiting plane as RAF jets zoomed overhead, making it look like child's play.

The various lines of the plane were explained, then I was boosted up into the cockpit—no easy stairs like the airliners use. The oxygen mask was fitted again (trouble again, small face) and it was turned on before we started, to avoid any stupidity on my part in twisting wrong levers. I was carefully warned not to touch; dozens of gauges and meters were vaguely explained (I do believe they assumed a mere woman would never really understand . . . I didn't, much) and I was shown the button that allowed me to talk to the pilot.

We were off! Four minutes it took to reach 20,000 feet but that hardly registered. I saw the clouds go by, but the height didn't impress me; I'm a bad judge of distance. My only gauge is the size of cars I remember—watching from the top of the Empire State Building in New York. Nor did I really take account of our speed. Only when we passed an ordinary type plane did I appreciate the speed—over 600 air speed, over 750 ground speed. There wasn't time to read the lettering on the plane as we passed.

We dropped "a few feet"—about 10,000, to be exact—and that was when I noticed the funny feeling in the tummy. On a dive or turn, my stomach left the plane completely. There seemed to be a terrific pressure pushing it out, and along with it went the face muscles. My eyelids gradually closed against stiff resistance on my part. It was almost as though I could feel my 23-year-old body turning into that of a 90-year-old, with sagging muscles and dropping frame. Dimly I heard Johnny Rainville talking into my ear. He didn't get any reply. We were up 40 minutes, in all. There were times when it seemed years . . .

A couple of steep turns—you have to turn steeply at a speed of 600 m.p.h.—just about did me in, so when we landed, I stretched out on the grass for a bit, then took it gently into the medics room, but finally had to cave in and go to bed.

As for the Indians, they're wonderful, the nicest bunch of men in the world. They held my head, washed my face, brought me dozens of pills, kept asking me how I felt (or just crept in to see for themselves), and looked after me like a baby. The poor press officer, Flt.-Lt. Alan Marshall, from Peterborough, Ont., was nearly beside himself. He seemed to think I might die. Small wonder. It seems my face had turned grey.

And me! I felt like the biggest sissy on the face of the earth. The pilots assured me they had all felt the same when they first flew in a jet, and the ground crew told me they'd never go up in one.

I'd go again, out of grim determination to be a better sport next time. Jets are here to stay, and I don't want to be left an age behind.

Wednesday, May 30, 1951

Dear Mum,
Did I tell you Tony has had another offer of a job from Oxford University Press? I wasn't in the least keen and somehow almost felt that if he took it, it would mean the end of us, as I don't think I'd like life in Oxford. However, it's his life and work, so I didn't say anything. Also it meant only 3 weeks' holidays a year and all desk work, which I can't imagine him liking—and 3 weeks would cut out any hope of getting to Canada, which of course I didn't like. He had said he'd take it and then took a few days to think it over. Last Thursday we went walking and he argued with me about everything under the sun—particularly my work on the Express, which he considers a corrupt paper—as it is, I know, but it's still brilliant. By the end of the evening I was so fed up I didn't bother talking at all and figured I'd probably seen the beginning of the end . . . Can you imagine how I felt on Saturday when he told me he had wired Oxford after he left me Thursday night and refused the job?

Friday, June 8, 1951

Dear Mum,

Boy what a full week this has been! Have been fired by the Sunday Express with one month's notice—which means I'm through now and get 4 weeks' pay. They tried to cut the pay by 3 guineas ($10) per week but I phoned the news editor and complained. Got a letter in Wednesday's post telling me I still did not have enough experience for the type of writing they require.

It's all rather funny actually for I was complaining to Alan Hoby only the day before that I was almost ashamed to say I worked for the Sunday Express because it is becoming such a scandal sheet under the managing editor. Lucky I said all that before being fired instead of after, as he would have thought it was sour grapes.

When I told Tony, he merely said "Congratulations" and that he is pleased as he doesn't like my long Saturday shifts. Guess I'm quite satisfied too when I think of it, as all my friends from the Sunday Express are gone, Prebble, Junor, etc. and I don't much like the new gang . . . Had I been the Sunday Express, I would have fired me long ago. I haven't done any decent amount of work for them in months.

Thursday, June 14, 1951, 8 p.m.

Well, I really am having a week! Tuesday went to Ascot—the most fashionable horse race meeting of the year with Liz, Marg, the Queen and whole shoot in attendance. That kept me busy until about 7 p.m., and Tony, plus a headache, came over about 8 p.m. He's had these headaches, or rather general depression feelings quite often lately. He looks terribly fit, but . . . he'd better get himself off to a doctor quick or he'll remain single for life.

By the way, what would you say to us skipping over to France to be married while Marion is visiting, or later. Since you and Dad can't be with us—providing we decide definitely—I'd rather not have anyone at all, but maybe just sort of a small "at home" sometime after, for friends over here. What do you think of that?

Tuesday, June 19, 1951, night

About the column: I'm sorry you don't like my "boring" stuff, but can you imagine how much more "boring" the whole thing is to me when it goes only to the same old people and brings in so miserably little each week? . . . I'm sorry, Mum, but the column has become more of a drudgery than a pleasure to me and after two years I'm beginning to find both my humour and my material running out. I believe I only keep it on because you get such a kick out it and now that doesn't seem to be true either.

As for the Sunday Express, I'm glad I'm through with them, for I wasn't enjoying it . . . hadn't been for ages . . . I'm not in the least worried about my work for the Evening Standard, who have me as a freelance and not a staff member, and would not keep me on if it were not satisfactory . . . Howard Clegg was fired by the Montreal Standard a couple of months ago, and I believe they are closing up their office here.

Saturday, June 23, 1951

Don't know whether I've ever told you, but Tony is almost as restless as I am. Don't know what kind of stability that provides for, none, I should imagine, so I'm not banking on a quiet normal married life with the bridge club set. I'd be bored stiff, I'm sure.

Funny, I haven't that ardent desire most females seem to have to cook, sew, darn, and look after a guy. I'd rather Tony looks after me. But I've never felt I wanted to share my life and live with any guy before. Heaven help him on the cooking and housekeeping end, we'll have to share that too, I guess.

Discovered the other day that Tony has been finding out a lot more about the Catholic faith than I thought he had. Say a couple of prayers, Mum, because there are times when I think he may think himself right into it. But that is some way off yet.

Saturday, June 23, 1951, evening [a second letter on the same day]

Dear Mum,

Just read your June 19 letter and shall answer it now, then write a couple of columns.

As to Tony, you are a bit right. He IS serious, far more so than most guys you meet these days, but he can enjoy good jokes and takes seriously only those aspects of life which require it . . . He has little time for society chatter and the antics of film stars and again prefers not to be told of their silly goings-on. I quite agree, most of their antics are too dumb to be true, but I am feline enough to listen to them! That's where we differ.

He likes my face because it has character and has little use for the pretty, vague English society and American college girls. He feels a girl should have something inside that shows on the outside—I always knew I must have something, since it wasn't looks, now I know. Next person I meet I'll say, "See my pretty character?"

I got a terrible dressing-down yesterday from Mrs. Greene [a neighbour in Richmond]—the only person I really talk to over here—for not being more affectionate or at least showing it. I never call him "dear" or anything because it sort of embarrasses me or I'm afraid he won't like it or something. My old rigidity I guess, although I often call him such terms when I'm walking along thinking to myself and he isn't there. But I have heard him call me "dear" and "darling" a couple of times but very softly and usually against my hair or something so I can hardly hear. I particularly remember one evening when I finally mustered enough courage to tell him that I loved him very much; he sort of held me at arm's length for a couple of minutes, looked square at me and almost incredulously said, "You know, I believe you really mean that."

Yesterday I went to meet him when he wasn't expecting me and he had to look the other way he grinned so hard and seemed terribly pleased. Gosh, Mum, I don't know what to do half the time, when I figure I'm being very showy in my affections I realize by most people's standards I'm an icicle. I think of so many things that I never have the courage to tell him and if I try they come out like a school girl reciting a lesson. I even sometimes rehearse the things I'd like to tell him but can never muster the courage when the time comes.

Wednesday, June 27, 1951, morning

Your letter re stopping the column came yesterday but as you no doubt know by now I have perked up a bit and sent off a few more columns. What do you honestly think about the column, Mum? . . . I like having the column appear and don't mind too much doing it, but don't really feel it is worthwhile. I might hang on until David Roberts gets back to see if the Gleaner [New Brunswick newspaper based in Fredericton] were in the least bit interested in the column. It's a pity to cut off from Canada completely, in a way, and yet there is no sense in beating my head against a stone wall forever.

Friday, June 29, 1951, morning

Hello again!
Got a bit delayed on this but everything is more settled now. I go up to Llangollen on Tuesday and return either Wednesday night or Thurs. morning—the latter if I have my way. As you mentioned, these choir boys can be good publicity for me, but I think it is much better to be a representative of an English national rather than on my own for a small NB paper. Am doing the whole job, even taking my own camera for some exclusive pictures. Should get a good show in the Gleaner indeed.[10]

As for the jet story, the delay is my fault but it may work out perfectly. Had the article half-written and had been mulling over phrases in my head for days. Your letter telling of your

---

[10] The Llangollen International Musical Eisteddfod, held annually in Wales attracts choirs and performers from all over the world. Ouida was covering it for the Evening Standard and The Fredericton Gleaner. Her primary interest was the St. Joseph's Boys Choir from New Brunswick.

phone call to the Gleaner about it scared me, so I finished the article . . . then had Tony go over it with me. He seemed to like it fine . . . It should be on its way by Monday at the latest. Then I'll get someone to phone Canadian Press and tell them after a few days and see if I can work anything there. Might as well make the most of the jet trip, as my tummy will never take another, I don't think.

Wednesday, July 4, 1951

Dear Mum,
It is now just after noon and I'm sitting in the festival tent at the press table at the Eisteddfod in Llangollen. The University choir from Helsinki is singing, No 4 on our programme, and St. Joseph's is No. 28. The festival is like any other, intimate and local with the announcer giving a pat on the shoulder to each solo contestant. But the atmosphere is the most colourful and electrifying I have ever seen. National costumes galore and a choir is liable to stop and burst into song anywhere . . . Now the Italians, all men, in brown suede jackets, open neck shirts and multicoloured pants are singing . . . German choir just came in—Italians were extremely good . . . Boy, don't ever let anyone tell you all Swedes, Norwegians, etc., are tall blonds—they are not by a long shot . . . The ugliest looking English girls' choir just came on and Mike Walsh of the Express just turned around and muttered "Perhaps they can cook." . . . St. Joseph's is next . . .

They've won! Boy, the excitement. Boys are half crazy. I shrieked right out. Just phoned the office.

Love, Ouida

Monday, July 9, 1951

As you can probably gather, I'm flat out for the Italians now and especially one big, tall rugged guy named Vittorio Tranquillini. He can't speak a word of English but he sings to me—or did—and they went and got a doctor (very nice children's specialist who came up on Friday from London where he had been on business) to come and interpret. Through this method I was told he liked the way I dressed and my red coat, but he wasn't a communist. (I wore a red duster coat which I had just finished making that Monday . . . with a small feather hat with two red roses on one side and white gloves and it seemed to catch everyone's eye.) The next day I was told that he liked me very much and please could I visit Trento when I go to Italy in August and he would be glad to show me his beautiful country. The doctor, Fausto Dorigatti, endorsed this on his own, saying they would love to have me visit them and would gladly take me on the lake etc.

Vittorio is a tall, brown-haired chap with a pleasant face, not handsome but has a bit of character (probably bad) and a wonderful smile. He's quite probably married with 40 kids, but the doctor had an honest face, and they would be genuinely pleased to see me, I'm sure. Anyway we may not get anywhere near to Trento. There was one sulky guy in the lot, a handsome dark-eyed character who made the first play and when I showed equal interest in the others, seemed to get rather sore. I took great delight in putting an amused expression on my face as though I was speaking a joke then saying the most outrageous things and they would laugh heartily.[11]

Today I love life—and my bed because I'm tired; yesterday I loved that Italian who flattered me so; tomorrow I'll love the whole St. Joseph boys again when they sing to the Beaver and me, too, I hope; Tuesday I see Tony again and I may even love him, you can't tell.

Sunday, July 15, 1951

Called Cunard [steamship line] and found out Marion may land on Thursday evening but shall keep in touch. I have been given a special press pass which will allow me on board the minute it ties up and as I have next Friday off, I'm all set. The following weekend will be a long one for me so I may take Marion up to Marie's or might make a stab for three days in either Scotland or Cornwall if my finances are anywhere near good, although I mustn't cut into our continental trip or the money I want to spend on Marion for whatever she wants. Am getting quite excited about my holidays, as I now think we should be able to go from here to Paris, then into Switzerland and down into Italy, then probably spend the third week recuperating in the south of France. We shall probably travel with rucksacks and a sleeping bag and just camp in someone's backyard wherever possible to cut costs, but with three of us—Shirley Reid [friend from Canada who lived in London for two years working as a model, canasta teacher, and Mayfair hairdresser] is coming too—we should have a barrel of fun, then join Tony for the last week maybe. Anyway I'll see how Marion takes to all this; she's a pretty good sport I imagine, if she's a true)MacLellan.

Friday, July 20, 1951, evening

Dear Mum,
Well, Marion is here and had a wonderful crossing. She spotted me from almost mid-Atlantic today (of course I was the only person in sight and wearing a red coat and white hat and standing on the end of the pier) and began that excited flappy waving of hers. She wasn't dif-

---

11 Ouida made several friendships among the Italian Men's choir from Trento that lasted for some fifty years. She and her sister Marion did visit Trento in August.

ficult to see. Her cabin companion was a Mrs. Spiers from Westmount who had taken great care of her and as she left said, "Come kiss your sea mother goodbye," which Marion did.

Wednesday, July 25, evening

Marion is being a great little trooper. While I'm tied up here in the office she gets herself out on her own and has managed to see quite a bit. She finds her way around very well indeed—like me, not you!

This afternoon we're going to book our passage to France for August 12 and tonight I think we had better make this an evening of washing, ironing, and tidying up.

Love, Ouida

"PERHAPS I HAVE AT LAST GROWN UP"
August–December 1951

Friday, Aug. 3, 1951

Gosh, all this talk about your sending the jet story off to everyone, I hope you haven't ruined things. Al Marshall [RCAF information officer] has taken the pictures along to Canadian Press (did the Gleaner use them?) and they are interested in releasing them but if you've sent the stuff out to everyone ahead of time, it's going to spoil it.

There was no use your sending the Welsh festival stuff to the Montreal Standard, Mum; they have told you before they can't use stuff printed in other papers. Good heavens, the Montreal papers would never admit they were beaten by the Fredericton Gleaner. Anything they accept must be original and exclusive.

Rather wish you'd let me do all this in my own way, because from the sound of things, phoning Fredericton, etc.,—and Marion tells me you do nothing but fiddle with the column—you'll get yourself the reputation of a nut. I don't mean this to be mean, Mum, but I also don't want people saying you're the push and that you're trying to drive me or that I am incapable of doing anything on my own.

Another thing, until I send you an official announcement that a wedding date has been set, please don't go on assuming that I'm contemplating marriage. Until a thing is definitely set, don't ever take a word I say seriously. There are a great many bridges before anyone gets me to the altar and any one of them could collapse. I would also appreciate it if you spread that view around Moncton, as I'm sick to death of people coming over here saying, "When are you getting married?" Also, please remove Tony's pix out of the front room. They were for family benefit, not public.

[During her August holiday on the Continent with her sister, Ouida's letters were primarily travel pieces and descriptions that she intended to use as column material.]

Monday, Sept. 10, 1951

Well, it's been pretty lonesome around here since Marion left on Thursday. I was getting pretty accustomed to having the bright face around when I came in—even though I didn't really show it, I'm afraid.

Saturday night I was invited to a party at Mike Skinner's. His folks (fishmongers) have a beautiful home down at Virginia Water, huge house, terraced gardens, etc. I had a riotous evening baiting an Englishman named "Arthur." He's one of the "By Jove, I say" types.

When my feet hurt after a lot of dancing, I went out into the garden, removed my shoes, and walked around in my bare feet. He came out after me, seemed a bit stunned at first, then decided it was "a jolly good idea" and took his shoes off, too. We wandered around in the dark in the garden when he decided to explore. I pointed out where the next set of steps were, but oh no he had to go his own way. He asked me what I thought was in front of him. I said it looked pretty dark and was possibly a hedge. "I say, By Jove, do you really think so"? And with that he stuck out his foot to see and stepped off a 4 foot wall. I roared so hard I could hardly even ask if he was hurt.

His line was terrific. Sitting beside me, he asked if I was cold, touched one arm and said, "Oh, I say, you're absolutely freezing. By Jove, is the other arm as cold as this one?" A Canadian boy would probably say something tactful like "Will you have my coat with or without my arms?" This guy would be deadly in big doses but sure amused me for one evening! I think he wanted to kiss and I couldn't help baiting him on, but when he got within breathing distance he couldn't seem to make up his mind how to go about it, so I discovered a grasshopper and went to examine "such a strange freak of nature." Boy, what a jerk! Must tell Tony, it should amuse him.

Wednesday, Sept. 11, 1951

You asked about Marion. She was perfectly fine over here but then there is no reason why she shouldn't be. I've known for some time, especially after my trip home Christmas that you and Marion are of completely different temperaments and friction between you is most probable. She was amazingly patient, didn't seem to mind when I'd ask her to do things I knew I really should be doing myself and never complained once about anything. She is an extremely nice girl, very young yet, but shaping up well. I know I am extremely difficult to live with and because Marion takes everything off me and never talks back, she probably found me unrewarding and mean at times. She said she felt unwanted a couple of times, which I knew at the time she did, but to be quite honest I was so terrified she'd get over-tired or have ear trouble or something would happen, I tried to discourage her from doing too much, but evidently went about it in an awkward manner.

Wednesday, Sept. 18, 1951, evening

I think that Tony and I are through. Have had a feeling for a long while now that it wasn't really going to work out. What he seemed willing to offer isn't what I want, or rather just isn't enough for me. A pity in a way, as I'm very fond of him. He has suggested we see a bit less of each other for a while and see if the old feeling will return. I have my doubts. There are so many little differences, not to mention the religion, and Tony just doesn't seem to have sufficient "give and take." There's no real companionship. Suppose I'm half to blame but I do think I've been fairly reasonable. Anyway, we shall see.

Sunday, Sept. 30, 1951

Saw the film "Showboat" the other night and although the picture wasn't much, there were some good parts and I thought the male wonderfully masterful. That night I spent the whole night dreaming I had a masterful man too and through the dream it was Vittorio. Imagine the "Ah, fate" feeling when I got to the office next morning to find a special delivery letter from him. Boy, if he keeps writing me . . . you never can tell what may happen. What would you say to a name like Ouida Tranquillini, Mum. Suppose it wouldn't really suit, for I'd never be able to spell it properly.

Yesterday Tony collected me from the office at 4:00 p.m. and we had a bit of tea, then went to the Empire Cinema in Leicester Square to see "An American in Paris"—a musical, and at his suggestion, despite the fact he ordinarily doesn't like musicals . . . Funny, but our evening out was like a first date, only a little sharper. Maybe this break we are experiencing will do us both good, either toward each other or toward others. I seem to feel very much more confident in my conversations and thoughts—more solid reasoning, individual thinking, and forming of opinion with some basis for reasons given. Suppose it's all part of the process of growing up and developing, which I sincerely hope I'm still doing. Less of the daydreaming and more of the facing of actual realities should do me some good . . .

You know, Mum, I rather wish life would take on some definite shape for me. I seem to be going about accomplishing nothing, heading toward nothing, with little or no future. It's a funny feeling, for I feel that by now I should have some aim, some ambition, some purpose in view, but there's nothing. There are lots of things I'd like to do, but even those don't really lead to anything. Oh well, I've never been stuck before, something will probably turn up sometime soon—I hope.

Sunday, Oct. 7, 1951

I think Tony is trying to bring me around to his way of thinking by treating me less often. He acts rather reserved, doesn't call me as often, and we are seeing much less of each other than we used to. My role is supposed to be that of the broken-hearted female dying for affection. Instead I'm having a delightful time. This week I have one date with a chap in the office who has been asking me out for ages . . . also I have a theatre date with Pat Archibald and have promised Chris an evening to celebrate his $9 a week raise. So that won't leave much time for Tony. He'll find that unless he books ahead, he'll be out of luck.

Don't know where it is going to end—suppose if I were sensible, I'd tell him now that I don't want to see him anymore, although I've never broken completely with any guy and hate losing a good friendship.

Wednesday, Oct. 10, 1951

Another election coming up over here and I almost hate to have to vote, as I have little use for either the Socialists or the Conservatives. The Socialists have accomplished a few things at the expense of many others. The Conservatives have yelled like stuck pigs but still offer no better solutions to the problems. Don't honestly think there will be much of a change and can't see what difference it would make if there was one. Britain is a third-rate power now and the quicker she gets used to it and begins thinking like one, the better for all.

Was my column on Italy ever used? I've been waiting for ages for a copy to send the choir in Trento as they requested. For gosh sakes, send one!

Tuesday, October 16, 1951

Dear Mum,
Ah ha! the 16th, payday! Well, today is my day off and I'm trying to get caught up on a few things before going up to a cocktail party at Lady Gainsborough's in Kensington—wrote Fausto Dorigatti, sending the column on Italy, which came in the second post today. Think I'll wear the nylons Frances sent me to this cocktail party tonight. Have been waiting for an opportunity and this looks like a good one. They are the ones with the butterfly painted on one leg and the three ladybugs on the other. Should provide some fun.

Must go have a bath now and look all spic and span for the party—although it is just a small one, and goodness only knows how dull it will probably be!

Love, Ouida

Sunday, Oct. 21, 1951

I hope you realize, Mum, that the more you natter on about the small-minded "doings" in Moncton, the more determined I am never to get stuck in a similar set-up myself. Fed up as I get at times, this place grows on you, you know. You'd be amazed at the number of

Portrait of the author by A.K. Browning, 1953, who titled it *Fierce Virgin*

Ouida's *Evening Standard* press pass, 1950

Writing home from Mrs. Bennett's kitchen.

The £5 hat

"Gorgeous Gussie" Moran in the lace-trimmed tennis outfit by designer Ted Tingling, at a press showing at the Dorchester. Ouida is far right.

In the green satin dress and the £5 hat at the Kinsman Trust cocktail party.

Wearing out soles and heels on the hotel beat.

Modelling a suit and hat at a fashion show.

Flt-Lt John Rainville and Ouida in the Meteor jet fighter before takeoff.

Studio portrait of Ouida by Wallace Heaton.

Beverley Nichols interviewing Ouida, from *Woman's Own* magazine, February, 1954

The Healey Silverstone, Rodney's "flashy red sports car."

Rodney and Ouida at the Conservative Ball.

Lord Beaverbrook and Ouida MacLellan before her wedding to Rodney Touche, London, April 30, 1955.

After the wedding, Rodney and Ouida Touche leave for the reception.

Ouida at home in Calgary, Alberta, 1984 from a magazine clipping.

both Canadians and Americans over here who will never return to the other side to live. Paris is lousy with Yanks and most of them clear-thinking, keen types. Europe, despite the wars, has so very much more to offer in so many ways, and I know that Canada and the United States are young yet, but the way they're going about life they'll never match the culture, arts, etc., there is here. Judging from the press the U.S. gets over here, it must be like living in a witch hunt of the Medieval ages with hysterical psychology cases branding everyone who thinks for himself as a communist. And to be confronted with Joe McCarthy on the cover of Time magazine this week and learn he was a so-called ardent Catholic made me sick. I suppose Time hopes to knock some sense into the sheep-like mobs that follow McCarthy's lies. Wonder if McCarthy ever reads the Commandments—like the one that says "Thou shalt not bear false witness against thy neighbour"?

Here I am at 24, with still no purpose or aim in view, no definite plans for future . . . just an aching, itching, restless feeling inside . . . There are times when I almost wish I could marry and settle down, yet I know I haven't yet met the man who is for me. At times I feel I've wasted a year on Tony, but I don't regret it, for I've learned so very much from and through him. I think, Mum, that perhaps I have at last grown up. Funnily enough, Chris remarked the other day on how very much I had grown up during the last year—for the better, he thinks.

Sunday, Oct. 28, 1951, evening

I met Tony at 4:30 p.m.—first time I had seen him in over three weeks—and we had a bit of tea then walked for a long while. He looks rather thin to me, has given up smoking in an attempt to clear his sinus trouble, and is a bag of nerves, fidgeting all the time, although possibly there was a reason, as we decided it was better to make it a clean break between us, as this letting it slide is doing no one any good. He says he realizes he could never marry a Catholic, especially after visiting Catholic countries like Spain and Portugal and seeing what goes on. Also that we have such very different views, and he rather wonders how we have kept it going so long now. He is sorry to have wasted a year of my life over here, etc., etc., etc.

I'm not sure of how I feel, although I've known this had to come. I suppose I've known it ever since the start, when we didn't agree on religion, but I'm not particularly sorry, for I feel I've learned quite a lot from Tony . . . Still it hurts to see the end of something I had almost hoped might work out, for I feel the need of something steadying and solid and just can't seem to find it.

Must get to bed now, as I'm dead beat.

Lots of Love, Ouida

Thursday, Nov. 8, 1951, evening

A cocktail party on Tuesday night proved both entertaining and interesting. Some good people present, and David Ross was terribly sweet to me. We had vaguely planned on going dancing afterwards, but instead stayed for supper then went for a walk on our own and by that time it was 11 p.m. and I came home . . . David is still quite fond of me—hope it remains just that, as I couldn't bear him to get sticky again.

Seem to be off all men these days. Seeing the end of Tony browned me off Chris as well and I haven't seen him, although he has phoned me several times. Now he goes back on nights so I probably shan't see him except for an odd cup of tea, which will suit me fine.

Thursday, Nov. 22, 1951

You ask what I do for the Gleaner—and now it is the Vancouver Sun as well. This week I've done a terrific lot. It should be bylined—at least some should be, I think. Did a story on the Mounties, just phoned over one on a naval dinner tonight, and an exclusive interview with Mrs. Brooke Claxton [wife of the Canadian Minister of Defence]—evidently I'm the first reporter ever to get her to talk, according to her husband. This afternoon—although it's my day off—I have an interview with Jim Armstrong at Ontario House; he is secretary of the Canada Club in London, of which Prince Philip was made an honorary member.

So I'm back in the groove again with the Overseas Service, so that should help some.

Wednesday, Nov. 28, 1951

Dear Mum,
Well it looks like I'm in a silly position and stuck with it. I had hoped to be able to say I'd be home for Christmas, but arrangements aren't panning out as planned. The office are quite agreeable to me having the time off, but transportation isn't forthcoming.

Originally I thought the RCAF could accommodate me on the homeward flight, and I have asked TCA again if they can help me get back on a Press pass. Haven't heard from TCA but RCAF, although seemingly quite willing, say their planes are loaded until after Christmas. Am going to try Pan American this afternoon, but free Press passages are pretty scarce!

The complete return fare is about $545. How much have I in the bank there? Very little, I should imagine!

Have tried ships, but none are going at a suitable time and even they cost money. I haven't a penny over here as I will need everything for income tax in March. So there you have it. Had hoped to get home during weekend before Christmas and back here again for Jan. 20.

Evidently I am getting bylines in the Vancouver Sun now, too. And yesterday David Roberts suggested a picture feature on me to be sold in Canada, so the future could be bright.

Called Pan American and have to call again tomorrow so hope not completely dashed yet. Any suggestions?

Lots of Love,

Ouida

[Pan American came through for Ouida. The next letter in the series is dated Jan. 4, 1952, on Pan American World Airways stationery from the airport in Gander.]

"MOST MEN THINK FEMALE JOURNALISTS ARE TARTS"
January–February 1952

Saturday, Jan. 4, 1952, 8 p.m. [on Pan American World Airways stationery]

Dear Mum and Dad,

Am sitting in Terminal 1 here at Gander and expect to take off in about one and a half hours. Weather is closing in so TCA are going to Goose Bay instead of here and I have been transferred to Trans World Airlines. This means I fly a Constellation, take off at 9 p.m. instead of midnight, fly straight to Shannon, bypassing Ireland, and should be in London about 9 a.m. So quite pleased. [The plane stopped in Ireland only to refuel.]

Sunday, Jan. 13, 1952

Dear Daddy,

. . . You bet I enjoyed my stay. It was really wonderful, and a few weeks with you at home at Christmas really sets me up for another year over here. Only wish I had had longer, as I came back with dozens of things I wanted to tell you.

The Constellation is bigger than the North Star that TCA uses and quieter. I had a double seat to myself, and the middle armrest is detachable so I used the whole seat. Carries about 50 passengers but wasn't full. However TWA can't touch TCA for service on the flight [TCA: Trans-Canada Airways, predecessor of Air Canada].

Had a nice day today when an Australian publisher took me driving and to lunch at a lovely riverside hotel at Marlow in Oxfordshire.

Lots of love, Ouida

Friday, Jan. 18, 1952

Dear Mum,

Tuesday afternoon I drove to North Luffenham—Canadian No. 1 Fighter Wing—with Al Marshall for some stories and information I want for both newspaper and radio.[12] Had quite a pleasant time, although I felt rugged Wednesday a.m. when I had a lot of walking and standing to do.

Have been invited up to their Valentine formal on Feb. 16 by Flight Officer Art Rayner, who seems quite a nice young man. Other than that, I know nothing about him. It was rather amusing. We (Doc, Padre, the Education Officer, Marshall, and me) were sitting at the dinner table when Rayner joined us. During conversation he asked me if I had heard of the Valentine dance. I replied, "Someone mentioned it last night. It's one of those things people tell me about beforehand, then a fortnight after ask me why I didn't attend."

"Then I'll put my question this way," replied Rayner, "would you like to come to the Valentine dance?" He suggested Al might bring me up by car, and the padre jumped in and invited Al and his wife to be his guests, then the Doc suggested I might bunk with the nurses in the officers' mess, so there I was, all fixed! Actually I'm quite pleased, as I'd love to go, and Rayner seems about the nicest of the pilots. He's probably just my age—if that—about 5 ft. 11 in., thick dark hair in slightly crewcut style, brown eyes, and very cut out and neat in appearance. He's going to call me before the dance.

I may be moving after all but probably not until April or later. Mrs. Bennett and Mollie are thinking of buying a farm. Think I shall try for a small service flat though, as I'm seldom in and would prefer someone else to clean, etc. One room and bath is almost enough and I'd just as soon not share unless I want to have friends in—but all that's a long way off.

Must close,

Lots of love, Ouida

Monday, Jan. 21, 1952, evening

Funny, but I am wondering already if I was wise to give up the column. The written word lasts much longer than the spoken one, you know, and it's amazing how far that column managed to get itself. The cutting services would send it all over the country, of course, and in that way people, even important ones that it concerned, would see it. Have had several stories lately that would have done for it but can easily adapt them to radio—if they'd only hurry up and give me the go-ahead or at least send me the blank tapes.

---

12 Ouida had decided to stop writing the column and wanted instead to do a regular radio program on tape for CKCW in Moncton.

Pretty, am I? Boy, you'd better watch out, I'll be believing all this malarkey—but not with Dad around to remind me that I have a bump on my nose, buck teeth that ruin a profile, pigeon-toed feet, and I pick my nose. But I do quite like my hair parted in the middle, and Mollie has given me a new trim, and it looks amazing good.

Saturday night I was originally invited to a party and asked David Ross to accompany me as he had last year to the same affair. But it was a "bottle party," which means everyone takes a bottle of something, usually gin. David and I compared finances—both nil—and then Aubrey Cousins, the Australian publisher, phoned to ask me out. That settled it. I phoned David and frankly told him I thought we'd be silly to spend our own money on a party we weren't sure we'd enjoy when this Aussie wanted to spend his money to entertain me, and besides David had some work to do. He roared at my bluntness and asked me to dinner at his home on Wednesday, so I went with the Aussie. What a night!

This guy is one of those rather silent characters; you can't quite tell what he is thinking. We saw a movie—"The African Queen," very good—then went to a Crete restaurant for a meal, when I am told he's really quite shy. We had a discussion about purposes in dating, and I frankly said I usually distrust a guy because my job surrounds me with a much more glamorous and wild reputation than I have, and rather than waste a guy's time, I usually give him time to think it over and call me again if he's still interested. He decides I have an inferiority complex and had it never occurred to me that I was a rather attractive person and quite good company? Rubbish! Most men think female journalists are tarts, and I know it—besides, you can usually tell by the look on a guy's face what he has in mind. I'm quite capable of sorting people out, thanks!

Anyway, I noticed that he made a habit of calling me "pet"—which I figured was some crazy Aussie idea and let it pass, although I loathe endearing terms used loosely, or at all, for that matter. Driving home—he has a new Morris car—I was daydreaming per usual, and can you imagine my surprise when suddenly he slipped one arm around my shoulder and called me "darling"? I wanted to hoot with laughter. He suddenly sounded like a guy who had it bad—silly ass, a grown man of at least 35 doesn't go overboard for a casual date who is as unencouraging as me. Anyway, I firmly said I had to go in and when he complained, retorted that he had moaned about being tired all evening, and I wasn't going to be accused of keeping him from his beauty sleep. He announced that he found me a very "womanish woman" (what did he expect?) and wished he could see my "big grey eyes" to find out what I was thinking. I snorted, "They're blue," which obviously wasn't the right answer, but then my mood wasn't a romantic one, so small wonder. The whole thing struck me as funny, so I doubt if he'll call again. Real femme fatale, eh! WOW!!

Lots of love, Ouida

Thursday, Jan 24, 1952

Got a kiss on one cheek from Max Caulfield last Saturday and on both cheeks from Alan Hoby—first time I'd seen them since my return and they made me blush furiously right in the middle of the restaurant. Still have John Prebble to see, although I was talking to him on the phone yesterday—what a guy! Then Tuesday, Alan suddenly popped up to me on the street when I was with Peter Wood of the Star (rival evening paper) and asked me out to dinner and to an ice pantomime with him one evening soon. He was probably kidding, but shall have to wait to see.

Have called an accountant and because I had some stories printed over here on my Canadian trip, he says I can have my fare home as my business expenses, which should be a big help. I'm going to need it if I'm to have to meet all my yearly taxes at once.

Monday, Jan. 28, 1952

So Marion considers me dumb, does she? You might remind her that it is one thing to "personalitize" your way into things, but it takes a bit more to keep yourself in once you get there. If you continue to let her make such remarks, people will soon start suggesting I have to make my way by "other" means and in Fleet Street that usually means the "bed route"—sleeping with the various editors. Surely I can depend on my own family to give me credit for a little bit of grey matter—there are enough outsiders ready to relieve me of any I might have! These so-called "cute" remarks can be unintentionally harmful.

Friday, Feb. 1, 1952

Dear Mum,
Your Monday letter came along with Daddy's Sunday one yesterday and you have me a bit worried. You say, "Still no word from CKCW." As I've already said, you won't have any word. I had a letter from Berkley [her contact at the station] on Tuesday—just one day over a week after I'd written him, so that's not bad. He said the program boss preferred the one 15-minute weekly program and he would try to get more blank tapes off to me shortly. Also, he hadn't as yet worked out a deal with either the Saint John or Antigonish stations but hoped to have further word regarding a sponsor and starting time by Feb 3. So he is on the job, but for goodness sake don't you worry him. This is something I've really got to handle on my own. Your job now is to get the column started again, as I guess I could manage all right by making a carbon copy of quite a few of the stories I do for the Evening Standard. The readers by now are quite willing to accept strictly English stuff, whereas the radio audience will have to be fed a lot of Canadian angles, for a start anyway.

Well, it looks as though I might be moving quite soon now. Mollie and Mary—the other woman who is going to share the farm—are negotiating for a property about eight miles from Southampton, and it looks quite hopeful for them.

There was an ad in the Times yesterday for a furnished room with kitchen/bath, electricity, heating, and telephone for 3 1/2 guineas a week in Knightsbridge. So I sent a letter in—only a box number given—and although the chances via a letter are pretty slim it sounds very much like what I'd like and the area is excellent. That price is about $10 a week, which is very good if the place is really anything decent.

Had lunch with Aube Cousins—the Aussie—on Wednesday (darn good feed too!). And am seeing him again tomorrow night and that will probably be the last, as he flies to New York on Monday. Over lunch he remarked "Gosh, those big blue-grey eyes, they really are beautiful, you know." I'm not completely immune to such trash, so probably just as well he is clearing out because although I'm flattered, I'm still not interested otherwise and don't really believe he is either.

At last it's Feb. so now I have only another fortnight to wait before I go up to the Valentine dance at North Luffenham. Wonder what the outcome will be? It'll be strange, an all-Canadian dance in England! Wonder if they'll stick to Canadian habits and try for corsages or follow the English customs.

Sunday, Feb. 3, 1951

Dear Mum,
Here it is February and gradually I am reducing my debts. Still owe the bank £40 and Mrs. Bennett £24, but another few weeks and that should be pretty well taken care of. Then of course there is the income tax, due about the first of April. Hope this radio thing materializes quickly, as I was rather planning on a bit of it to help with my taxes so I could get rid of them quickly then settle down to put some money aside.

My future home is still undecided but judging from the present prices, think I'll stay here with Mrs. Bennett until I am forced to leave, as this is as cheap as anything I could find—unless something exceptionally good presents itself.

Yesterday about 12:15 p.m. the commissionaire in the front hall at the Standard phoned to tell me there was a Mr. Ryan to see me. Down I went, and there was Joe, closely resembling a tweedy tramp but not caring two hoots and in a carefree mood. [Joe Ryan was a friend from Moncton studying medicine in England.] He finally left to fetch his brother and they returned about 1:45 p.m. and took me to lunch. The brother John is no improvement on Joe and between them they had me in fits of laughter. Joe is through at Southend

Hospital and thinks he will take a course at the Royal College [of Medicine] for a while, which means he is back in London, so I can see more of him. He keeps insisting I should get married—lack of other ideas for conversation, I should judge.

The brother likes London but occasionally the Englishmen annoy him so he takes the mickey out of them. At a restaurant recently—posh places practically lick the floor for would-be dollar customers—the waiters made so much fuss (once they heard his accent) he finally fixed them by peering around the room through a hole in his serviette. At the motor car show, he stood at the back of a group of bowler-hatted Englishmen peering at a new Rolls Royce and shouted at the salesman, "Hey Mac, how many dollars?" The salesman rushed him to the front and promised him delivery in New York in a fortnight, while young John (who said, "Imagine showing a guy like me a Rolls Royce") just stood around and found fault with the car, size, lines, speed, etc.

I asked Joe Ryan about Marion coming to study medicine here and he said, "Good idea, their schools are good here." She would go right into hospital training here and take both Canadian and British exams at the finish. Joe says McGill Med. School has gone down.

Art Rayner got me by phone this morning and everything is fixed for the Valentine Ball on Feb. 16. It was rather sweet, for very "a la Canuck," he asked what colour dress I would be wearing and what kind of a corsage I would like—so he could rush back and plant it now. I'll wear the black with red, and like a man he said, "Something pink, then," at which I shrieked! I imagine it will be red carnations, as he suggested them, but I said nothing big, so I can possibly tape it on my bare shoulder.

Wednesday, Feb. 6, 1952, 4:30 p.m.

Dear Mum,
This has been one day to end all days. It started calmly, then came the announcement of the King's death at 10:45 a.m. and it blew up. Indigestion over lunch, jamming telephones, screaming editors, rush of copy—in short, a completely mad atmosphere. My head is aching, my brain in a whirl, and I'm dog tired.

Thursday [added]

I was so exhausted yesterday I didn't even finish this letter. Don't know what the next few weeks will bring but sure hope my long weekend won't be cancelled, as I'm so looking forward to a rest with Marie and Bill. Suppose there is a good chance of the Valentine Ball next week being cancelled.

We are now awaiting the arrival of the new Queen. Just had my picture taken for a police pass, as we all must carry special passes throughout the pre-funeral period. Haven't seen the result yet.

Have to dash so shall close.

Lots of love,

Ouida

Monday, Feb. 11, 1952, morning

Dear Mum,
Am back in the office today, as my day off was cancelled because of the arrival of the King's body in London. I'm to go shortly to Buckingham Palace to await the arrival there of Queen Elizabeth, the Queen Mother, and Princess Margaret. They are travelling from Sandringham in the funeral train but are not in the procession from the station to Westminster Hall.

Friday will be a truly hectic day, as the funeral procession begins at 9:30 a.m. and so we shall probably be out and about long before that.

Have just been told the Valentine Ball has been cancelled for Saturday—no social functions at Luffenham for a month. So that will probably be the end of Art Rayner, as he's bound to meet someone closer to home or new in that time. I was just a "date" to him, I'm quite sure, so I'll probably not see him again unless I go up there on business.

Thanks for all the nice things you said in your Monday and Wednesday letters. I sometimes feel I'm a completely incompetent dunderhead who does have a butterfly brain and has so far managed on pure luck. It's a sore point with me, I'm afraid, and I like a bit of "talking out of it."

5:30 p.m. [added]

Last Friday spent the whole day outside St. James Palace and saw Elizabeth proclaimed Queen by the heralds on the balcony. Today I saw her enter Buckingham Palace for the first time as Queen—also Queen Mother, Margaret, Queen Mary, Princess Royal, Gloucester, and the Duke of Kent.

Mike Smart just phoned and has asked me out to dinner tonight—free meal, hurrah!

Wednesday, Feb. 13, 1952

Had a grand time the other evening with Mike Smart. Always have liked Mike, but he would never chisel in on Chris's territory before now. But with Chris now dating Kate, Mike and I are both free operators and quite enjoyed ourselves.

Sunday, Feb. 17, 1952

Dear Mum,

This is one of those weekends when I feel I am going insane! Mrs. Bennett is in one of her moods when she barely speaks to me and gives the impression I am in the way and everything she does is my fault. There is work I should do but I really can't face staying in all day in this atmosphere . . . I phoned yesterday, as I rather wanted to ask Mike Smart in for the evening but was told "Oh, no, George and Jean are coming" (her nephew and his wife). There are two lounges in this house, but the thought of offering to allow me to light the fire in the second one never occurs.

Yesterday Marius Pope, music critic in the office, told me of a friend of his who is hoping for a job abroad. If he gets it (he'll know next week) he will sublet his flat near Sloane Square, and Marius asked if I'd like it. It sounds ideal. One large room, kitchen, bathroom, and small entrance hall, completely self-contained—in a block of flats, I gather—and a telephone operated through a switchboard where messages could be taken. The price is wonderful, for Sloane is very central, and furnished I could have it for about 30 shillings a week ($4.60). That would be even better than sharing an unfurnished place, so if I get the chance, I'll grab it quick.

The Express syndication service is selling some feature articles on the funeral by Rebecca West [English author and journalist]—she's a big name, you know. It was a riot yesterday as David Roberts told me he went to Windsor with her and she came back into the hotel room after the funeral to say, "I'm sorry but I didn't see a thing except rows of the backs of distinguished heads." David nearly blew up, for he had already sold her piece everywhere. So he calmed her down, then sat down and discussed everything with her and finally convinced her she had seen quite a lot, and with the help of reports of other reporters, finally got her story written. He said it was really good in the end.

I saw the funeral procession from Horse Guards Parade, an excellent spot. The Duke of Windsor looked quite drunk, but as I think it over now, realize he was probably horribly nervous and uneasy. Monday I spent outside Buckingham Palace; Tuesday, Clarence House; Wednesday, off and washed hair; Thursday, inside and outside Westminster Hall; and Friday, the funeral. Yesterday was at Clarence House again for the morning.

Thursday night, cinema and dinner with Mike Smart and two other couples and had such a headache and felt so tired I let Mike and the others talk me into staying at his house overnight, as I had to be up early for the funeral the next day. He phoned his mother and when we reached his home he was very sweet, got everything ready and laid out lovely silk pyjamas of his own for me. Had a very nice sleep and felt much better next day. Mike goes back to Germany on Thursday or Saturday of this week.

Must close,

Lots of love, Ouida

Wednesday, Feb. 20, 1952

Dear Mum,
Golly, I'm gone again! Saw Mike Smart two evenings last week and thoroughly enjoyed them. Then saw him again last night—this time we were on our own—and had a wonderful evening. We just seemed to click and it was fun . . . I'm starry-eyed for a while again and always enjoy it! . . . I like him fine and enjoy being with him—but he's a pilot and a non-Catholic and I really don't know him too well—AND I'M DETERMINED to remain fancy-free for a while!

I've had a letter from Art Rayner and it's sooo Canadian, I roared! Typical male scrawl, paper folded unevenly and talk plain. Says he was disappointed about the dance but that wasn't his prime interest, as "getting to know you seemed like it could be much more fun"! He says he is really quite keen to date me, so he's giving me fair warning and he'll ring me on the Wednesday prior to his next London visit. He realizes an Englishman would submit written permission a month in advance but Canadians are a more impromptu crowd. How little he knows! Beside Mike Smart, Art's slow!

Sunday, Feb. 24, 1952

Well Mike's gone back to Germany . . . He didn't say a thing about writing, coming over in May, or anything else except for me to take care of myself. So I know absolutely nothing but am hoping he will get around to writing.

That ugly old "if only" is staring me in the face again. If only he were a Catholic! Mike's as solid as the rock of Gibraltar, straightforward, honest, and under an occasional gruff or bullying manner, there is extreme thoughtfulness, kindness, and consideration. He's making the air force his career, is a Flt. Lt. now, and hopes to have his own squadron one day. That means plenty of postings and living in a variety of places and conditions. Mike realizes this and knows he must have a wife who can take it all—he told me all this and said he had seen wives ruin so many careers for the fellows and become the victims of so much gossip it would take a very wise and understanding woman to keep her head through it all and still like it. So at least I know he has thought it out carefully.

Feel in a mix-up again but like it. By the way, Mike brought on this feeling without doing any more than holding my hand. For about the first time in my life I very much wanted a guy to kiss me, but no sir, he kept his distance. At the same time, from the way he looked at me and the way he gripped my hand or my arm when we were walking, I'm pretty sure he was aware of the fact that I exist. Oh, blast—life can be stinking.

Must dash now, sorry about all this drivel!

Lots of love, Ouida

Wednesday Feb. 27, 1952

Tell Marion not to worry about not being asked to dance. I well recall sitting out a variety of dances, and I had the misfortune of my face in repose appearing sulky. So either I sat and grinned and looked like an idiot, or looked angry. As for Marion's friend Norma, she's a much more self-contained girl—physically. She, I should imagine, has a well-developed line of patter and flattery and also has a more alive-looking face. It's all a highly developed art. I find I've polished up tremendously ever since coming over here. Also, working as young as I did made me more at ease in meeting people than Marion probably is. But I was always classified at home as a bit of a "stick in the mud" for my ideals, etc. Tell Marion a sweet, fresh, and nice personality takes longer to uncover but it also lasts much longer. The whole social set-up is completely artificial but if you can treat it as a game and a chance at play-acting, it can be amusing. Why not dream up a few lines—you can help her, Mum—and see which boys are easiest to fell and on what ground? It can be very funny, for some are such fools!

Love, Ouida

"FLAT BEHAVIOUR"
March–May 1952

Wednesday, March 5, 1952, evening

This is my long weekend and so I am going up to Marie's on the 4:30 p.m. train Friday (arrives Diss 6:58 p.m.) to stay until Monday evening.[13] Phoned Marie last night and she said she had been waiting since Sunday to hear from me. The new Catholic church is opening in Diss on Sunday, and Marie says we are going to the bishop's tea on Sunday afternoon—it ought to be fun!

Yesterday Eileen Ashcroft, our fashion editor, told me of a friend of hers who has a flat to share in Cheney Walk, Chelsea. The woman, about 30, is separated from her husband (one of the war marriages, and she had been supporting him ever since, according to Eileen). She has a nice flat facing the Thames with a little garden at the back. Evidently there are two bed-sitting rooms with adjoining bathrooms, a kitchen and dinette . . . The woman is a harpist and musician. Sounds like a good set-up to me. My own room and bath, and company at hand if so desired. The garden particularly tempts me, and the area is excellent. Eileen is going to see the woman tonight, but I've heard of so many things and nothing has panned out yet, so I'm not banking on it.

Friday, March 7, 1952

Dear Mum,

The more I think of the idea of you and Dad coming over next year, the more excited I get, for I see no reason at all why you shouldn't come. How I would love to have a family life for a while again and how I should love to show you London and the Continent.

According to reports today, the latter part of May or early June seems the most likely time for the Coronation. You could sail early in May (or fly, as prices may be about equal by then). I would rent a flat for 3 or 6 months or as long as you would stay. We could even fly Marion over the day college closes so we could all be together.

---

[13] When Bill Fraser left the air force, he and Marie bought a farm in Norfolk, near the village of Diss, about a hundred miles from London.

You know, Mum, Marion and I are old enough now to be able to look after our own futures and I see little point in you and Daddy fretting about your future. What is the use of money in the bank or insurance that pays off after you're dead if you don't make the most of life?

I know that when Joanie was alive you did have to make certain of her future. But now certainly I am—or should be—economically independent, and if Marion is good to her word, with scholarships she should be, too. Then what is to stop you from enjoying yourselves?

And it wouldn't really be that expensive. You would be my guests over here, for I should be well able to take care of everything easily by then and nothing would give me greater pleasure than a chance to take my own turn in providing a bit of the wonderful family life you and Dad have always given us.

Do think about it, Mum, and write soon and tell me you are coming.

Lots of Love,

Ouida

Monday, March 10, 1952, morning

Dear Mum,

Am sitting at Marie's dining room table in New House Farm, typing this on my own typewriter, which I brought up this weekend with good intentions of doing some work. But you know where most of my good intentions go, and somehow country air and work just don't seem to go together. It's so relaxing and restful I can't work up any enthusiasm up here unless it is for feeding chicks or doing something quite alien to my London occupations.

Marie thinks my suggestion for you and Dad coming over next year an excellent one and has already asked me if I thought Dad would like it up here. He'd love it, for Bill wanders about all day in rugged old clothes doing everything to his heart's content, and when you're your own boss, it's a pleasure to work yourself to the bone.

They have two sows ready to pig in April and one of them should produce about April 21st, which is when my next long weekend should be due, so I intend to hie myself right back up here, as I've never seen brand-new piglets.

Marie has just gone hustling through to get her bee veil. She got her first swarm on Thursday night and is as excited as a kid with a new doll.

Up here we rarely go to bed later than 10 p.m. so I get about 10 hours a night—last night I got 12, as we went to bed by 9 p.m.!

Thursday, March 13, 1952

Dear Mum,

Funny how something always turns up to save a new week from being dull and ordinary. Started this week with a blank diary page, but a phone call Tuesday night from North Luffenham livened it up considerably.

It seems at last that I am to keep that date with Art Rayner. He called to say the whole squadron is coming to London on Friday for the weekend, and could I keep it free or break any date I might have for Saturday in particular? They are to arrive Friday afternoon in time for the evening performance of "South Pacific"—I've seen it twice. He'll call me as soon as they get in and he would like to arrange something for after the show but since it does not end until 10:30 p.m. I may suggest we wait until Saturday. Anyway, the weekend looks like fun—and being hectic.

Monday, March 17, 1952

Dear Mum,

Well, I'm flabbergasted! The weekend turned out very well, I fell for Art quite thoroughly—not that it would ever be serious or even anything other than "fun" or "amusing"—still he was able to convey to me a wonderful feeling of "life is fun" and "good to be living," something I haven't experienced for a long time—and I loved him for it. Golly, that guy seems capable of enjoying everything—such a wonderful change from most of the deadly, bored jerks I meet in this job. Maybe it's just that he's young yet—24 in February—but it would be a pity if he were to lose his outlook.

He flattered me blind. Kept saying he felt he was way out of my class. You'd think he was dating Princess Margaret. Evidently he was amazed when I accepted his invite to the ball as I seemed a "pretty sharp girl who had been around a lot" and would never bother with him. He seemed to think I was somebody!!

Just got in from the office, and your Wednesday letter was here. Pleased you are seeing things my way about next year. Now I can start looking for a flat with something more definite in mind.

But be definite about it quick, for I must apply for tickets for the Coronation parade seats through Canada House right away, as the booking agents here are already offering seats at fantastic prices.

Wednesday, March 19, 1952

I'll be glad when the next few weeks are over, for I've still got £20 to pay off from Christmas, the flat to find and move into, and my income tax to save for. That is going to be steep and I sure wish I had a few dollars coming in to fall back on, for I may need a big sum in a rush.

For heaven sake, phone Berkley and see if he's dead. Still no word about the radio program and I'm nearly wild, for I need every penny I can get. I take back what I said about no interference, guess I can't manage alone, letters aren't enough.

Tuesday, March 25, 1952

Dear Mum,
Have been held up a bit in my letter writing. Sunday, Shirley [Shirley Reid, with whom she went to France the previous summer] and I spent flat-hunting and saw some adorable mews places but they are horribly expensive. By chance I stopped to look at some ads in an estate office window, when I noticed a chap inside. I remembered meeting him at a party two years ago, so went in to chat. He mentioned one studio flat quite near the office here. He put my name down and said he'd call. I forgot about him, when he suddenly phoned today and said the flat was vacant and was I interested.

I said sure, so he is going to try to arrange for me to see the place tomorrow evening. It is within walking distance of the office and sounds OK if it is all this fellow says.

Boy, it was sure a relief to hear of your conversation with Berkley about the radio job, but I wish to heck he'd hurry up and fix things, for I must have some money behind me somewhere to face this income tax if it suddenly comes.

Thursday, March 27, 1952

Dear Mum and Dad,
Am thrilled to bits today, for it seems as though Lady Luck intends to stick by me a while longer. I've got the most adorable flat imaginable! Such a pet and ideal for me! It's the one I mentioned that is only a two penny bus ride from the office—or a 10-minute walk. Went last night to see it and phoned the agent first thing today to say I'd take it—and I'm quite sure the girl who owns it liked me enough to let me have it, so it should be all set by tomorrow.

Shirley came with me. The entrance is just a doorway between two shops, and the three flights up are very dull and dingy. As we climbed, we both became more disheartened. Then you reach the front door, open it and have another flight of stairs up into the flat—that means that you're above everyone and will not be disturbed by people just outside your door.

Then you come into the flat, and my heart sang! Suppose it is really the attic of the building and the roof is pointed, but how charmingly it is decorated. The owner is Margaret Gordon, Edinburgh-born actress who looks very like the actress Pamela Brown. She is going to join a Scottish theatrical company and plans to tour South Africa with them next year. There is always the chance that could fall through, but she said it didn't seem likely.

Anyway, the flat—it is one huge room, but the stairs coming up in the centre rather divides it into two sections. In the front with the big main window facing south is the lounge bit with a window seat, two upholstered chairs, a round table, and a white chest of drawers which serves as a table. On it she had a plain vase with two branches of red-rust leaves that filled the corner and looked terrifically effective.

On the other side of the stairs—which come up facing a set of bookshelves—is the bed, which is a divan with an excellent mattress, and with a lamp at the head and a shelf there, too, for the telephone, and a white sheepskin rug by the side of it and a second window to the right of the head of the bed.

Taking up the other end of this half of the room is the kitchen-bathroom, very compact, with just the bathtub in the kitchen. The lavatory is downstairs on the same level as the flat door. That is the only inconvenient bit but doesn't really matter much.

The whole flat is painted in a light cream colour, with a dark rug on the lounge floor and dark stain on the kitchen-bedroom side. On the walls are a few well-chosen prints and sketches very nicely framed. The flat is high enough above Oxford Street to avoid the noise of traffic and also to catch all the sun. There is a tiny balcony out back where one can sit in summer and hang clothes.

It's a perfect size for just me, not too big to have to keep clean, and the window seat is plenty big enough to put someone up on if I want to. Oh yes, there is a skylight as well, lighting is good, and the girl says it is easy to heat and keeps warm in winter and in summer windows at either end of the room can create good circulation of air. This Miss Gordon was very sweet, said she would introduce me to her butcher, grocer, etc., and was quite frank about costs above the rent. Rent will be 4 guineas a week—about $12.50, which is very good. She will not be moving until the end of April, which suits me fine, for I want to get everything paid off out here in Richmond and the first month's rent ahead before leaving.

Must get this in the post and maybe it will go out tonight. Did I tell you the address of the flat is 70 New Oxford Street, so you can look it up on that map. Think I'll try to buy me a pressure cooker so I can have meals quickly.

Lots of love, Ouida

Thursday, April 3, 1952

Have been making a few notes of recipes I'd like and here is the present list, if you could please jot them down for me: peas and bacon scallop; tomato scallop; plain white cookies; upside-down pineapple cake; stew with the "dough boys"; clear vegetable soup; tea biscuits.

Things you can always pop in a parcel that would be more than welcome: brown, white, and icing sugar; Jello and puddings; butter; meat; cake mixes; pancake flour. Glad to hear there is maple sugar on the way—good old Daddy!

Still nothing from Berkley, oh gosh, how I wish I could get started with that. And nothing from Grainger about starting up the column again, so they must be trying to think up some way to outwit me on the financial end.

Saturday, April 19, 1952

Dear Mum and Dad,
This has been some day! Mr. Hyde let me have the morning off to go to Bernard's wedding [Bernard Mooney]. Got back into the office at 1:00 p.m. and noticed a piece in the early papers about two RCAF jets colliding in mid-air. No names, but a note came through on the wires a few minutes later and Al Marshall, who had been phoning me since last night, came through. The result is Art Rayner is dead. He got out of his plane and landed alive but badly injured in the water. A plane saw him wave but from there on, the stories vary. One says boats took 25 minutes, another, an hour and a half to reach him. He died anyway from loss of blood and injuries before they got him to a hospital.

Al has asked me about going up for the funeral but that depends on when it is. I'd rather like to, for I liked Art a lot, he was a wonderful guy with a rare and happy view of life. I offered to write his folks, as he talked so much about them and very obviously had a home life very similar to my own. Al grabbed at my offer very gratefully. I did it because I felt you would appreciate hearing from Art or anyone else if I had been in that plane. Am I right?

Funny, Art was the only pilot I've dated out of all the numbers I've met and he wouldn't have been either, except for the ball. Yet he gave me such a good time with his fresh personality and I was really looking forward to his next visit, which I was told only yesterday would be the end of the month.

Tuesday, April 22, 1952

Dear Mum,
It will be hard to equal the events and feelings of the last few days!

Art's funeral is at 2 p.m. today, and until last night, I was going up with Al Marshall. But when he had to cancel the trip, I couldn't face the long train journey on my own and so had to scrap it.

Remember I told you it had been ages since I'd had a crush on a new guy so I was pulling all stops out on Rayner and loving it—knowing of course that it would undoubtedly wear off shortly. Guess I didn't realize how many stops I had pulled, for I can't believe he's really gone and have found myself suddenly bursting into tears on a couple of occasions, which is pretty peculiar for me. I had steeled myself to face this funeral today, which might have been for the best, as nothing could impress the finality more. Now, with not going—I sent flowers today instead—it seems to be all the harder.

We still don't know exactly what happened except that they collided during the slip-over in a turn. Art, it seems, used his ejector seat, got out alive, and after being in the sea for some time, was picked up, still alive. But he had been injured somehow and died before they got him to hospital.

I move to the new flat next Wednesday, the 30th.

Tuesday, April 29, 1952

Dear Mum,
Well, the Coronation day has been named—June 2 [1953]—so now it's up to you and Daddy to make plans accordingly. I am applying here immediately for seats, as nothing could be done until the date was named. You realize, of course, it will mean seats or places along the route, not inside the Abbey. Only the high and mighty go in there.

Spent Sunday afternoon playing tennis and suffered a few stiff muscles yesterday. Went back with Noel Jackson (Tony's best friend) for coffee on the way home and was amazed to hear that Tony is rather bitter about our breaking up, although Noel agrees with me that Tony in his present state is not ready for marriage.

Can't really understand how he can feel bitter, for I let him break it off so he couldn't accuse me of throwing him over. But then, Tony is good at seeing the faults in someone else's backyard. Tony's main worry is that he is 32, the eldest in the family, and still not married. He seems to feel he should be, and his strong affection for children only makes it worse.

Sorry about the delay in getting a column off to you, but shall make a dead set for Thursday or Friday, as I should be settled and independent then.[14]

---

14 Ouida's mother had suggested that offering a sample column or two would show that she was willing to start up again.

I'm also most anxious to get back into some hard work and contacts with Canada. Still nothing from Berkley, though. If there is any way of stirring him up, use it. Arrangements over here to record the programs for shipping to Canada were completed within 2 weeks of my arrival back. All we need are the tapes and the green light! I want to work, and work hard again. Feel it would do me good!

One thing about being up in town, I'll have a much better choice of churches and some—like Farm Street [Jesuit church in Mayfair]—have some excellent speakers, while just around the corner will be the Italian one where visiting Italian celebrity singers often sing at the masses. And the Cathedral with the excellent boys' choir is on the route of a bus that passes my front door.

Must get this off,

Lots of love, Ouida

Saturday, May 3, 1952, afternoon

Dear Mum,

Hope you have noticed the mistake in my address that I gave you—it's WC1 instead of W1—it seems to be delaying things a bit.

Am feeling very proud today. Made a potato scallop last night and it turned out beautifully—or I should say deliciously. Tonight Shirley is cooking the meal—salmon with a mushroom sauce—and we are entertaining Chris and the two Ryan brothers to dinner. Should be a good evening, as the Ryans alone are worth their party chatter.

Shall try to take a couple of pictures of the flat for you so you can see what my present abode is. Hope you have written Mrs. Bennett, for although I could never be sure if she liked or loathed me, that's no reason for you to neglect good taste and thank her anyway, for she did provide a home for me, even though it was trying at times.

Chris seems to be turning up rather a lot these days, and although he was certainly a wonderful help on the moving, I'm going to have to discourage him again, for I just can't stand it. I'm terribly rude to him and know it must hurt but can't help it. I hate to even have him touch me, even to guiding me across the street, and he's so darned kind-hearted and gentle, it's pretty trying. He asked last night if he could come to dinner tonight and doesn't yet know I've asked the Ryans too, as I just couldn't take another evening with him alone.

Sunday, May 4, 1952

Dear Mum,

The enclosed column is possibly a bit long, so shall mark some stuff you can leave out if it is. Have tried to make it informative as well as descriptive and readable. Hope you like it. Am typing with a big burn on my middle finger left hand—result of taking a tray out of the oven without a pot holder. Let me know right away what you think, and in the meantime I'll bang out another one you can use immediately or save as filler for a later one.

Dinner last night went very well and both Joe and John Ryan were very taken with the flat. We were late eating—Shirley had volunteered to get the meal, but was delayed and only got in about 10 minutes before the boys. It's probably just as well she's going back to Winnipeg this month and not sharing with me permanently, as she is much slower than I am and as much as I try not to notice, it bothers me a lot. When I decide to go to bed, I go, but it takes Shirley at least another half or three-quarters of an hour.

Al Marshall just called me. He's been up at North Luffenham all week. Guess Art's roommate Frank Sylvester is taking the accident pretty hard. The pilots up there now are all young kids, post-war products, and as Al remarked "They figured the war had ended about six years ago," which means they are unaccustomed to sudden deaths as the wartime men are, and take it pretty hard.

Was talking to Marie on the phone yesterday. Susie let them down by producing 9 piglets, but one was scrawny and died, and she laid on two and did them in. Marie says Susie was so upset she was off her food for a couple of days. Phoebe produced only 6 piglets, but on the other hand, Bill put up a little sign announcing potatoes for sale and duck eggs and had more orders than he could fill!

Must get on to more work,

Lots of love, Ouida

Thursday, May 8, 1952, evening

Am settling in nicely to the new flat, which is a honey. Everyone who has seen it has been enchanted! Today I had Mrs. Bennett to lunch, and boy did I work. Cleaned and dusted every little nook and cranny and had the place spotless—not that I don't keep it tidy anyway! Then I cooked. Made a very good potato scallop, hard-boiled eggs, and mixed sandwich spread with the yolks then re-stuffed them. This was set on lettuce with a tomato for colour and for meat used a small luncheon meat (like Prem) which I baked in the oven after covering it with a paste made of brown sugar, mustard, and vinegar. It takes the ordinary taste away from the luncheon meat and makes it quite delicious. Luckily I gave her such a heaping plate she couldn't go for any more than the lemon tea for dessert—lucky, because I had forgotten what it was that I intended having. Anyway, the meat was a big success, and afterwards I helped her buy a lovely purse at Harrods on my purchase tax coupons, so I'm in the good books.

Tomorrow night I entertain David Ross and his mother—have to be salmon in a mushroom sauce with boiled rice and a side salad, as it's Friday. On Monday evening, Isabel Greene comes to supper and on Tuesday I have Bob Greene (American photographer) and his fashion model wife, Barbara. So I'm not stuck for company just yet. And I still have several people I want to have in.

Also, today I met Elizabeth Welch, negro actress and singer who has—I think—one of the loveliest faces I have ever seen. It has so much animation and expression, and she's a terrific personality. She's playing in a show called "Penny Plain" in a theatre not far from here and has promised to come over one night for supper after the show. She's the kind of person I love to know, for she's got so much to offer to this old world.

Saturday, May 10, 1952, afternoon

Norman Nash [a social friend and a member of the Queen's Household Guards] phoned me yesterday for the London Scottish Rugger Club dinner dance at the Savoy on Friday week—formal do, which should be fun. And I'm taking the Greenes to hear Yma Sumac on May 31. Was most surprised to see her advertise for a London concert, but sure won't miss it, even for the novelty if nothing else.

Mr. Hyde took me to lunch today, a quaint Italian place in Soho where the meal was excellent, and afterward we wandered through the street markets while he did some shopping—he cooks the Sunday meal at home. It was most enjoyable and a great help to me toward getting over that half-terrified feeling of him—although he still puzzles me.

Dinner with David Ross and his mother last night went exceptionally well (she's a White Russian and most amusing), and David even helped me write a letter in Italian to Vittorio Tranquillini, who sent his Easter greetings all in Italian.

Tomorrow at 2:00 p.m. I play tennis at the "Mah Deah! The Hurlingham Club"—terribly fashionable, with a South African girl, Hazel May. It might prove quite fun.

It looks as if living in town might prove quite successful socially.

Lots of love, Ouida

Sunday, May 11, 1952

Dear Mum,

Well, here is a column. It couldn't be a more British subject, being about the Coronation, and I thought that perhaps as many people were rather waiting for me to send columns on this subject, it may be as well to start with it. Haven't enlarged too much on anything, as there are several good possibilities for future stories here—such as Coronation robes, etc. But it should give a bit of taste of what is to come, enough I hope to tempt Grainger to start up the column again.

Went out to the Hurlingham Club for tea—tennis cancelled because of rain—and it was quite pleasant. Certainly is a beautiful club, with 23 tennis courts, about five croquet games, miniature golf, swimming pool, a small stream with ducks and swans running through the grounds, and everything beautifully kept. Tea dance every Sunday, regular dances on Saturday evenings, and big functions at various times through the year.

Could you please send me some menus? I seem to be out of ideas for what to have on different days.

Love, Ouida

Monday, May 12, 1952, evening

Thanks for the advice about men and "flat behaviour." Also, I'm aware of how high my own emotions can run in one heated moment. Don't know of any girl with a sharper conscience or more brutal examples to live by.

As I think I told you, I went pretty soft on Rayner that weekend he was down, and when we had a long—and expensive—taxi ride home, he remarked, "Gee, I wish you had your flat now." He meant it purely in that he'd have liked some place where we could sit down and relax and not have to keep getting out as places closed. That statement stuck, and at the back of my mind when I found this place was the thought that I'd be in here by the time Art got down to London again. Yet I was a little afraid of my own feelings, knowing that I would either behave coolly toward him and probably either puzzle or hurt him, or remain fairly soft and feel guilty about it.

One of my first thoughts after the shock of the accident was—no need of the flat now, for I shan't be entertaining him in London again—which was a purely selfish attitude, yet it showed me how much I have been planning on the two together. It was a lesson, harsh, but indeed a lesson.

Tuesday, May 20, 1952

Dear Mum,

Sorry about the several days' silence but a weekend like the one just past is a rarity.

It all started with the London Scottish Ball on Friday. Wore the black net with red earrings but no necklace—instead a single red rose taped to my shoulder, which caused quite a sensation. Norman Nash is an absolute honey and a perfect escort. We were in a party of 12—all Hurlingham Club except me!! Felt rather strange at first, as the others are rather a "gang," but a couple of the girls melted, and Norman didn't really give me much of a chance to feel too lost. We danced downstairs at the Savoy and then sneaked upstairs to watch the cabaret. Bill Saville's band was playing for us (I had met him when on nights at the Sunday Express), and didn't he wave, call us over to say "Hello," and later told Norman and David Ross he thought I was the prettiest girl in the room!! Such blarney! And when he asked Norman if he was my husband, the devil said "yes." [Bill Saville's Orchestra was a favourite at high-society functions.]

From the Savoy we went out to the Carousel night club [in St. James's Street]. I got to bed at 4:40 a.m. after refusing a game of tennis for Saturday but agreeing to meet Norman at the Hurlingham at 6 p.m. Sunday. Went to work at 8 a.m. Saturday and to the tennis club in Richmond about 7 p.m. Played two sets of tennis, then stayed for the dance. Had several grand dances with John Delanghe, then my feet gave out about 11 p.m., so I left. Sunday, out to Mass at 8 a.m. and spent the morning measuring a dress hem for Mollie and altering suit sleeves for Mrs. Bennett (had stayed the nite with them in Kew).

On Saturday at the office, Hazel May (the South African girl) said she was going away, but Elizabeth Owen of the Manchester Guardian had taken over the court booked at the Hurlingham and wanted me to play and could I get two others. Said I'd try. Turned to Clive Baxter (Beverley Baxter's son) sitting next to me in the office and jokingly asked if he'd like to play. Nearly collapsed when he accepted delightedly and phoned Edward Hardwicke (Sir Cecil Hardwicke's son) for a fourth.[15]

So, on Sunday I went to the Hurlingham at 2 p.m., played two sets, then we went swimming in a terrific pool in the club grounds. Saw Norman, who was playing, and said I'd meet him later. He finally found me at about 6:30 p.m. and invited others in to his place for a drink. Elizabeth, who had only shorts with her, left about 8 p.m. but Clive and Edward stuck on and even had a salad supper with us. I was rather annoyed and had a terrific headache (unusual for me). Felt they were perhaps sponging a bit and said so to Norman.

---

[15] Beverley Baxter, a Canadian, had been editor of the *Daily Express*, was a theatre critic for the *Evening Standard*, and a Member of Parliament. Clive went back to Canada to work at the *Financial Post*. In 1956, he said that there was a job there for me. Ouida and I moved to Canada.

Imagine my horror when on climbing into bed the phone rang, and there was Clive Baxter inviting me to his 21st birthday party this Friday to be held at the Café de Paris.[16] He had already asked Norman. Luckily I had bought a piece of white material several weeks ago for a bargain ($4) and find I have enough to make a dress for the party—6 yards. Isobel Greene was in last night and helped me out with the skirt, which was the tricky part.

Norman has also asked me to the Honorary Artillery Company Ball on July 4, so may have to scour for something new for that as well. This boy looks like producing some nice dates, as the ball is one of the swankiest balls of the season.

Your Saturday letter came this morning, and naturally I am disappointed about Grainger deciding not to continue publishing the column, but quite expected it. However, now no holds are barred so how about offering it to the Telegraph[17] from the angle of the coming Coronation year, and say that I can now work it in. Ask $7 or $7.50, not more, as these are small papers. We could also try Sydney and Halifax again on the strength of 3 years here and the coming events. Honest, Mum, I'm going to need this money badly if my income tax suddenly comes due.

About Marion—all hospitals tell me they are filled for this year. They take applications in October '53. The Royal Free Hospital—famous for women—is very interested in her. Will try some more yet. May even ask Beaverbrook to help me.

Lots of love, Ouida

Monday, May 26, 1952

Friday at the Café de Paris, Clive greeted me as "Ah, here she is, the guest of honour." His father said he had heard a great deal about me from his son—all very good. As I was introduced to Beverley, his Sealyham terrier "Dissy" got under the hoop of my long skirt and nipped at my ankle, then found it couldn't get out and starting running around under the hoop until I hitched up the dress and booted it out, feeling a perfect fool.

Later in the evening Beverley Baxter called me over to sit next to him, saying, "If you're going to be my daughter-in-law, I may as well get to know you"! I gasped, and he went on, "You are going to marry my son aren't you?" I replied jokingly, "Well no, not within the next half hour." He said, "Why not, you must marry someone and he's a nice lad."

---

[16] The Café de Paris was a high-society favourite.

[17] The *Telegraph* was a rival paper to the *Moncton Times*.

At which I changed the subject.[18] All this left Norman and me a bit confused, as Clive had placed me on his right with Norman a couple of seats away on the other side of the table, had started dancing with me, and had given me one of the two roses the cabaret singer Hildegarde gave him. When we left the Café de Paris, he gave his sister their car and piled in with Norman and me to go to some chap's flat for further drinks, and when we left, seemed quite upset that Norman drove him home first. Don't know what this is all about.

Wednesday, May 28, 1952, evening

Last night Clive Baxter took me to a movie. He's really quite good company and an intelligent chap, quick thinker.

Mike Smart phoned tonight. He's in town for a few hours only, for a stag theatre party with the other 22 pilots in his squadron. But he'll be down for the Whitsun weekend and a party is planned for Saturday night, which should be rare. I have the Yma Sumac concert first with the Greene family, but shall go on from there to Mike and be lucky to get back for breakfast, I should imagine. He sounds the same as ever.

Love, Ouida

---

[18] Clive later married the Canadian heiress, Cynthia Molson.

"EITHER A FEAST OR A FAMINE"
June–August 1952

Sunday, June 1, 1952, evening

So Dad's getting snooty, eh? Thanks for your advice, Mum, but it really isn't difficult to be "nice" to the "Baxter lad" (His name is Clive, for the record). He's a very nice guy, good talker, and very intelligent. The kind I get along with easily. He came up for supper Tuesday evening and we went to a movie after—pleasant evening. We're playing tennis with Hazel May and John Hillaby (Clive's friend) on Wednesday and I plan to have them back here afterward for some grilled steaks. (Have been polishing up my butcher and saving my ration.) Could be a good evening, and Clive has invited me to his house to see the rebroadcast of Beaverbrook's talk on TV. So guess I'll be OK.

As for Mike—don't worry anymore. Went to the party he and Chris threw last night at his house and have never been so browned off or bored before. I got fed up and left about midnight when it was supposed to last until 2 a.m. at least. Separately they're pleasant enough guys but together they're juvenile delinquents and quite impossible.

Heard Yma Sumac last night. Her voice is certainly terrific but she used a mike all the time, which means lack of power. Also there is no expression or emotion in her singing and once the novelty has worn off it could be boring, for her songs vary only slightly. [Sumac had a range of nearly five octaves.] We nearly passed out when she introduced her husband, conductor, arranger, assistant arranger—and her dress designer—all from the stage of the Royal Albert Hall!!!!!

Keep your fingers crossed, Mum, for I go to see Lord Beaverbrook at 7 p.m. on Tuesday about Marion. I want advice for her and also about a lecture tour for me but only one at a time, so shall concentrate on her and see how it goes.

Sunday, June 8, 1952

Now about Marion. Lord Beaverbrook says for her to send all her qualifications to Sir Daniel Davies including birth certificate. By qualifications, he means actual certificates, such as school reports or copies etc. Joe Ryan says for her to stress her experience, such as extra chemistry (she was in the Chemistry Club wasn't she?) and any possible medical experience, courses, etc. And even say she is spending the summer in a hospital—he says they'll never check up to make sure she did. But don't try to pull a fast one on the Old Man. He'd be wild if you did. The Beaver said if her qualifications are suitable, Davies would take her in. Joe says Davies does as the Old Man says, but even if she can't make it this year, she'd be set for next.

Davies' address is Sir Daniel Davies, K.C.V.O., M.D., F.R.C.P., 36 Wimpole St., London W1. Tell him you wish to apply for entrance to the medical school of the Royal Free Hospital and I suppose you mention that Lord Beaverbrook advised you to apply to him. (You address him as Sir Daniel.) The only thing we can do now is wait and hope.

Lots of love and luck, Ouida

Thursday, June 26, 1952

Maybe this is Marion's lucky day. The Royal Free Hospital phoned me this morning to say they had the application from Sir Daniel and are checking to see if her qualifications are enough for London University or if she will have to take two further exams here. No hint of her not being accepted at all.

When on Monday I received your letter calling Sir Daniel "Dr." I was ready to quit. In England a "Dr." is a mere general practitioner. A specialist is always "Mr." and of course Davies is knighted. I figured if you had made the same mistake and called him "Dr." in your letter to him, you'd have deserved to be slung out.

Monday, June 30, evening [added]

Gosh, has this ever been held up! My life these days is so hectic I do nothing save sleep every chance I get. Have been doing Wimbledon from the news angle and have evidently been a great success—front page stories five days running, and most of them good news stories no one else has had until much later. But I'm completely exhausted and still five days to go.

The weather has been terrific—85 degrees—and with up to 29,000 people milling about, it's pretty killing at times. My success has been in making friends with the players and wives and lining up my stories the afternoon before. Then I take the car and chauffeur and a photographer and do all my work before they leave town for Wimbledon, whereas other papers wait and catch people down there. Of course, my method means waiting until play is pretty well finished to see what the most likely stories will be. Start in the office at 8 a.m. and rarely get home before 9:30 p.m. so it's a long day. Am thoroughly enjoying it but am sure planning on this weekend at Marie's to recover.

Today saw the warden and secretary of the Royal Free Hospital, as she had written me to come. They are very pleased with Marion's marks and she will be writing you. New regulations require advance work in 2 subjects, preferably chemistry and physics, so she advises Marion to set her aim for 1953. She will tell her exactly how to go about qualifying for these exams and says she will waive the personal interview to allow Marion another year at home while she takes the courses. They seem anxious to have her—it's six and one half years of study—so it looks as though she will be all set for a year this fall.

Monday, July 7, 1952, morning [from the Fraser farm in Norfolk]

I go back to London from Marie's tonight and must wash my hair, as I'm going to a tea-dance at the Café de Paris with Noel Coward as the cabaret star. It's a Baxter-organized "do" with Norman Nash included, as well as some Canadian sailors and a chap named Tony Jay I met at Wimbledon. His father is Ernest Jay, the actor. He went to St. Paul's School, and has just finished at Cambridge. Tall, rather pleasant-looking, and good company, we had dinner together the other evening—before I knew he was going to be in this party tomorrow. I fear I'm going to have a tricky time if I want to keep them all—and encourage an Australian navy officer I quite liked at Clive's party. Guess I'll have to plead a headache, leave early, and go home by myself. Same old story, either a feast or a famine!

The Honorable Artillery Company Ball was on Friday and a truly glorious affair. Right in the heart of the City (the Wall Street of London) is the green field—really a cricket field for the Honorable Artillery Company. A huge marquee covered a dance floor above which hung huge pots of chrysanthemums and hydrangeas. On either side were bar and buffet tents. Artillery House was thrown open, a most historic building, and at the far end of the field was a fair merry-go-round, swings, electric bumper cars and all. Can you imagine the sight of women in flowing evening gowns riding side saddle on the merry-go-round with men in uniform—crimson coats and tight black trousers with a red stripe down the side and a Sam Browne belt with silver medal things on it. Even met four couples there that I know—funny now how I am beginning to know someone everywhere I go.

Saturday, July 12, 1952

The Ethel I have mentioned before is Ethel Young from Vancouver who has spent 3 years in France and came to London in April. She has a job now with an advertising firm and lives in a maisonette in Mayfair. She's a very intelligent girl—about 26 or 28, I think—and I find her good company. She's shortish, fair-haired, and not a "good-looker" but with a pleasant face and a wonderful smile, which gives her a charming expression. She's natural as well as frank, and we get on very well after a corny start—we didn't like each other at first at all.

Thursday, July 17, 1952

Tonight I am going out with John Russell, who is the Sunday Times art critic. Only met him on Sunday. He has quite a stutter but seems intelligent and pleasant. Anyway, tonight will tell.

Saturday I'm going to a theatre with Todd Dodswell, an Australian navy lieutenant. He leaves for a two-month tour of Canada next Wednesday so I'll ask him to see you if he's down your way. He's young, but a nice guy.

This morning I had a long-distance call from North Luffenham. There is a new press officer for the station and he was checking that I am coming up next week. Then I'll be darned if he didn't tell me there is a formal dance on Friday night—the 26th—and could I come. I explained that being a single girl, I don't travel to formal "dos" alone and he replied that he would be delighted to escort me. When I thought it over I realized that was probably why the guy called. Lots of fellows up there could tell him what I'm like and he possibly knows about Rayner asking me out of the blue, so wants to get the bid in before I reach the station next Tuesday. Al Marshall says he's a "good guy," tall, about 24, and nice. But gee, here I've been roped in on a half-blind date (I meet him next Tuesday really) and I think his name is John!!!

Later

Had a most amusing and enjoyable evening with this John Russell. It is now 11 p.m. and I've just come in. He arrived 10 minutes late and announced he had locked himself out of his flat. Funnier still, his cook had left us a meal, which was also locked in. After frantic phoning, he got her address and we took a taxi to fetch her key (taxi cost about $2). He has a lovely flat, a good meal, then a cinema—we left before the end, as it got lousy. But he is a perfect gentleman, aged 33, Oxford (he said I was the youngest person he'd spoken to in months), and very good company and a sense of humour. He goes on holiday next week but has asked to phone me again.

Sunday, July 28, 1952, evening

Went up to Luffenham on Tuesday and stayed until Wednesday night doing stories—five good ones David Roberts was very pleased with for syndication, and a couple for the Standard out of it. Which means payment and good expenses—I hope! Trip was most successful. John Ruck (my date for the Friday dance) seemed quite pleasant, and the Commanding Officer was charming as usual and entertained me at his table to lunch on Wednesday. We talked about the Miramichi [river in New Brunswick] and fishing a blue streak.

Then I dashed madly for the train again Friday at 1:45 p.m., and Doris and Garney Brine [an RCAF pilot and his wife who was a friend of Ouida's from Moncton] met me at Stamford at 4:04 p.m.

Doris looks great, and we gabbed madly and were still lallygagging about, getting dressed, when John Ruck arrived. He was wearing mess kit and although I know it is proper, I felt it was a bit corny for a summertime cadet to wear it when all the regular officers were in uniforms with dress shirts and bow ties, and besides I didn't think the pants fit properly—only consolation, the Wing Commander's looked much worse!

Well, you can gather he was a dismal failure as an escort. Oh, he was gentlemanly and all that, but deadly dull, a lousy dancer and he kept hovering around me until I felt like screaming. I bore with him until suppertime, when I seemed to find myself talking quite a bit to Air Vice Marshall Atcherley. After supper we traded a dance with Doris and Garney.

Garney is a very good dancer and I so enjoyed it. I figured "frig on this—I'm going to have a good time." The stag line was pretty strong—and interesting—so I cut loose—except that John just wouldn't be cut and kept just hanging around. Every so often he'd butt in and I'd have to circle the floor with him in agony. Strongest competitors were Flt. Lt. John Marion—shy as anything but a honey from Winnipeg—and bright-eyed, crew-cutted FO Frank Sylvester (Art Rayner's roommate) from Toronto. Had a whale of a time and ended up with five characters asking to take me home. Of course, I had to go home with John but we were in Garney's car so it wasn't too bad, but you should have seen the faces the other guys pulled when I said I was leaving with the guy who brought me. I was lapping it up and loving it—needless to say. Chris says I'm becoming a flirt, and do you know, I think he may be quite right! And am I having fun!

As for the art critic—I discovered he's an Oxford man and considered a terrific intellectual. And yesterday my next-door neighbour told me I may be 24 in years but mentally I'm much older—that was why he enjoys coming over to my flat. So maybe John Russell and The Times considers me intelligent too—well, I can fool some of them some of the time can't I?

Caught a train at 7:30 a.m. from Luffenham and got into the office at 10:15 a.m.—15 minutes late. But Mr. Hyde didn't seem to mind, for he invited me out to lunch (was wearing my snazzy white creation) and it cost him $7.50. I was hungry so I had melon, then roast duck with port wine and orange sauce (scrumptious) and fresh pineapple, and coffee, and ginger ale! He seemed to be kept quite entertained by my conversation, which was always proper—if just a little bit leg-pulling at times.

Friday, Aug. 1, 1952

Dear Mum,

Another busy week and no day off! But did fly an airplane, even though it was for only a few minutes. Now I'm thinking of taking flying lessons.

Wednesday was sent up to Lincolnshire to cover the passing out parade at the RAF College at Cranwell. We flew up in a VIP Valetta—the kind the Queen and Princess often fly in. On the return trip, I was in the co-pilot's seat all the way and the pilot let me handle the controls for a bit. But he took over again when he said I was liable to make the others ill if I let it get too rough.

Met the Canadian air cadets up there—25, but no Monctoners. Lord Alexander was the receiving officer and shook hands with all the Canadian boys.

Monday, Aug. 11, 1952

What a wacky weekend this was. Friday night Doris Brine called me about 10 p.m., as she and Garney were down for one night only. She mentioned that Frank Sylvester and Len "Speed" Bentham were down for the weekend. They were Art Rayner's best pals.

Saturday morning I phoned Frank, as it was raining and miserable, and an unorganized Saturday night in London can be deadly. Simply told him that if they were stuck for the eve, I had vague intentions of laying on a hot-dog party and they would be welcome. He phoned me back in an hour and said they'd love to come.

I had originally been invited to a supper party at Sir George Bolton's [Banker and former Director of the Bank of England] and when I phoned his daughter Sheila to say I couldn't make it, she said I'd have to, as she only had 8 people going. It ended up with us all going, Ethel, Frank, Len and I, and it was a most enjoyable party with a mixed but most interesting collection of people. Our boys fitted in very well indeed, and Ethel and I are feeling very pleased with them as "Canadians."

Back here at the flat afterward, the boys insisted on having their hot dogs (Ethel was staying the night and in fact is staying all this week), so Len and I got them ready. They stayed until about 3:30 a.m. and said they hoped to see us again soon—asked when I would next be up at Luffenham. We said we'd all celebrate my birthday together, as it's on Labour Day, and the pilots get all the Canadian as well as the British holidays. But we'll have to see if that comes off. Anyway, Bentham is a pretty sweet character—think I'm off again!! Frank does the solo aerobatics in the squadron and Len is in the team of 4 who do formation aerobatics, so they must be fairly good pilots.

Monday, Aug. 18, 1952

Saturday night, Ethel and I had a sort of dinner party—steaks broiled with a half peach on top. That developed because John Ruck had phoned to ask me out and I didn't want to go, yet felt I should pay him back for the dance, so invited him in. Todd (Australian navy Sub. Lt.) was coming in anyway, then the butcher gave me so much steak, we asked Liz and Nino, too. (Liz—Elizabeth Eccles from Southern Rhodesia—great fun, and her boyfriend Nino, Count Nino Milesi, Italian count, English mother, a charming guy, also great fun.) John was his usual conceited and boring self, and impossible to insult. Todd was his usual sweet self—a real honey of a guy.

While I think of it, any chance of some more butter, please? Am running pretty low and would sure appreciate some—and some cake mixes, if you can manage, please.

Tuesday, Aug. 19 1952

Yesterday I attended the opening of the International Horse Show at the White City [stadium in Shepherds Bush]. It was raining and most miserable but I had a most exciting interview with Foxhunter, the famous show jumper (horse class) who won Britain's only gold medal in the Olympics. He behaves remarkably like a person with horse sense! [Harry Llewellen was the rider.]

Sunday, Aug. 31, 1952

Poor Norman Nash! Ethel dropped rather a bomb on him last night, and I've never seen a guy so shaken! He kept insisting we should go to the Guard's Chapel one Sunday morning for the service, as it was most impressive. I asked him what was so impressive, etc., and said we wouldn't mind going if it was to be really worth it—you know, pageantry, etc., but not if it was just a good sermon.

Norman jokingly said, "You're both C of E, aren't you?" To which Ethel replied, "No, neither of us is. I'm a complete agnostic and heathen, and Ouida's a Roman Catholic." She said it plainly so Norman didn't believe her and said "You're not, you're Presbyterian, I'll bet, and you can still come to the chapel—so long as you're not Roman Catholic."

He didn't know whether to believe us or not. I said nary a word and let him stew. He's accused me before of being a Presbyterian but I've never told him what I am because he never asked and it had no bearing on anything, since I have no intention whatever of marrying the guy. Ethel nearly split trying not to laugh, for here was the guy twice as worried about one of us being a Catholic as about one being a heathen. It'll take him a long while to recover from that one. Funny, isn't it—he had quite accepted me as a person (not that I cared), yet I'll bet he cools off now. Actually, it will be just as well, as I'm not half as interested as he is.

Love, Ouida

"GOOD FUN WITH NO SERIOUSNESS THROWN IN"
September–December 1952

Tuesday, Sept. 2, 1952

Dear Folks,
Am well launched into my 26th year now. Todd (the Australian navy lieutenant) was in for dinner last night, and the guy from next door, Eardley Iremonger, who is very nice indeed. My butcher produced the most delicious steaks imaginable, and Ethel cooked them with a braised peach on top. Todd turned up with a lovely box of sultanas and currants his father had sent—home grown in Australia. Ethel came in with a most amusing book on French cooking—she's determined I'm going to be good—and a lovely box of cherry chocolates in liqueur. Todd brought me some chocolates from the Continent as well. And your cable came—tanks muchas!

Thursday, Sept. 18, 1952

This turned out to be quite a weekend. Arrived at the officers' mess in North Luffenham just in time to rush through lunch and then attend a briefing for a pre-Battle of Britain Day flypast by the three squadrons. [Battle of Britain Day is commemorated each year in mid-September.] That drifted into a cocktail party which was OK for a while, then I got bored—press people always drink until all the drinks are gone, and that's usually much too long for me. Found a good system of flitting from one crowd to another by eating all the cherries out of everybody's Manhattans, but I grew tired of that, too, so left the party with Flt. Lt. Bill Bliss (he led the flypast) and went over to the officers' mess. Had seen Frank Sylvester at noon, but Speed Bentham came in while I was waiting in the hall and I went in to supper with him. The press boys (about 18 of us in all) went into the bar before coming in to supper, so I was finished by the time they arrived. Speed excused himself and went to change, saying he would see me a bit later. Frank turned up again, and as I had a stuffy head, suggested we go for a walk.

Frank and I walked into Luffenham village, looked over the church, and he showed me Art's grave in the churchyard, something I had wanted to see for a long while but didn't have the chance. Later, as we walked into the front hall of the mess, Wally Matheson, the Canadair representative [Canadian military aircraft manufacturer], asked if we'd like to go to a movie in Uppingham, so we piled into a car with Wally and the dentist and drove off. It was a crummy movie but good for laughs.

Back in the mess, the press crowd were still hard at it and a couple were nearing the saturation point. A few minutes later Speed came in and eventually drove me back to the hotel at 1:15 a.m. Up at 8 a.m. Went to the mess and then down to the grounds where the station's annual Canadian Carnival was being held. Got my story, phoned it through (they used all of it word for word) and was then free until Monday morning. First time I've really been able to knock about with the boys instead of the top brass. After lunch I got carried off to help with the booths at the carnival and then wandered about until Speed came about 3:30 and collected me. He never left me after that, supper in the mess, party afterwards until wee small hours, car drive around Rutland by moonlight, watched the dawn break over a gypsy encampment, breakfast in Stamford, and church at 8:30 a.m.

As you can gather, Speed Bentham is quite a guy. He has a friendly, easygoing manner and a love of dancing and music, with an unhandsome but manly appeal and a quick smile and deep voice. And he's a Catholic, loves the air force, comes from outside Windsor, Ont., and is a true-blue Canadian who plans to retire there eventually. He's just over 6 feet tall, crew cut, blue eyes, calm manner, and huge feet!

Thursday, Sept. 25, 1952

Am meeting Ethel in half an hour to go to a French movie and Frank Sylvester is phoning about 7:30 p.m. to see what I want to do over the weekend. Did I tell you he stayed in town with us (Ethel and me) last weekend, stayed in the flat next door, as the two chaps who occupy it were away. He's a very sweet guy and on the Saturday night we had a birthday cake for him (his 21st on Friday), and he got quite a kick out if it as well as a surprise. Sunday we had a late pokey breakfast then wandered up to Hyde Park Corner to hear the soapbox orators, and it was great fun. He has now moved into a club in town, so won't need a place to stay again. On Saturday evening we invited Nino too (the Italian count, friend of Ethel's roommate), and Frank ended up teaching us all to play bridge. Must drag him off to more of the quaint old places in London before he goes back to Luffenham.

Funny, someone just pushed my doorbell (which means I run down 55 steps), and there was a letter from Speed—signed "Len," so guess he's going to stick to his intentions not to be called "Speed." As I guessed, he hopes to get down next weekend—my long one, naturally, and I had hoped to get up to Marie's! Had a feeling that would happen, now I'll have to see if he'd like to come farming with me or else stay here in London for the weekend. Oh well, it'll mean a really good chance to see if my first impressions last or if I was pipe-dreaming; I may as well know now as later.

Sunday, Sept. 28, 8:30 p.m.

Ethel and I went to the Italian church this morning and the music was wonderful—full, rich voices filling every nook and cranny of the church to the extent that I sometimes thought the roof would burst off. There was a snappy 15-minute sermon, with the priest taking only one breath that we heard—what a flow of words, all Italian too!!!

Todd (the Australian) took us and Frank Sylvester driving down thru Kent this afternoon and the scenery was lovely but it poured rain almost the whole time—and it's still pouring while Ethel's curry finishes cooking. The banana cream pie looks terrific and there is fresh melon already on the table.

With Frank to a musical last night, "Love from Judy," which was very good indeed and I thoroughly enjoyed it.

Thursday, Oct. 2, 1952

Speed—he seems to be insisting that I call him Len—phoned Tuesday night. He is not off this weekend after all but will be down the weekend of Oct. 19—four days free and I shall be working three of them. Oh well, maybe we'll be bored stiff with each other by then—time will tell. Meanwhile, Frank Sylvester has asked me for a theatre next week.

But the best news of all is, of course, your sailing dates. Now I can really think ahead a bit. Shall try for my holidays during that time, but may have to make it early May or July—probably the former, as I'm quite certain we will not be allowed time off during the Coronation period—anyway, plenty of time to worry about that.

Just phoned and think I can get tickets for the opening night of the all-negro production of "Porgy and Bess" next week. It should be good. I like Gershwin and with an authentic negro cast—it is the New York production—should be OK.

Len, when he phoned, asked if I could save my holidays and take 60 days next year—he has 28 days owing now, too—but that would be impossible—honeymoon, I wonder??? He also said a couple of the fellows had returned from Ireland and liked it very much—???? I always have a good time in Ireland!!!!

Saturday, Oct. 11, 1952

Dear Mum,

Feeling really sleepy today after a couple of late nights. "Porgy and Bess" was wonderful. We thoroughly enjoyed it—Frank had never seen an opera before. The production was excellent and all the voices good. And it was a star-studded audience, Douglas Fairbanks sweeping about in a great, black opera cloak, Lord Hambledon in a midnight-blue velvet dinner jacket, Marian Anderson in the front row—and even Lord Beaverbrook himself, although I didn't actually see him.

Ethel, Frank, and Al Bremel (Ethel's date) got a kick out of seeing so many and I must admit I got a kick out of knowing so many—all the press crowd, critics, etc., called out "Hello," some stopped to talk, Lord Hambledon (he's one of Margaret's frequent escorts) came to chat, as did several others. Terrific gowns, and we had seats well back and could see everything.

Frank casually mentioned that they would be having a New Year's party at Luffenham again this year. Must tread carefully, as I really would prefer Speed to ask me—I think—and I've been caught before with the wrong guy asking me too early. Frank is a honey and I'm very fond of him but 21 is a bit young so there is no need of even thinking of starting anything.

Todd has asked me out for Wednesday. Haven't seen him for a couple of weeks. And Dev (an Aussie journalist who is great fun) phoned me for dinner last evening but I couldn't manage. And Leslie Finer has asked me to the staff dinner-dance on Dec. 12—so I am not hard up for escorts, all of them good fun with no seriousness thrown in, which is what I much prefer.

Ethel has been staying with me most of the time. If the flat were just a bit bigger, I think we would probably share.

Could do with a bit more butter, if you could manage, then I can make a white Christmas cake. Rather assuming you'll send us a dark one. Should be quite a Christmas, as I gather some of the boys from Luffenham will be down. Ethel and I are vaguely talking of taking over her maisonette (as everyone else will be away) and having a house party. There'll be plenty of room.

Lots of love, Ouida

Saturday, Oct. 18, 1952

Well, I'm on another loss of appetite binge! Speed arrived last night to stay until Monday night and so far my first impression still holds. It was a panic last night, he ate no supper at all and I downed an omelet made of one egg. Had only a banana and a glass of milk at noon. Speed picked up an apple but quit after two bites. We didn't do a thing but went for a walk down through Soho to watch the goings-on. Afraid I'm at a bit of a loss. I don't particularly want to do anything, but to be with him. Can't get to know him if we sit in theatres. But tonight we are supposed to be going to see "Call Me Madam" with Frank and Ethel. I haven't heard from Frank yet, and he met Speed last night and didn't say a word about the show to him. Frank did ask Speed what he was doing last night, and Speed simply answered that he had a date.

In fact I suppose it all adds up to "I'm off again," Mum!

Last Sunday Ethel, Frank, and I went to the zoo to see the Canadian cougar, mascot of the 410 Squadron. The keeper took us inside, let us pet the animal through the cage and in one case took us into the cheetah cage to pat it. The thing purred like a cat.

Must post this, Love, Ouida

[There were no letters from October 18 to November 23 while Ouida was visiting her family in Moncton. She had evidently come to Canada on an RCAF flight. While in Montreal, she was interviewed by the *Herald*. The following report appeared.]

NB SCRIBE FINDS COVERING ROYALTY CAN PROVIDE EMBARRASSING MOMENTS

One Canadian girl who won't have much trouble getting a ring-side seat on coronation proceedings next year is Ouida MacLellan of Moncton, NB, who looks like and has been mistaken for the Duchess of Kent.

The fact that she might double for the Duchess has nothing to do with it, however, while the fact that she covers many Royal Family functions for the *London Evening Standard* has everything to do with it, Ouida explained in an interview last week. This trip to Canada is her third in four years of work in London . . .

Her first Royal assignment was to cover Princess Margaret's attendance at a St. John's Ambulance function. "Like everybody else," Ouida says, "I was surprised at how tiny she is, a little over 5 feet, and at how pretty. No picture does justice either to Margaret or to Elizabeth. A lot of their beauty depends on their colouring." Margaret dresses very attractively, Ouida says, and wears really beautiful colors. Both the Princess and the Queen are expected to wear outstanding colours, Ouida explains, so that the public can pick them out easily. "Margaret's preference is actually black," Ouida says. "She often wears a black dress under a coloured coat."

According to Ouida, the death of King George was a tragedy for Margaret, who had been very close to him. "She seems to have lost some of her high spirits," Ouida says.

Ouida's resemblance to the Duchess of Kent has proved embarrassing at times. Once when she was covering the Duchess's attendance at a theatre in London, the theatre manager in tie and tails came rushing toward Ouida, wreathed in smiles. "It wasn't very hard to understand what had happened," Ouida says. "I signalled frantically no, no, and an embarrassing few minutes were had by all."

Ouida, who plans eventually to return to Canada, hopes to be assigned to the Royal Tour of Australia.

[She did not get the assignment]

Sunday, Nov. 30, 1952

Dear Mum,
Speed phoned Saturday morning. He asked me up for New Year's and is coming down for Christmas. So is Frank, and Speed has suggested two other pilots to join us as well, so it should be great fun. Speed also brought down the things Frank's mother sent him for the white fruitcake Ethel's going to make.

We saw "Porgy and Bess" Saturday afternoon after a morning of shopping. I thoroughly enjoyed it again. Got the groceries and talked of eating out but it was raining with a smattering of sleet, cold and windy, so we eventually ate at home, listened to the radio, and talked.

Speed came back about 1:30 p.m. today, spent part of the afternoon mending broken dishes for me. We ate (potato scallop and baked ham) about 5 p.m. and he caught the 6 p.m. train back. I have tomorrow off from work so must finish up so many things left over during my time away. Thursday I'm at home but having a dinner party. Noel and Eleanor Jackson, an American teacher, Joe Hillary, and Tony Cheetham. Phoned Tony last Sunday evening and he jumped at the invitation and seemed delighted to be asked. I want Ethel to meet him—not matchmaking, but the idea didn't completely escape me. It will be nice seeing Tony again, as his company—if he is on form—is always an asset. It will also be interesting to see how Speed compares with the intellectual qualities I admired in Tony—and if I remember them correctly.

At the start of the weekend I was wondering what it was I saw in Speed, but he certainly has the right method of handling me—be it conscious or unconscious—and he improves with age, for I found myself hating to see him leave tonight. Although I still don't think for a minute I am completely gone on him.

Friday, Dec. 5, 1952, evening

Dear Mum,
This has been a corny week. I've been early reporter in the office (7:30 a.m.), still have a cold, a headache today, and the weather outside is terrible, thick fog that makes me feel my insides must be coated with black by this time and leaves a horrid taste in the mouth all the time. It was even foggy inside our office. Thought my glasses were dirty at first.[19]

---

[19] Fog from coal fires was so bad at times that it was described as "not seeing one's hand in front of one's face." It left soot in the bathtub.

Thursday evening—last night—we had the dinner party I mentioned before. Ethel turned out a marvellous French meal with veal cooked in white wine that had Tony's admiration hanging out, for he is quite a connoisseur of food. It was a very pleasant evening, although puzzling, for somehow it seemed as though I had seen Tony only a day or so before and imagine my astonishment to learn his sister has a six-months-old baby. Can't quite explain why I asked him—just felt like seeing him I guess, or perhaps it was some deep-rooted desire to see if what I liked in him was correct or imagination . . . Ethel was very taken with Tony—he always makes an excellent impression and is, of course, a very nice person—and I am completely at sea. I felt simply quite natural and at home with him, no burning desire, no dashed dreams, only a faint feeling that I vaguely miss his kind of company and had better be careful when I go to Luffenham this weekend because too much analyzing could perhaps spoil my Christmas and New Year's. Guess you could say it made me think, and that never hurts anyone—so long as it does not go on too long.

The Christmas party seems to be shaping up but I only realized the other day that these characters will obviously eat on the other three days besides Christmas and that's going to mean a whale of a lot of cooking and food! A turkey for 10 (about) ought to be terrific.

Wednesday, Dec. 10, 1952, noon

We are having no less than five pilots for Christmas, so it should be fun. The only blot now is that our friend Jackie has invited a 37-year-old dry cleaning managing director from Nottingham to join us. He was a wartime bomber pilot, a bachelor, filthy rich and usually stays at London's more expensive and exclusive hotels. I just can't imagine him with our batch of youngsters, and post-war jet-age fighter pilots will have little in common with a bomber wartime guy who loves to "reminisce"! Ugh. Surely to heaven he'll refuse to come!!

Yesterday was quite a day. The Canadian Defence Minister arrived at Luffenham at 10 a.m., toured the station, cocktails, etc., and lunch in the officers' mess. I was—per usual—the only female in existence, and per usual loved it. As I was travelling back to London anyway, dropped the hint that I wouldn't mind flying, and the invite was forthcoming, so in I get with Defence Minister Claxton, Air Commodore Martin Costello, and a few other miserable wing commanders.

We flew to Langer, the new supply base near Nottingham, toured the place, where Costello suddenly took it upon himself to escort me and I travelled with him in the second car while the other less notables travelled behind. He was quite cute, for in one place—airmen's quarters—he told me to wait, rushed ahead and looked around, then waved for me to come on. He had been afraid they were going to walk me into the airmen's lavatory!

Played rummy (with my baby cards I always carry) with Claxton's aide Major LaPlante all the way to London in the private RCAF minister's plane (lush job), was warmly greeted by the Northolt Airport group captain on arrival (old friend from last year), and invited to drive into town by the colonel waiting for the party, before Costello could get his bid in, which I had to refuse. Quite a day for a small-town girl.

Love, Ouida

Tuesday, Dec. 16, 1952

Had lunch with Mrs. Bennett today. She has sent you a Christmas pudding. Seemed very glad to see me and showed more interest in all the people I've talked about for so long than she ever did before, so maybe she did like me.

Quite a time last week. I told you about Luffenham and flying back in the Defence Minister's plane. Well, Thursday evening was Canadian Finance Minister Doug Abbott's party and who turned up as well but Prime Minister Louis St. Laurent and his eldest son Jean-Paul—both quite charming and fascinating. Thoroughly enjoyed the party, had a great chat with St. Laurent. And the Canadian pressmen seemed to like me OK too.

On from there to Norman Nash's cocktail party, which was fun too, but so different as it was all social as opposed to all intellectual and business.

My sleeping bag arrived just this minute from Marie's, so I sleep in it now and send all sheets to the laundry to prepare for Christmas. The first chap arrives from Paris tomorrow but he is staying at a hotel. All house guests come on the 24th.

Suddenly realized last night that we have invited thousands for Boxing Day and have very few glasses. What a life! Have at last planned our menus. Marie is sending two boiling fowl, as Ethel figured she would prefer them to a goose, and I have asked for all my bacon ration to be put toward a big boiling piece (ham) so we'll be able to have plenty of cold meat for snacks, etc. Now, so long as none of our pilots gets "duty officer" over Christmas we should be OK. Looks like it could be lots of fun.

Thursday, Dec. 18, 1952

The flat is a shambles now, as I'm sewing again and we're leaving everything go until the weekend and have one grand clean-up. That way, we (or I at least) figured we wouldn't invite anyone in, and we do so need the rest and break. Am remodelling the red velvet gown for New Year's and it's beginning to look pretty sharp—I think. Made it strapless style and trimmed the top with white fur with a halter neckline, also in fur. Having earrings made of a small, circular buckle with white fur covering the bar in the middle so they will match. These will dangle and I hope be quite striking looking.

Yesterday struggled with some shopping—tumblers, mainly, as we realized that after inviting everyone and his cousin to our open house we only had about six glasses and we will be nine in residence.

Three boiling fowl arrived yesterday from Marie and I carted them off to the butcher to be cleaned and dressed and stored and had a look at our turkey, which is already there and waiting.

If everyone turns up at our open house at the same time, it should produce a riot, as we'll be short of glasses and everything else but most of those coming are good types, so we should manage and by that time our own lot should be enough like a big family to be able to cope and see the funny side of it as well.

Tuesday, Dec. 23, 1952, evening

Ethel will be over soon with her friend (Canadian) from Paris, Charles Moore (he's on a scholarship over here), who has at least turned up, and Frank, Speed, and company should put in an appearance sometime tonight. They will all have to bunk in the flat next door tonight, as the girls don't leave the maisonette until tomorrow. Will be crowded but we'll manage.

Ethel went off early yesterday to get a Christmas tree in Covent Garden market and had her wallet stolen out of her purse with £9 and a $12 Canadian cheque. She was terribly upset but at her office they took up a collection and gave her £5. She was embarrassed but very flattered.

Wednesday, Dec. 24, morning [added]

I bought a tree today, had four men cutting and fixing it for me and one carried it home. But still no word from the boys—the wretches.

Lots of love, Ouida

Sunday, Dec. 27, 1952

Christmas dinner, nine sat down, we ate in the lounge at a long table covered with white tablecloths, red candles in Chianti bottles, and the lights on the tree the only illumination. The tree, by the way, had real one-penny candles in little holders. Ethel had seen them in France, and they gave the tree a fairy-like appearance.

We had a lovely turkey, which Speed carved, turnips, Waldorf salad, creamed potatoes, onion stuffing, cranberry jelly, gravy, accompanied by red French wine and ginger pears for desert. There was plenty for all and they ate to their heart's content . . . In the evening we did nothing but sat around and talked, joked, and chatted, but still didn't have a very early night.

Friday, Boxing Day, we were up about noon—Ethel and I made it a bit earlier and I tore off to my flat, as I wanted to change. We had invited our friends in for "A" drink and "A" piece of fruitcake (Ethel had made a terrific white one crammed with fruit, and we had your dark one.) Well, the first arrived about 2:30 p.m. and I heard Chris and Mike say goodbye about 1 a.m. when I had been in bed for half an hour. People poured in, few left after the anticipated half hour, some phoned other friends to come, people I had never seen before turned up, there seemed to be about three groups in all, everyone remarked on what a terrific "party," while Ethel and I maintained it wasn't supposed to be a party. Ethel went off to the ballet with Charlie Moore about 7 p.m., thinking it was all over, when another dozen rolled in. We finally got them out about 10 p.m. when Ethel returned with three French Canadians who spoke almost no English, and Frank and Al came back with Chris, Mike, and three others.

Guess the secret of a successful party is to not plan on having one, for people are still phoning to thank us, saying it was one of the best they have been to in ages. Of course, our boys were a great help, for they are easy to talk to, were always around to look after new arrivals, and, as Ethel said that night, "I wouldn't trade one of ours for anyone here today."

Saturday I was in the office by 7:30 a.m., was sent out on a late-morning job, phoned back to the office to be told I needn't come back in so joined the gang for a movie. Started out for a French one but the queue was so long, half of us got discouraged. Frank, Len, Ethel, Bob, and I went to "The Man Who Watched the Trains Go By," which was so-so, and with it was a lousy Yankee gangster one—but Len held my hand so I didn't mind, as I adore holding hands in movies (I did have to tell him to at first, but he didn't seem to need coaxing.)

Had a French meal "tournedos" (steaks) Saturday evening, which was excellent, and afterward we all stretched out on the floor around a couple of candles and talked again. Finally the boys got to bed about 6 a.m. (Ethel had managed it a bit earlier after the boys had demanded to be kissed goodnight and she obliged amid howls of laughter from all—the whole weekend seemed to be one long laugh with few dull moments.) But Len and I didn't manage bed at all and went out to mass at 8 a.m. Came back to my flat for breakfast and then collapsed on my divan and window seat and slept for a couple of hours, getting back to Ethel's in Stanhope Row about 1:30 p.m. as most of the boys were beginning to wake up.

So there you have it—quite a Christmas. Not an intimate family affair but the best of its kind for being away from home.

Off to mass (12 noon) so must close,

Lots of love, Ouida

"GETTING SCOOPS"
January–July 1953

Tuesday, Jan. 6, 1953, evening

Dear Mum,

Got a little gen [information] for you! Next time someone tells you reporters lead such interesting lives, go to such interesting places, and meet such interesting people—put a bee in their ear for me!! I have been to the sales. That statement should stand on its own, but the rest is too good to lose.

Started at 7:30 a.m. yesterday (Monday—always a blue day). Felt as though I'd been let in on the inside of a mental institution when I met two women who had been queuing 19 and a half hours!! One wanted to buy a five-guinea beaver lamb coat ($15) which had been reduced from 12 guineas ($37). Can you imagine the quality of coat for even $37—in a country where all furs are imported??

The doors opened and I got knocked into a side aisle then pushed back again. I stood like a great elephant huddled in a corner, holding onto my own purse, the photographer's case and hat and gloves, and trying to keep eager women from pulling my own hat off my head. Stood it for half an hour then beat it home.

Phoned the office to report—and was told to walk around and have a look at the other stores' sales. Not on your life! I stayed home, cleaned and tidied the flat, listened to the radio, wrote a couple of letters, phoned the shops having the sales and asked questions from a safe distance, then put over a further story.

Still I was condemned to the streets, so I went over to Ethel's for some lunch, took my umbrella to Harrods to be repaired—a nice store with no sale—and bought me a new wastepaper basket.

Thursday, Jan. 8 [added]

Now something much more exciting has happened. I am flying to Edinburgh tonight for Earl Dalkeith's wedding on Saturday.[20] Shall have three nights in Scotland, returning

---

[20] Earl Dalkeith, later the ninth Duke of Buccleuch, was marrying Jane MacNeill, a fashion model.

Sunday noon—and double expenses, as the Sunday Express have asked me to help their reporter out as well. Am really quite excited about it all and hope everything goes well. My jobs seem to keep getting bigger and better, and my stories receive more space and attention—and, of course, I love it.

Tuesday, Jan. 12, 1953

The Dalkeith wedding was quite a "do." Flew to Glasgow Thursday night, as Edinburgh was fogged in. Spent the night in a hotel room the size of a museum with private bath, etc. Caught the 7:30 a.m. train to Edinburgh.

Wore my velvet hat, fuschia rose, and gloves to the wedding and guess it looked quite good. Jane looked really beautiful and it was a truly lovely wedding. I had to dash out during the signing of the register and phone in the story, thus didn't get to the reception. But then nor did several hundred others, as the crush was terrific.

Caught the overnight train back—1st-class sleeper, private compartment—as we were afraid planes would be grounded—and so did the honeymooners. In the morning I opened my compartment door just as Dalkeith walked by—they had come to the front from the rear of the train to get off quickly. Jane moaned as she saw me, but I grinned and said I was now a private citizen, not Press, and felt quite sorry for them. We stood and chatted for 20 minutes until the train got in about the wedding and everything. Both are very pleasant indeed.

But I near passed out when Jane suddenly turned to me and said, "Were you cold last night? My compartment was freezing and I nearly froze all night." Maybe husbands—especially new ones—are not much use after all!!!!

Mum, I have not yet sent any columns out to anyone. Everything has been so rushed—and probably I'm so lazy, too. Not sure now whether to get a couple off quick or forget all about it. Suppose I should get some off or they will never trust me again. Suppose I ought to be more conscientious.

Thursday, Jan. 15, 1953, noon

Dear Mum,
Well, the ground has opened beneath my feet again. Margaret Gordon phoned last night and although she has no definite job, she rather thinks she will be returning to London in early March—which, of course, means a move for me. It couldn't come at a worse time because everyone is jumping prices for the wretched Coronation period and accommodation is becoming more than scarce.

But this morning I saw an ad in our paper (luckily I see it before it hits the streets) and there is a maisonette going, newly decorated and not more than a couple of blocks from here. My main problem is location. I do not want to move out of central London again and the closer I get to the office the better. I must try to stay close enough to be able to get home for lunch because that cuts my expenses terrifically.

This place—which I am to see tomorrow—is actually in Soho, quite a colourful area indeed which would probably shock some of my "snooty" friends. But it has a sitting room, kitchen, large double bedroom and bath—according to the agent. I would have to pay $22 a week (against $13 now) plus gas, electricity, and phone, which is the same as now. BUT Ethel is quite keen to share with me and divided between two it would work out at slightly less than I pay now and, of course, give much more actual space. It would also be much better for you and Dad because, although we could have managed here, it would really have been pretty crowded.

Sunday, Jan 18, 5 p.m. [added]

Now at Marie's. Saw the Soho place. I don't think it's too bad, but Ethel wasn't too impressed. It is newly decorated but hasn't everything necessary and a double instead of twin beds. But the agent said he will have a two bedroom place available which is also new and sounds quite nice and is in the same area. We're not in a rush, so we're going to keep looking.

Wednesday, Jan. 21, 1953

Dear Mum,
Received a bit of a shock today. The Syndicate desk phoned—Douglas Cobham—to ask if I would do some work and I jokingly asked if David Roberts was around, or had he died off? Nearly passed out when Douglas told me David died a fortnight ago of a kidney ailment. Douglas has taken over as editor. Knew David was unwell, but not dying!

A letter from Speed yesterday said he has a car for the week of Feb. 23rd. With a car at our disposal, it's a good chance for a look at Cornwall, which I have never seen. And before you get the wind up, Mum, remember I'm a MacLellan, 25, and—I hope—not a fool. And I quite like FO Bentham (who is Canadian and not English in outlook) so not liable to chance anything that would lose his present respect for me!

Thursday, Jan. 29, 1953

This flat hunting is driving us crazy! Have spoken for a new one that is to be finished in about a month in the middle of Soho. We'll be surrounded by all foreign restaurants, prostitutes, and heaven only knows what else—but the place is quite nice and very central, though a trifle expensive. Would you be afraid or ashamed to live in such an area? Ethel and I find it quite fascinating, and this flat is on the third floor so above it all. The area will not bother us at all—but I can see some of our friends raising eyebrows!

Tuesday, Feb. 10, 1953

Dear Mum,

Well, Ma'am, you'll be living in Chelsea in an authentic artist's studio when you visit your elder daughter in April. We have finally decided on a place, will move heavy stuff this weekend, and ourselves probably about the middle of next week.

So my address from, say, Sunday onwards, will be 59 Glebe Place, Chelsea, SW3. The telephone for the time being will be FLAxman 9969—it is an extension of Mrs. Dugdale's [her new landlady], but I am trying for a private line of my own and hope to have one before too long.

Now the story. There has been quite a gap in letters but trust my clippings have explained the trouble.

[During the exceptionally severe winter of 1953, a massive tidal surge in February in the Thames Estuary had cut off the Isle of Sheppey from the mainland. Ouida was assigned to cover the story.]

Last Tuesday I started out from here at 4 a.m., reached the town of Iwade on the Kent coast about 6 a.m., and left almost immediately in an open navy duck (amphibious tank) for the cut-off Isle of Sheppey—2 1/2 hours and three miles across flooded marshlands away. It was bitterly cold, windy, raining—in fact, nature threw the book at us—but we managed to be successful and I was heartily complimented by Mr. Hyde and several reporters on my story.

The next day I went back with the Duchess of Kent. She travelled in a small police launch, but not me! I went with the commander-in-chief of Chatham Naval Base, Admiral Sir Douglas–Tennant in his minesweeper, and he shared his sandwich lunch and coffee with me. I sneaked in and used the one emergency line from the island to the mainland when other reporters were not looking, so got my story off about two hours before them, then rushed back to the minesweeper in time to be taken back again, and as the admiral brought the head of the St. John's Ambulance, and a couple of her colleagues along too, there was no room for any other reporters except me. We even passed HRH in her launch on the way back. It was quite a trip—and of course I HATE getting scoops and being squired around!!!

Thursday I went to Sandhurst, the country's biggest military academy for the passing out parade, which included King Hussein of Jordan. His fiancé-to-be, Princess Dina, was there and I chatted with both. Again a pleasant day—but terrible cold again too and I had to sit along with everyone else in the wind for 1/2 hours. Boy, are my snuggies [flannel underwear from Canada] coming in handy—Ethel refuses to take hers off even indoors! We shock the natives!

Friday I glanced at Thursday's Times and saw the ad for the Chelsea studio and phoned the number just for fun as I was certain it would be too expensive or already gone. The woman who answered asked if I was an artist, as she wanted to let the place to an artist. I replied that I was not but that I was a writer who is forced to paint with a pen through lack of talent to enable me to use a brush. She seemed to like the sound of me, so said I might come to see the place.

I took Saturday afternoon off—Ethel had looked at a couple of places that morning—and we went along. She turned out to be A.K. Browning, a painter in her own right and widow of T.C. Dugdale, the Royal Academy portrait painter who died last November. She is absolutely sweet and seems very pleased with us, for she said there was an Australian woman artist who wanted the place and she felt guilty not giving it to an artist, but if we wanted it we could have it. I liked it immensely and although Ethel didn't care for the walls, which she claims are grey, she was keen on taking it. But we almost think we took it because we were completely charmed by Mrs. Dugdale and feel we will enjoy knowing her. She has never rented a place before and therefore is not a cheat.[21]

To our astonishment she asked if we would mind if she gave us silver plate, as the sterling is away in the vaults! Everyone else supplies tin! The studio is completely detached and self-contained. We have our own walk up to the front door, which is set back from the street—Mrs. D's house/studio fronts on the street. There is an entrance hall, a bedroom, bathroom, and kitchen in addition to the studio, which is 23 by 22 feet. The kitchen is being fitted in new—she said Ethel could go help her pick out a stove. It will be tiny but that's Ethel's domain and she is happy.

And it should be warm, for there is a large Quebec stove type thing. It takes coal (which she supplies) and has a pipe which goes up and then out of the wall, and Mrs. D says it really keeps very warm. The floor is inlaid cork. Furnishings are sparse at present but she had a six-bedroom house in the country which she must give up and we can have what we like from there. We figure Ethel and I can sleep on divans in the studio when you are here—and we could even put others up if we wished. Either way, we'll be able to entertain when we like, as we have no one above or below us and our own front door—and we can provide sleeping accommodation for friends when necessary.

Speed was down for the weekend and has asked me up to the Valentine dance this Saturday but I don't think I'll go, as I must save some money to meet the first rent payment and shall need time to get packed and moved. I plan to go up to Marie's next Thursday eve-

---

[21] Amy Katherine Browning, 1881–1979, was an associate of suffragist Sylvia Pankhurst. Ouida kept in touch with her until her death in 1979. Ouida had to sit through several sessions of having her portrait painted.

ning, and Speed can drive over there from Luffenham on Friday night. We'll probably stay until Sunday and start for Cornwall from there. That will give me a couple of days' quiet before we do any hard driving. But boy, if this weather keeps up I'm going to be tempted to inspect all the scenery from the inside of the car.

Thursday, Feb. 12, 1953

Dear Mum,

Boy, yesterday took an unexpected and exciting turn! Adrian Lighter, a friend whom I hadn't seen since before going home, phoned about 3 p.m. to say he had just been given tickets for last night's French Film Festival Gala performance to be attended by the Queen. It was strictly a formal "do," so I bought me a new pair of white kid evening gloves, got my red velvet back from the cleaners, sewed on the white fur, and was ready to be collected at 6:30 p.m.

He took me to dinner at Martinez, a Spanish restaurant which served a very nice meal indeed. I quite forgot to take any money at all and had to ask for money to go to the cloakroom. Tremendous crowds outside the Rialto Cinema and tons of starry names wandering about in the foyer, stalls, etc. all staring at everyone else.

I absolutely love such an occasion and do just twice as much staring as everyone else. Laurence Olivier introduced the French stars Martine Carol and Gerard Philipe (who is quite fascinating), and there were dozens of other stage and film stars around such as Douglas Fairbanks, Jack Hawkins (sitting behind me), Trevor Howard and his wife Helen Cherry, Yvonne de Carlo, and about six other French actors and actresses including Simone Simon and Simone Signoret—the latter I find most attractive and fascinating.

The Queen wore a grayish-champagne-coloured lace dress and was dripping with diamonds, while Prince Philip looked most original in dinner jacket and black bow tie. It was all extremely glamorous, and I'm afraid I—quite lacking in sophistication—didn't miss a trick.

The film, "La Belles de Nuit," a comedy by Rene Clair, was delightful and I thoroughly enjoyed it. A good French film is miles ahead of anything Hollywood turns out; what masters of mime they are, so much expression and meaning in so few words, and the acting is always so very good.

Ethel's French is, of course, very good; mine, slipshod as everything else I do is. She is very keen on French films and I must admit the ones we have seen lately have been excellent and I should imagine good for my vocabulary and understanding.

But later in the evening—which I think Adrian quite enjoyed too—he said something about the coldness of the night and remarked that he now has a hot water bottle but he's not spending another winter on his own. He intends to get him a wife—I rather gulped and sincerely hoped he was just passing remarks that have no connection with me. He's quite pleasant and a good escort—a half-pound box of chocolates for me—built rather long and lean but with heavy black horn-rimmed glasses, a black Anthony Eden hat, and oh so very English!

One of the girls just phoned from the office—I forgot my red snuggies there last night and it seems someone brought them out of the ladies' cloakroom and put them in one of the men's drawers (desk). Facing that outfit tomorrow is going to be rather embarrassing!

Lots of love, Ouida

Friday, Feb. 13, 1953

Have to laugh at Ethel. In my own inimitable way I just happen to ask her every so often what she thinks of Speed. She says she never really sees enough of him or talks to him long enough to know him at all. When I think about it, I suppose she's quite correct. He doesn't really make a tremendous impression either way, favourable or unfavourable.

You get the idea that he's a nice guy, pleasant, friendly, but he doesn't strike you as being good-looking, brilliant conversationalist, clever, dumb, noisy, boring—you find yourself left with no opinions about him at all. He's not inclined to be argumentative and thus doesn't stimulate lively conversations, he's a bit big in size and as he's inclined to be lean, he terrifies me that he'll break something; he wasn't built to be a fairy and is not particularly athletic. If in fact, if he runs, which is very occasionally—he looks rather as though his arms and legs might leave his body in exasperation. I am becoming accustomed to him and that takes away half the fun, I think. But he is quite good company and I hope I still think so at the end of this holiday.

It's all jolly well you nattering on about getting tickets for Wimbledon etc. while you're here, but I'm not the chief ticket-issuer, so don't bank on too much. Glad to hear Dad will be looking sharp when he sets foot on British soil. I've been telling everyone that my Dad is really very handsome and I get my beautiful countenance—except for my bumpy nose and crooked mouth—from him. So I expect him to live up to his reputation.

Received the agreement from Mrs. Dugdale's lawyers yesterday and have our company lawyer going over it. Evidently there will be a slight delay in our moving in as there has been a holdup on the kitchen, but I still want us to move out of here on the 18th, as I shall leave for holiday the next day anyway and there is no sense in paying rent for an empty flat here. We are still moving our heavy luggage this weekend.

Friday, Feb. 27, 1953

Dear Mum,

As I sit writing this the sun is streaming in on me. We have been so fortunate in the weather, not a drop of rain and yesterday was glorious. We are walking about with only suits on and yesterday stretched out for a while on the top of a grassy cliff to watch the sea beating against the rocks and the gulls and our suit coats were almost too warm.

Speed reached Marie's about 6 p.m. on Saturday. That night we took Marie and Bill in to Diss to a movie—lousy one, "I'll See You in My Dreams"—and on Sunday, Speed took Marie and me and two Irish children and their aunt all in to Church. After lunch Speed and I drove to the coast, Southwold and Lowestoft, getting back about tea time.

Monday we started south. On the way we crossed the Salisbury Plain Dad is always talking about. On the hillside—it's a very chalky area—are carved in the soil and chalk regimental crests, about 10 of them. [Her father had been stationed there in 1915 before being sent to the Front.]

We stopped in Redruth for lunch on the way to Penzance, and on the recommendation of a grocer we had a "really expensive" meal at 4 shillings and sixpence in a place where a curtain separated us from a tap dancing class. The meal was bacon, egg, baked beans and potatoes.

On Wednesday we drove down to Land's End and sat for a while partway down the cliff face. It was quite terrifying to see the sea roar in against the rocks below, sending the spray up almost to our feet—but very thrilling too.

Saturday, March 7, 1953

Now, about accommodations for Marion. I, of course, will provide a home for her but I really feel it might be better for her to live in one of the university girls' residences. There are three near the hospital. But she must apply for a place now, so I shall get the addresses off as soon as I have checked the places to find the nicest. If you disagree, say so, but I think she will have more of a college life that way.

Our new studio is now quite charming and we are very pleased with it. Ethel did a lot of furniture shifting on Saturday and improved the place immediately.

Speed stayed until Wednesday after our return from Cornwall and slept here while Ethel and I slept at the old place; he did all our moving for us—which entailed about 15 trips up and down the 4 flights of stairs—and left behind a pair of shoes size 13!! He was an absolute honey, working like a pack horse.

Lots of love, Ouida

Thursday, March 12, 1953

Perhaps flying is like being a glorified bus driver to many, but Speed joined the air force because he wanted to fly; he loves the life. That I admire much more than the men who do the humdrum everyday jobs with which they are bored. By far I prefer the man who does what he wishes, no matter what that may be, to the man who simply does a dull task because it pays well or brings home the bacon.

I've come to realize that happiness is a very important thing. One can tackle almost anything—so long as one is happy in it.

Marg's suggestion that I need someone above me—I presume she means mentally—doesn't hold. I once thought it did—and met Tony. He probably did me a world of good in the thinking quarter—but he almost stamped out that wonderful butterfly feeling I get in my stomach when I'm happy. It's when I feel like dancing or singing or shouting and I know the guy with me will understand that I'm content. Perhaps he doesn't shout too—but he doesn't try to stop me.

Best of all, I think, is the kind of guy who has an alert brain, intelligent, who can go along with me—but is kind, thoughtful, considerate too, for these latter qualities make the difference between a business partner and a husband.

By the way, Ethel announced the other day she was quite certain Len would propose but it sure wouldn't be all moonlight and roses, as he just isn't the kind. More likely it would be in the midst of a traffic jam—but I'm pretty sure it won't occur at all or certainly not for quite some time. Mr. Bentham is no fool and he has already remarked that he'll never propose to any girl unless he's fairly certain of what her answer will be.

Ethel says she likes Speed more, the more she sees of him—but she still doesn't think he's quite the answer. The only one with no opinion is me—and I'm not in such a hurry as everyone else to decide about the future.

Must go to whip up a birthday cake for Ethel—expertly, out of your cake-mix box!!

Lots of love, Ouida

[Miriam MacLellan's letters to Ouida in these years have been lost, but one from March 17, 1953, illustrates that the frankness between daughter and mother went both ways. She says in the letter:

"Grand letter, dated 12th, arrived this a.m. and has been read at least four times. You make me smile when you rave on about Len. Same old angle, would love to have your cake but dare not take the first bite! I, like Ethel, do not think Len is your big moment: you would not have to stop and wonder, either one of you; there comes a force over which neither have any control and you go right ahead until you land at the altar. Until that experience comes, just enjoy life as it is.

"I know what happiness is and you certainly described it . . . perfect contentment, no matter what you are doing or what you may have to do without, as long as you can be with your beloved."]

Monday, March 23, 1953

About our seats for the Coronation. Are you certain this Father Leopold's seats are for INSIDE the Abbey? I can't for the life of me think of how he would be entitled to them. The peers in this country had to ballot for seats and many are left outside so scarce is the space. The ordinary civilians inside will be the representative ones, like one Boy Scout, one Girl Guide, of all the leading organizations. It is much more probable he will have two seats on the route—which (I hope) you and Dad will also have, so don't let that story circulate.

Logically, Mum, what possible reason would there be for an unknown CATHOLIC priest from Canada to be invited to the Coronation? Canada will be represented by St. Laurent [Prime Minister], probably Mike Pearson [Lester Pearson, Minister of External Affairs], and a couple of others. What about Catholics, you say? That would surely be the apostolic delegate from Rome—as a government representative. Find out, for if your story is true, then it is a terrific story I wouldn't mind having—but I'm certain you'll discover he has seats on the route.

Thursday, March 26, 1953, evening

Did a short two-minute BBC radio newsreel talk yesterday outside Marlborough House. Luckily it was just used on the overseas service, for if Mr. Hyde had heard it, he'd probably have passed out—me being paid to stand guard as a journalist outside Marlborough House because of Queen Mary's death, for the Evening Standard, and in fact I'm around the corner being an "overseas student" telling BBC audiences that I'm there because of my great respect for the old girl.

Oh yes, think I've stuck my rather long neck out again! A chap in the sports department in the office named Gus Hinds—brown eyes, heavy-set, blond wavy hair, and quite nice—sits near where I hang up my coat. I always say "Hello" when I come and go and got to know him quite well. He's been kidding me about taking him to lunch for quite a while now, so the other day I said he could jolly well take me, after all his talk—was a bit short of cash that day. He's been beaming ever since and today hung up in the middle of a telephone conversation to ask me as I was passing if I'd have lunch with him again. The boy's a bit keen!!

Love, Ouida

Monday, April 13, 1953, morning

Dear Mum,

Speed turned up Saturday in time for lunch with Ethel, then came to pick me up after work. We did some shopping on the way home, butchers, grocers, etc. He had come down with another officer named Len Fine and had asked him to join us for the evening. With Ethel, we went to a play then to dinner at the Chez Auguste and finally back home for coffee.

Speed slept in the studio, Ethel and I in the bedroom. Our new phone is in the studio with the extension of the old one still in the bedroom. Sunday morning about 9:15 a.m., I used the extension, let the phone ring in the studio until Speed answered, then asked for breakfast in bed. I didn't get it.

Sunday, April 19, 1953

Mike Smart has asked my plans for Coronation week and the week previous, which looks as though he may be home then. That could be fun—if I survive. Chris has asked me to "THE" Coronation night ball at the Savoy, but I would so like to go in a party or with someone else. I like Chris but not in big doses. Would much prefer Mike for a partner, so shall suggest it to him. I feel Chris ought to take a completely new girl because there is no sense him hanging around me when his case is hopeless. Had also better sound Speed out for his plans during the Coronation period, but think he will be flying and thus confined to base.

Your ship is due at Southampton at 6:45 a.m. on the Monday so don't look for me on the quay! Also I shall have to wangle some time off to meet the boat train, as I'm due to work that day, but shall give a good sob story to get off.

Did a feature on a ballet school in Guildford this week and have another on American servicewomen over here lined up for next week. I'm thrilled to bits about getting more feature work and they seem pleased with what I turn in, and I sure love doing it.

Sure hope you are bringing some BUTTER! Love, Ouida

[No more letters while Ouida's parents were on their ten-week visit. They stayed with her in London and visited Bill and Marie Fraser in Norfolk. Ouida was with them for twelve days in the south of France. In London, they saw the Coronation parade and attended a Garden Party at Buckingham Palace. Ouida's father went with her to Wimbledon and with Chris Dobson to cricket at Lords: he was concerned when Chris was late until he heard that the match lasted five days.]

"A CANADIAN AND AN ENGLISHMAN"
August 1953–August 1954

Wednesday, August 12, 1953, evening

Had Monday and Tuesday off this week—in lieu of the day off I missed during Coronation week. Lazed around Sunday and went to the Greene's for tea and did just about the same on Monday. It was nice to relax with no worries. Tuesday I went to Brighton with Chris and Mrs. Dobson and we had a nice day at the seaside—beautifully warm.

Last Saturday Mr. Hyde took me out to lunch, then took me shopping in Soho; the chauffeur picked us up and drove me home and Hyde gave me the rest of the afternoon off. He came in to see the studio—he was one of my references—and thank heavens Ethel was home, as I wouldn't have wanted him here alone. She found him most interesting.[22]

Next Wednesday we are having a "Dior Party" with Bob and Barb Greene supplying most of the guests and eats, and we are supplying the hall. I have asked a few people but don't intend to make it very many as I don't really feel in a party mood and would prefer something when Speed is down to help out.

He and Frank Sylvester gave an aerobatic display in Holland recently. His oxygen mask cut out and he couldn't breathe, so had to break away from Frank and fix it. Then Frank's wheels fell down and he had to slow down to almost a stall. As Frank was going by the crowd slowly, Speed got his mask fixed and roared by and straight up in some spiral rolls. It seems the crowd thought it was all part of the act and loved it.

Mike Smart had another crash in Germany—a miracle. His engine failed when he was 10 feet up in takeoff (the speed then is pretty terrific) and down he came, port wing touched first and broke, undercarriage broke and he slid across the runway on his belly—and with overloaded (530 gallon) tanks. Evidently there were plenty of sparks but no explosion or fire, and lucky Mike stepped out without a scratch.

---

[22] Ronnie Hyde, the news editor, very suave and handsome, told me he would like to be the butler in a large country house.

Thursday, Sept. 3, 1953, morning

I had my birthday card from Nana stuck up on the writing desk last Friday when Speed was here and he looked at it and said, "Whose is this?" I said my grandmother's. "To her?" "No, her to me." "A bit premature isn't it?" [Ouida's birthday was Sept. 1.] So when he thinks my birthday is, I'm not sure. Ethel said she felt it was only fair for her to drop him a reminder, but I wouldn't let her. Of course, now that I think of it, I had only just met Speed last year when my birthday came round and there is no reason at all for him to remember when it is.

Of course, I don't deserve anything from him either, because I was in one of those cantankerous moods over the weekend and picked at him about his hair, size of feet, suit, etc. Last night when he called I said I'd been feeling rather guilty and he quietly replied, "Oh you weren't any worse than usual and I guess I'm pretty used to it now." Not sure whether to take that as a dig or a compliment!!

Oh yes, Speed, being his usual romantic self, suddenly asked me the other night if I realized how much I was worth over here because an officer gets an extra overseas allowance for a wife and the air force pays her way back to Canada. Of course he didn't suggest I should become an air force wife or anything like that and it does seem a bit hard on a guy, I pointed out, to burden him with a wife while he is here just to get him some extra pay. And what would happen to this unfortunate woman when she was landed on Canadian shores if she was only valuable over here? Boy, what a guy! Romeo could take lessons! But it does suggest he may have honourable intentions.

[Added next morning.]

Well! A birthday card arrived this morning from Sir Lancelot and believe it or not, it included a poem! Boy, what an effort!

A single card, a simple rhyme,

A simple man, a single hope,

That joys will not decrease with time

And time store nothing you can't cope.

I hope this little poem of mine

Can equal yours of old

But even if it lacks in rhyme,

For me it's getting pretty bold.

Monday, Sept. 21, 1953, morning [written from Marie and Bill's farm]

Dear Mum,

Guess I'm probably in disgrace by now with this long silence, but so much has been happening. First of all, I'm being really worked hard at the office and last week had only one evening off and then made a skirt.

And the weekend was pretty eventful. On Friday Al Marshall's secretary phoned to ask if I would mind "terribly" if I had to fly to Luffenham for the Battle of Britain Day celebrations with Gary Cooper instead of the rest of the press group. I thought she must be nuts but managed to calmly say I wouldn't mind too much.

Of course I had to get to the RAF aerodrome at Biggin Hill in Kent for that, but by luck our helicopter was going down, and Mr. Hyde said I could go in that. Quite an entrance we made, me welcomed by the CO; then Wing Commander Lindsey from North Luffenham arrived in an Expeditor [Beechcraft] to pick up Cooper and me. But at Luffenham the fun started. On landing, a crosswind hit us and we tipped up on one side, damaging the wing and tail. I thought we had lost a wheel and the thought went through my head "Golly, we're going to crash. I've never been in a plane crash before." I wasn't at all afraid but felt shaky later when Speed told me that tipping was a good way of "writing off" a plane.

Gary Cooper was very funny. He was sitting in the co-pilot's seat and after Lindsay got the plane righted and we taxied along, Cooper turned to me and said "I thought for sure I had my foot on something wrong—I didn't, did I?" he asked Lindsay.

A mere 30,000 people watched our arrival heralded by the bagpipe band. I could have fainted and felt a fool getting out of the aircraft and slipped as quickly as possible into the crowd and up into the control tower, where I was greeted by Air Commodore Costello and General Smith. Had a lovely view of the show—didn't see the rest of the Press until they were leaving.

Speed told me later that as he was getting into his plane, an airman ran up and told him his girl had just arrived with Gary Cooper.

Speed gave me a very attractive sterling silver ring for my birthday, but I nearly died of heart failure when he pulled out the box. Then later—after the dance about 5 a.m.—he said something about us becoming a habit and it was just as well we didn't see too much of each other, as we'd never make a pair, and he'd get posted, and that would be the end of it and I'd have wasted a lot of valuable time. Whether he expected me to contradict or not I do not know, but I had to leap out of the car and run, as I was suddenly violently ill to my stomach. Felt a perfect fool, and I think he was a bit embarrassed too.

He came on Sunday to take me to the station and looked a bit sheepish. When I asked him if his remarks the night before meant he thought we ought to break it off, he said "Gosh, no"—so how am I to know what is in his lousy head!!

My tummy is still upset today, so Marie called the office to say I wouldn't be down for tomorrow. Feeling pretty tired too, so no sense rushing back into the fray.

Will be back to meet Marion on Thursday though for sure. [Marion came to study medicine.]

Love, Ouida

[There are no letters to hand covering the next eight months. For the *Evening Standard*, she wrote a series about former fashion models and another about London society hostesses. The following was published on November 3.]

HOSTESSES OF 1953 by Ouida MacLellan

There are never flowers on the table at the Belgravia home of Mrs. Gerald Legge, wife of the nephew of the Earl of Dartmouth. Mrs. Legge suffers from hay fever, so in place of flowers she has candles in gilt holders for her dinner guests to admire.

The raspberry-walled dining room has a glass showcase of white and gold Staffordshire china. The refectory oak table glows with the deep patina of centuries, for it was made in the reign of Charles II: the narrow serving table once did duty in a public house.

Mrs. Legge will explain jokingly that guests always number six, because she has only eight chairs, and "it's a bore trying to borrow more." If you are invited to the Legge's you can be late for cocktails (poured by Mr. Legge because his wife is a non-drinker) but you must be on time for dinner, always served promptly at 8:15 p.m.—for even London's top hostesses have servant problems. Servants must not be kept up too late, nor overworked on weekends, so Saturday and Sunday night parties are out.

The main course will be most original, for the West Indian cook composes the dishes as she goes along. "She tries out new ideas and writes down the recipes, afterwards, if we like them," Mrs. Legge explains.

You will not bring out your cigarette case if you have a habit of smoking between courses. Non-smoker Mrs. Legge would not approve. But you *will* play cards, preferably canasta. Otherwise you would not have been invited, for Mrs. Legge thinks it is "too, too dreadful if one has to make conversation for a whole evening."

[In February 1954, Ouida was interviewed in her flat by Beverley Nichols for *Woman's Own*, a weekly magazine. He was a very well-established author, playwright, and journalist. The piece appeared on February 25, 1954.]

MY WORLD by Beverley Nichols

Whenever I ring a new front door bell, my heart beats a fraction faster... particularly if there is reason to suppose that the door may be opened by an attractive young female. No exception to this rule was the evening I had been asked to dine by Ouida MacLellan at her flat in Chelsea. If that name means nothing to you at the moment, the time may come when it will mean a great deal.

Stand on the doorstep and ring the bell with me. There is a moment's pause, the sound of footsteps, and a girl's laugh. Then the door opens. There is a blaze of red. A positive conflagration of carnation-coloured velvet. No—nothing has exploded. It is merely the effect of a dress. Inside the dress, which is low cut and sweeping, there is a young lady of twenty-five, tall, dark, and slim.

In this first split-second impression I make a note of deep-set eyes, a beautifully curved neck... (necks are very important, though women and ostriches often forget the fact)... lovely hands, and a general sense of grace. Ouida is a Canadian journalist, and a brilliant one too. She has carved her way in and out of an astonishing number of front-page stories, pleasant and unpleasant. And she hasn't done this merely by the light of nature. She's worked.

My word, how that girl has worked. She's studied ballet, music and dramatics; she's modelled dresses; she was probably the first Canadian woman to fly in a jet fighter plane; she has had published a history of 42 towns in her native New Brunswick; she hitchhiked around Europe, wrote and broadcast her own radio programme series, gave talks on Britain to Canadian clubs, and she made a dress overnight for a Buckingham Palace garden party.

It will be generally agreed that a girl with all that experience ought to have some pretty shrewd observations to make about the male... particularly the British male. And that was the subject to which I directed the conversation after dinner. Ouida, with her Canadian forthrightness—and journalist's flair—pinpointed the whole of this gigantic subject with a single illustration. A bunch of flowers. In Canadian language, a "corsage."

"You asked me the difference between a Canadian and an Englishman? Well there it is. In that corsage."

"Which corsage"

"The one you didn't bring me tonight."

She laughed infectiously, "Please don't look embarrassed. I know it isn't 'done' over here. But in Canada..."

This subject is so totally new to me—and I guess to you too—that I'm going to devote the rest of the article to it. Here then is . . . "The Story of the Corsage."

In Canada a corsage is a "must" for any formal affair. It needn't be very grand or expensive . . . a couple of roses with a little maidenhair, or three carnations with a silver ribbon . . . though even these, in Canada, cost the English equivalent of ten shillings, which is quite a hole in a young man's pocket. But no Canadian boy who was taking his girl out to a dance or a party would dare to ring the doorbell unless he had that little Cellophane package in his hands. As for the girl, she'd consider herself insulted, and if she consented to go out without one—which is improbable—she'd feel improperly dressed.

A whole code of romantic etiquette, which I find quite enchanting, has grown up round this corsage business. Firstly, the boy has to find out what dress his girl is going to wear . . . and that means all sorts of pleasant little intrigues. If he's an experienced young man, he'll have the flowers delivered beforehand . . . "Then a girl can get them safely anchored on," said Ouida.

"What d'you mean . . . anchored on?"

She laughed. "It's obvious you've never sent a girl a corsage," she said. "Pinned in the right place, of course. It's not always too easy. And there are times when you have to make sure that they'll fall off."

She saw my look of mystification. She explained that if the boy had been careless, and hadn't rung up the mother or the girlfriend, he might arrive with something quite frightful, like pink carnations for an orange dress. And then . . . well, while they were dancing, the pin had to come loose!

Now please don't get the idea that Ouida doesn't like Englishmen, just because of the flower business. She does . . . indeed, she nearly married one.

Ouida believes that the story of the corsage is significant of the fact that in Canada a girl gets a better deal. "All men put women on pedestals, at some time or other in their lives," she said. "But in England, one sometimes has a feeling that the pedestal has been bought on the hire-purchase system, and sent back to the store after the first payment."

Two more "quotes" from Ouida: "In England," she said, "if a man makes money, you can tell it by looking at him. In Canada, you tell it by looking at his wife."

Cynical? But there is more than a grain of truth in it.

Again . . . "A Canadian likes to feel proud of the woman he takes out. And he's mighty pleased if she's admired and made a fuss of. The Englishman isn't. If the girl he's with is the centre of attention, he's inclined to resent it."

Is that so far from the truth?

Thursday, June 3, 1954 [Just days before her departure to Canada for a cross-country train trip.]

Dear Mum,

Everything is happening to me at once.

First of all, I casually asked for an extra three weeks' holiday and to my astonishment got it. That gives me a full seven weeks. I ought to be able to "see Naples and die" in that time. It'll probably be of starvation I die, too, unless they give away food for free!

Secondly, a chap at the BBC arranged for me to have a TV test on Tuesday and they were quite enthusiastic about the results. I had wanted it especially to know if I was photogenic enough to try for something while in Canada. Then yesterday I saw Andy Cowan, CBC chief here, and he was most encouraging. He is writing the TV chiefs in both Montreal and Toronto and was very sweet about advising me on the best kind of material to try on them.

BOAC [British Overseas Airways Corporation] meanwhile have sent out a press handout on me to Montreal—not that I expect anyone to get killed in the rush to see me. However, it does present possibilities and I would surely love to make a little pocket money to carry me over the seven weeks.

And Speed goes to Moose Jaw. He had hoped, as I told you, to get further west, nearer the Rockies, but guess the Air Force isn't taking his views into consideration. He plans to meet me in Montreal and drive me to his parents' home in Windsor. From there on, I'm in a fog, as to plans.

[During her stay in Montreal in June of 1954, Ouida was interviewed by the *Montreal Star*. The interview appeared in the paper on June 16.]

CANADIAN GIRL BECOMES EXPERT ON STYLING by Zoe Bieler

When it comes to spotting a really pretty girl, Miss Ouida MacLellan, originally from Moncton, N.B., has a quick discerning eye. She's just completed a survey of pretty girls in London offices for the *Evening Standard*, a newspaper controlled by fellow Maritimer Lord Beaverbrook.

"It all began when one of the British Members of Parliament, John Baker White, a merchant, claimed that his business had a monopoly on London's pretty girls," Miss MacLellan explained in an interview here this week. "Of course this remark aroused some controversy, and my paper sent me to find out if he was right."

It took her six months, during which time she interviewed thousands of girls in every type of business from stores, telephone exchanges, the civil service, and private businesses. In one place she looked at 2,500 girls, selected six to be photographed, discarded four of the photographs, showed two to her editor, and he selected one for publication in the paper."

"It meant quite a lot for a girl to be chosen as one of our pretty girls," Miss MacLellan says. "One of them got four proposals the day after her picture appeared in the paper and another got a good modelling job."

Many of the men on the *Evening Standard* envied Miss MacLellan her job but the editors decided that when it came to judging one pretty girl from another, a woman was more likely to be unbiased. Although she started her survey with no definite age limit, Miss MacLellan, who is 26 years old herself, finally set 25 as the maximum age for prettiness—"after that, the lines being to show, especially in press photos," she declares.

By the time she completed her assignment Miss MacLellan decided that there were more pretty girls in the telephone exchanges than in any other type of London business. John Baker White's store—"it wasn't bad, there were quite a number of slightly above-average looking girls there, but the British on the whole are not a beautiful race and the average isn't high."

According to Ouida MacLellan, the average British girl has little idea of good grooming. "It's odd, but I soon realized that if a girl had a neat back to her head there was something wrong with her face. And if her face was pretty, she neglected her hair. Very few of the girls I interviewed really knew how to handle make-up. All too often they were heavily made-up from forehead to chin and then forgot their necks." She also complains that London business girls show a tendency to overdress. "I was always encouraging them to peel off layers of loose jackets, extra sweaters, little scarves, and surplus brooches."

A tall, slim brunette who dresses smartly and has a face that she would probably classify as "slightly above average good looks but not tops photogenically," Ouida MacLellan is back in Canada to take a good look at Canadian women. She also wants to spend a holiday with her parents in Moncton. "And I want to settle the question of where I belong," she says. "After five years in England, it's time to decide whether I'm going to stay there indefinitely or come back to Canada."

She arrived in Montreal this week by air and from here plans a trip to the West Coast—she's never been farther west than Toronto before. She hopes to gather material for a series of articles on Canadian women and also investigate Canadian television.

Thursday, July 12, 1954, 8:30 a.m. [written on-board the train]

Dear Dad,

At last a letter. Should imagine you've given me up as a bad job by this time. Shall post this in Jasper. As Mum probably told you, I had intended stopping over in Winnipeg. Got off there yesterday. It was cold and damp and somehow Winnipeg seemed like a friendless city so I just put myself back on the train and shall be in Vancouver tomorrow morning.

The conductor has just given me the leaflet on the trip through the Rockies, with the map and notes on places to see. Haven't minded the trip at all so far. There was a very pleasant Scots family on with two kids, boys aged 2 and 3, until Edmonton and I enjoyed talking to them. Also, my seat companion to Edmonton was an RCAF Sgt. who was very pleasant. I fed him and he bought the coffee and other things we wanted en route. Then last night a French chap also in the air force and being posted to Edmonton joined us to play rummy and it was amusing. The three of us went for a walk in Saskatoon, where we had 40 minutes.

I have asked for a lower berth for tonight if there is one available because we reach Vancouver at 7 a.m. and I'm afraid I'll miss all the scenery if I'm tucked away in an upper berth.

Trees, trees and more trees is all I can see now. This could be anywhere.

Still don't know how long I'll be anywhere or for that matter where I'm liable to be.

Bye for now, be seein' you.

Love, Ouida

Friday, July 2, 1954, 6 p.m. [Vancouver]

Dear Mum,

My staggering experiences continue! Arrived here at 8 a.m. By 10 a.m. I was having tea with Ethel's mother, and by 3:35 I had met Peter McDonald, TV Director here; by 3:30 I was doing a rush test before camera, and by 4:10 I was in war paint again doing an audition for "Tabloid," which is due to start here as a new programme in about two weeks' time.

The girl they hire will do probably 3 shows a week, work roughly two hours a day for which she'd get about $60 to carry home I gather. ($25 a show.) And she'd be free to do any other work she liked—radio, writing, and more TV. I liked the man Bill Bellam, who is to be the M.C., and he'd be nice to work with. So he's to decide definitely within the next week—and I, in the meantime, am quite staggered. As you know the Toronto TV job won't be known until September and I'm still employed in England. Still, Vancouver is certainly a pretty place and the CBC man makes it sound progressive and interesting.

Still, maybe fate will intervene again and I won't have to make my own decision. I'm fascinated by the speed of action here—as everywhere in Canada—and wondering if being the one to start "Tabloid" here might not be better than stepping into the shoes of someone who has been a success. Also being in at the start and going through the "teething troubles" would be darned good experience for me.

So there you have it—I'm here for a week at least.

Love, Ouida

Sunday, Aug. 8, 1954 [back in London]

Dear Mum and Dad,
Guess by this time I'm in disgrace, but it has been such a crazy week I've been unable to sort out my thoughts and so couldn't think of what to write. Whereas normally when I return from Canada I feel as though I had never been away, this time I felt as though I hadn't come back. Ever tried carrying on a full week's work when you didn't feel as though you were even in the country? It's quite difficult.

Monday was a bank holiday here anyway and a deadly day in the office, and right off, the boss invited me to lunch. I had no choice, as I had forgotten my wallet at home and thus had no money except a few pennies which I needed for the bus fare home. He was lucky, I only cost him £1:7:6—at Simpson's in the Strand—a most elegant place where one tips the carver who wheels his little trolley to your table and carves off whatever you wish right there! Luckily for me, the server's conversation was above average and mostly he questioned me about life in Canada, so I was on safe ground—I even quoted meat prices in Montreal straight from my notes.

Tuesday I spent most of the day in Norman Hartnell's salon selecting clothes from his collection to be photographed. [Hartnell was Dressmaker to the Queen.] Made friends with one of his delicious-looking blonde models, and did it ever pay off! Saturday morning she phoned to tell me she was being married very quietly and no one knew but at the last minute she decided to tell me in case I was interested in a picture. I sure was!

Wednesday I was in Hastings all day where the Evening Standard was sponsoring a fashion show. It was a lovely, sunshiny day and I thoroughly enjoyed it—even though it meant working until 9 p.m. and missing a first-night theatre [production] Chris had been going to take me to. Instead we got some supper then just walked around the West End and along Piccadilly looking at the shops and the people. I always enjoy that.

Friday I spent down at Henley on Thames meeting and interviewing Beatrice Lillie. It was our first encounter, and although she is a seemingly strange and rather shy person, I like her and she must have liked me reasonably well, as she showed me all over her house, which is really three Queen Anne cottages knocked into one huge house. The main lounge has the old original beams all uncovered. Then there are lovely grounds and gardens, a boathouse and motor-driven gondola-like boat. Her mother was there too—she was 79 yesterday—quite active but I fear going slightly around the bend conversationally.

Friday evening there was a party at Al Marshall's house. He leaves on Tuesday, going back to Canada and he's not very happy about it. Andy Cowan of the CBC left last Tuesday after 10 years here, so the crowd is rather breaking up.

Last night Ethel had a theatre and dinner date, so I was left on my own. Quite a change for me and I'm not sure my nose wasn't slightly out of joint. Chris invited me to join him and his pals in a pub but that isn't really my style and I was too tired to face it.

Monday, Aug. 9, 1954

Dear Daddy,
. . . Several people have said they think I'm nuts not to try for something in TV over here, which I suppose in a way is true. I do enjoy living over here, love being so close to the rest of Europe, and am not all certain I would like living in Toronto as much. I'm well fixed, house, interests, friends, and everything is very conveniently arranged and I'm well enough off to be able to enjoy it all. Am thinking of looking around for a little car, maybe, but there is no panic.

Dear Mum,
Saw the BBC TV producer today but I wasn't very encouraged. He gave me several people to write to and wants me to think up ideas for him. Guess the CBC almost chasing me rather spoiled me! I realize I should try a little harder but somehow I feel so incompetent when trying to "sell" myself for something.

I'm still hearing results of my press interviews in Montreal and Vancouver. One clipping from the Calgary Herald and another from the Canada Review here—and they get worse with each rewriting!

On Wednesday night we have a dinner party that has snowballed into 10 people. What I'd ever do without Ethel to plan the meal I do not know.

Thursday, Aug. 26, 1954

My day off today and it looks like being a lovely one so I am scheming to be taken to Richmond Park this afternoon. Ron Moody, one of the stars of a musical review who is a close friend of Al Bermel (Toronto), is coming to lunch, and as his show isn't until 8:30 p.m., I hope he'll take me out.[23]

The dinner party yesterday was an interesting lesson. I shall never invite 10 again, it's too many to be cosy and not enough to form several small groups for talking. It was the very good meal and the way we served it—buffet style with everyone going to fetch their own—that kept the party going.

I think it would be a mistake for Marion to try to come live with us again. Our age difference is still too great and always will be until she stops being a student and goes to work.

[added later that day]

Came in to find your note. I must admit I've been wondering too about the Toronto job. McLean did say I wouldn't hear anything until the end of August so guess I'll have to give him another week or so and then write.

As for not having settled anything, how could I without a definite offer to settle? And I was NOT "requested" to return to Toronto as you say. I was simply told to look in if I happened back—but that is one of those casual remarks. I don't want to appear over-anxious, especially since I am not at all certain as to what I want to do myself.

Now, to Marion. She did fail. I have talked with the hospital and there is no chance whatever of her getting back in. That much is definite. Hospital openings are much too scarce here for them to make an exception BUT Marion may be able to get her first MB [Bachelor of Medicine] outside the hospital and still accomplish her year by writing a second set of exams.

Love, Ouida

---

[23] Ron Moody later played Fagan in *Oliver!* on stage and in the film.

"YES"
September–December 1954

Wednesday, Sept 1, 1954

Dear Mum and Dad,

Golly, 27 today—and I had to run to catch the bus, jump off at the traffic lights, and run to the office. But guess that goes in the family so I should be able to keep it up until I'm 60 at least. But there won't be any celebrating tonight—I'm going to bed early. I've just had two late nights and very long, hard days, so it's bed tonight. Besides, I hate a fuss, and more than anything I hate others trying to be gay and celebrate something I don't see any point in celebrating myself.

I'm off to Marie's on Friday evening for the weekend and do I ever need the rest! All the fashion shows I've been covering have been getting me down and today when our publicity manager rang to tell me of a mistake I'd made, I ended up in tears and had to hang up on him. So hurrah for the country air.

Love, Ouida

Monday, Sept. 13, 1954

Believe it or not, I managed to cook a chicken dinner AND make a delicious deep apple pie yesterday! Not even Chris (who ate it) was more surprised than I was at the result!

Thursday Sept. 16 [added]

Got a bit delayed, but lots more news now. I have managed to get Marion back into Chelsea College again for her first MB, which should mean no time lost at all. AND the principal of College Hall has agreed to make an exception to take her in this year. So she'll be in the residence for London University, where she will be with Royal Free Hospital students and thus make certain her work is OK. Although it will mean a daily journey for her from Russell Square station to Chelsea, I feel it will do her a lot of good to be with the other students.

Tomorrow I go to a cocktail party, then on to meet Ron Moody after his show at the Criterion Theatre. Ron is taking me to Churchill's night club, where he is doing cabaret. It should be fun.

Wednesday, Sept. 29, 1954

Marion seems to be settling down OK in the new residence. I haven't seen the place yet but expect I shall one of these days.

Marie and Bill are coming to stay over Monday night, and I have booked tickets for "The Boy Friend" which is an excellent 1920s musical.

More than anything, I want a car now, so shall manage somehow. If you hear of any rich relatives inquiring about Christmas gifts please mention a car instead of hankies or aprons, and all donations will be more than gratefully accepted.

Met an interesting chap last week at a party. He is 6 ft. 3 and an actor. His hand was all cut because he had been fighting a duel with Errol Flynn, and Flynn is a poor shot. Bumped into him again at the "Don Giovanni" performance by the Vienna State Opera Company (it was wonderful), and he came home for a bite to eat. It turned out that one of the principals in the company is his music teacher, and Christopher himself (name is Christopher Lee) pops off to Stockholm every once in a while and sings in the opera there.

So while I heated some soup he wandered around the studio singing arias in a lovely bass-baritone voice from Otello, Marriage of Figaro, Don Giovanni, Barber of Seville, etc.—and in the natural languages, German, Italian etc. Astonishing the people one meets—a brief encounter with a chance acquaintance.[24]

Tomorrow is my day off, and Mrs. Dugdale has me sitting for that portrait again.[25] I must admit I'm getting a bit sick of the darned thing but shall have to see it through now.

I start a new series on Monday—or, rather, a new series I'm doing starts—the girls on the amateur stage. Sort of another "pretty girl" thing—but I hope a bit more news value this time.

Sunday, Oct. 10, 1954

Dear Mum,

Having a thoroughly lazy day and am I ever enjoying it after a near-frantic week! Crept out to church at 8 a.m. but went right back to bed again and finally got up and had breakfast at noon.

Am invited to a theatrical cocktail party 5:30–8:30—all the cast of "The Boy Friend," which might be amusing. Marion phoned this morning to ask me to tea, but I have this party, so arranged to go next Sunday instead.

---

[24] Sir Christopher Lee later became famous for his roles in a string of horror films.

[25] Mrs. Dugdale called it *The Fierce Virgin*. Ouida always told people the title.

We started the new series, "Girls on the Amateur Stage" last Monday and I've been run off my feet ever since, working all six days and one night. It is unbelievable, some of the females who have been sent to me as "pretty girls." One was a woman in her 30s, very pregnant, so buck-toothed she couldn't close her mouth, a too-big nose and no chin! I didn't know what to say. So many people confuse nice personalities with photogenic looks. Guess it's just as well, for if people saw us as the cold, hard camera does, we wouldn't stand much of a chance.

By the way, I sure hope you took in that remark of mine re Christmas inquiries because a car dealer Mr. Greene put me onto rang Friday to say he thinks he can get me a new Morris Minor convertible in about a month. He is ringing again tomorrow to see if I want it, and from all inquiries it sounds an excellent buy for me. And since the present waiting list for a Morris is about a year, the second-hand value isn't liable to drop very soon, so I could always resell it. Of course it will put a kink in my budget, but the office gives a car allowance of 6 pence a mile, and since you can get about 45 miles to the gallon at 5 shillings 6 pence a gallon with a Morris, I shall make good on it.

Shall buy the car on the hire-purchase but I feel that is OK with a luxury item I can sell if necessary—so you see why all donations would be much appreciated.

Monday, Oct. 18, 1954

I went to Marion's to tea yesterday. I like her roommate very much and the hall is a very nice place. She seems delighted with the whole set-up and very happy.

Tonight I am going with Rodney Touche (father is an MP and Rodney is on the paper) to a party at the Russian embassy. He has a flashy red sports car and we are going out to dinner somewhere late. Should be fun.

Wednesday, Oct. 20 [added]

Tasted vodka, ate caviar, terrific spread of food, roasts, chicken, etc. Embassy is a delightful place, and the Russians were thoroughly charming. After, we went for a drive—Rodney's car touched 110 mph on the dual carriageway. I loved it, wasn't a bit frightened, as I am in ordinary cars.

Love, Ouida

Saturday, Oct. 23, 1954, morning

Dear Mum and Dad,

Am at Marie's and my hands and ankles are stinging—got stung by nettles this afternoon. But I discovered at the same time (I was chasing the 4 pigs who got into the neighbour's field) that walking thro' nettles is an excellent way to clean lint off black velvet slacks.

After more careful thought—and an argument with Rodney—I have cancelled the car. I guess the idea of 18 months or more under a financial cloud is too much of a tie and worry. Also, I'd be too broke for too long, no running off to Italy for Easter or Canada when I feel like it. Also, I wouldn't be able to find a garage, and leaving a new car out is not a good idea.

So I bought a new tweed suit, a blouse, skirt, and hat and decided to concentrate on new boyfriends with cars.

Norman Nash has been around a fair bit lately (he's mobile) and there are a couple more on the horizon. Met two interesting males at a farewell party for Clive Baxter on Thursday evening. Clive left Friday for Toronto—he is joining MacLean's [magazine] for a year. One chap, a Canadian, is going home in a week, but the other, John Hillaby, whom I first met three years ago, said he would phone me.

Thursday, Oct. 28, 1954

Dear Folks,

Had a letter from CBC Toronto yesterday addressed "Dear Ouida" and signed "Ross" (MacLean). He still thinks he is going to be able to tempt me to return and wants to know if we can "keep in touch with one another." The next move is his. We shall see what he can produce. His letter sounded rather like a young smart-aleck boy to me. Smart humour stuff!

The weekend at Marie's was very pleasant—except that she fries a lot of things, and since I have been off fats for over 3 weeks on doctor's orders, it was a bit tricky. Nothing serious. I've just had indigestion for 3 weeks and the office doc thought it was affecting my appendix. Now Bart's Hospital [St. Bartholomew's Hospital] medics are testing me.

I'm in the office right now—the only place I get any peace these days. Tonight I'm going out with Rodney Touche again—he is the chap who took me to the Russian embassy. He was invited and took me with him. His father is Sir Gordon Touche, Tory MP for Dorking, Surrey, and his uncle is a Baron [baronet, not a baron]. Not sure if we are going to a theatre or the Motor Show tonight.

Went to see Ingrid Bergman in "Joan of Arc at the Stake" last night. It was a very boring show. Her husband [Roberto Rossellini] is the producer and is rather like a genius gone mad. Ingrid is a beautiful woman of the big Scandinavian type. But the production is dull and uninteresting and the words terribly ugly at times. Chris and a chap named Kenneth Bales came with us. Chris is just back from 3 weeks in Majorca and is terrifically tanned. He got a raise and is due for a promotion in jobs. The boy is really steaming ahead.

Saturday, Oct. 30, 1954

Dear Mum,
Oh dear, it looks as though I'm being pursued again. This Rodney Touche took me out to dinner on Thursday night and when I got in last night he had already rung up. We went to the Motor Show (he drives a racing car and goes in for motorcycle racing) and ate after.

He already knew my day off is Tuesday and has asked me down to his home near Dorking in Surrey. And still when he walked me to the door he wanted to know how soon he could see me again!

It really rather worries me. He is very nice but if he rushes me I'll get fed up very quickly, and it is awkward when I have to work with him in the office. Guess I need a slowpoke like Speed to provide me with a little of the fun of the chase!

Rodney, it seems, is an only son, went to Marlborough School and Oxford, and refused to join the family chartered accountancy firm. I gather the family is fairly wealthy, father a director of quite a few companies. They are Scots descent, all in Who's Who, etc. And it seems his father may be due for a Baronetcy if he stays on in Parliament. He is only a knight now, so his "Sir" is not hereditary. By the way the name is pronounced as "Toosh"—it used to be Touch but the grandfather, a Scot, objected to sounding like an easy bet and added the "e" when the family moved to London.

I also gather Rodney's parents don't get on too well and his father insists on him sticking around. Rodney wanted to go to South Africa and teach school after Oxford but his Pa said no.

Saturday, Nov. 6, 1954

Had a letter from Mrs. Bennett this week asking when I am going down to their farm. Had thought of going down this weekend but I'm still under doctor's orders, taking a foul medicine and on a dreary diet, so said I would go next weekend when I hope to be better company.

Rodney and I went to see a most delightful musical last night—"Salad Days"—and loved it. Wednesday night Rodney and I are taking Gus Hinds and his wife (sports writer in the office) to one of my amateur musicals.

Then Friday night I go to a Scottish dance with John Osborne and some of the old Richmond gang, which should be fun. And on Saturday Rodney is driving me down to Mrs. Bennett's for the weekend. He has asked me to go over to visit his family on the Sunday. Haven't met his father yet, so I may go just for tea—but I shall have to ask Mrs. Bennett first.

Friday, Nov. 12, 1954

I'm going to Mrs. Bennett's tomorrow for the weekend. Rodney is driving me down as it isn't too far from his home.

And next weekend I am to spend at his home. On Friday night there is a big Conservative Ball to which his parents go, as his Pa is the MP. They always take a party, which of course must include the only son. He was funny when he asked me. He said it might be a bit stuffy and dull but he would like me to go if I would. We are to come up for work on the Saturday then go down again for the rest of the weekend. Evidently he also has a Danish scientist friend (male) who is a Catholic going for the weekend, too—sounds interesting. I told Rodney I too am a Catholic.

Wednesday, Nov. 17, 1954

Marion came in after school while Rodney and I were having tea but she couldn't stay long. She said she is dining tonight at the head table with the residence chiefs.

Oh, while I think of it, could you please send me earmuffs. If I'm going to keep on driving in Rodney's open car all winter I'll need them! He could probably use a pair too.

I'm off duty tomorrow and plan to sleep all day in preparation for the weekend, if I can! We drive down to Dorking after work on Friday afternoon. The ball is from 10 p.m. to 3 a.m. I think—and we shall have to leave at 6:30 a.m. for Rodney to be in the office at 7:30. Then we go back again after work on Saturday for the remainder of the weekend. It should be most amusing.

On Monday evening Rodney came to supper, then we sat by the fire playing his Paul Robeson records—he has 16 of them. And several speeches from "Hamlet" by Laurence Olivier.

On the way to Mrs. Bennett's on Saturday we were discussing literature, and Rodney quoted T.E. Lawrence's dedication poem from "The Seven Pillars of Wisdom." It was really rather amusing to be breezing along in a red racing car having poetry quoted to me. He has quite a few surprises in him.

Tonight Ethel and I dine with her boss. Ethel is going to Germany for Christmas. Guess I'll go to Marie's.

Love, Ouida

[First verse of "The Seven Pillars of Wisdom" dedication:

I loved you, so I drew these tides of men into my hands
    and wrote my will across the sky in stars
To earn your Freedom, the seven-pillared worthy house,
    that your eyes might be shining for me
When we came.

The third verse is:

Love, the way-weary, groped to your body, our brief wage
    ours for the moment
Before earth's soft hand explored your shape, and the blind
    worms grew fat upon
Your substance.]

Monday, Nov. 22, 1954

Well, the weekend is over and it was really great fun—except that I sure didn't get much sleep. Rodney and I drove down through fog, arriving about 7:20 p.m. on Friday. We were the last to arrive and just had time to bathe and change into our evening clothes before dinner. I wore my black net with the black and red polka dot stole and red gloves. I wasn't too keen on the other girl, Jackie Cavaliero, at first but got to quite like her as the weekend wore on. I had Rodney's room and since there are three bathrooms, there was no queuing.

[Ouida had been to the house in early November when she came to tea and suggested that a red ceiling in my bedroom would make it seem warmer in the winter. It was painted red by the time she came to stay for the ball. My father being a Conservative MP did not approve of Socialist red and joked that the house could not be sold. It was an improvement.]

We had soup to start with for dinner, which was prepared by the Austrian cook, and then pheasant to follow and delicious apple strudel for dessert and several kinds of cheese (one homemade, as was the butter).

The dance started at 9 p.m. and we arrived about 10 p.m. and of course Sir Gordon had the main table. The other girl made a terrific fuss over Pa Touche and seemed terribly impressed at being with "the member." I'm afraid I found him rather a bore and what I consider a "typical" Tory—which isn't really very flattering at all! But I still like Lady Touche very much. [Ruby Touche was the daughter of a colonial administrator in India.]

The ball was pleasant, not wildly exciting, and we got about 3 hours' sleep before driving to work for 7:30 a.m. Got down on Saturday night about 7:10 p.m. and had a quiet evening talking and watching TV. Bed about 11:30 p.m.

Eric Faulkner, science master at Beaumont Boys' School, another house guest, took me to church on Sunday morning and we (females) stretched out by the fire in the afternoon while the males pottered with cars. Rodney and Eric played squash in the early evening. Jackie and I watched, then dinner with Susan and John, two cousins of Rodney's, coming in as well. We had wienerschnitzel.

Tuesday Nov. 23 [added]

Didn't get this finished yesterday.

Rodney and I drove up to work for 8 a.m. yesterday and he came home to dinner last night. But I put him out at 9 p.m. and went to bed dog-tired. My bed is far more comfortable than his!

Afraid life is going to be difficult. Rodney seems to have fallen pretty hard and said so, which is a fatal thing to do with me. Once sure of my ground I lose interest—will I ever alter, I wonder? And smack in the middle of Rodney being affectionate the other evening, I thought of Speed. They are rather alike, but where Speed said and told me nothing, Rodney tells me everything.

I am going out with Chris tonight.

Thursday, Dec. 2, 1954

Don't worry about Rodney. He isn't as dumb as I was afraid, in fact he can look after himself quite all right. He has asked for night turn next week so he can drive up to Marie's early Monday and fetch me back.

Friday, Dec. 3 [added]

Had a very amusing thing happen the other day. The Editor's secretary brought me a letter written by a young man in West Ham. It asked the Editor to help him trace a girl he had met at a dance the previous Saturday. His only clues were that the girl was studying medicine, was a Canadian, and had a sister, a journalist, on the Evening Standard. I asked Marion last night and she giggled like mad, said the boy had seemed very nice and that it had actually been the only dance she had. The letter was very nicely written indeed so I have written asking the boy, William F. Gilbert Jr. to our annual Christmas tea party on Dec. 12, Sunday week. It's rather exciting, and I'm so glad Marion has had something happen to her for a change and with no help from me. Marion has decided to come with me to Marie's for Christmas. It'll be fun to have her at the farm.

Our tea party seems to be shaping up well and should be fun. Probably have about 40 people in the end. Did I tell you Rodney's father gave Ethel and me tickets to the House of Commons on Wednesday, and we heard Churchill speak?

Love, Ouida

Wednesday, Dec. 8, 1954

Dear Daddy,
Thank you for the slap on the wrist about eating meat on Friday at Dorking—but what was one to do? I couldn't really insult my hostess by refusing to eat her meal, and to say I was not hungry would surely have been a lie. Eric ate it too. I'm sure Lady Touche would have felt terrible had she realized, and I wouldn't have gained anything by waving my religion at her in the midst of a formal dinner party. Never mind, I'll manage it OK.

I have ordered a magnum of champagne to take up to Marie's for Christmas—just a slight change from the usual. I want to take a few really out-of-the-ordinary things for them.

The other day—Churchill's birthday—a picture arrived in our office of the crowds and photographers at No. 10 Downing Street, and there up on a ladder well above everyone else was me! It got a good laugh! The picture was in one of the papers here, will see if I can get a copy for you.

Glad to hear about the earmuffs, thanks. Also Rodney is having a hood made. He came up to Marie's to fetch me back on Monday, 104 miles each way!

Lots of love, Ouida

Friday, December 10, 1954

I shall go to Diss on Thursday the 23rd, returning the 27th. Believe Rodney will come up on the Sunday and bring me back on Monday. Rodney's father has asked us to the Hunt Ball (white tie and tails) in Dorking on Friday after New Year's. It should be quite a "do."

Saturday, Dec. 11, 1954

Golly, Marion just phoned to say a lovely bunch of lilies of the valley have arrived for me and could she and Ethel see who they are from. But she couldn't find a card, so I told her to ring up the shop. It seems a young man sent them and said no card, but from the description it must be Rodney, round face and glasses.

Golly, I'll not be able to hold out much longer. I suppose the flowers are for our tea party tomorrow. But what a sweet thought and he has evidently noted that I like flowers that smell.

Last night he turned up with a completely windproof new hood for the car to keep me warm, a new specially made leather cover for the gearbox and gearshift so I won't get grease on my clothes, and even a new rear-view mirror because I scold him for screwing his head around to see what is behind. A girl could hardly help but be flattered. He shows such excellent taste I can hardly wait to see what Christmas will bring.

Today I decided to spend New Year's in Paris and to take Marion as my Christmas present to her. We will fly over the night of Thurs. Dec. 30 and back on Mon. Jan. 3. She sounded pleased, and it should be fun.

Tuesday, Dec. 14, 1954

Dear Mum,
The cake arrived in time for our party, which was a terrific success. Thank you very much. We eventually had 44 people at our party. Mrs. Robinson and her daughter handled the tea and Ethel and I coped with the guests. Ethel had made coffee, chocolate, and sponge cakes, date squares, coconut squares, and banana and nut bread—icing on the chocolate cake and a dab of whipped cream on the coffee cake and, oh yes, éclairs, too. It all tasted wonderful and we had Tak Tanabe, a young Canadian artist on scholarship here, put up some oils and watercolours. They made a good talking point and he made a sale.[26]

Could have murdered the first man, an Australian opera singer, who came at 3 p.m. (we said 3:30 at the earliest). Phyllis was still arranging decorations, Ethel was not changed and still icing a cake, and I was running around in my bare feet.

We invited Chris, Rodney, Suzette Stone, and two others to stay for supper, but the others didn't leave until 8:30 p.m.—and the opera singer was the last to leave!!!

Everyone seemed to agree that it was a wonderful party—if it wasn't, they sure were dopey to stay so long!

---

[26] Tak has been a successful artist for more than sixty years. He and Ouida kept in touch.

Monday, Dec. 20, 1954

Dear Mum,

You seem a bit off the beaten track: you call Rodney's mother Lady George (she is Lady Touche—Lady George is my next door neighbour!) and you expect Marion to be invited to the Hunt Ball too—why? I have been invited as a partner for her son; her daughter and husband are making up the party. Where would Marion fit in?

As for us "showing off each other" you must be dreaming! So my face is no longer "fresh and young," eh? I need Marion in my social life like I need a hole in the head. And she needs me about as much. She is doing very well as far as I can see—got in at 3 a.m. last Sunday morning and had had a "wonderful evening" with a boy I liked very much. I wasn't too impressed with William F. Gilbert Jr. and neither was Marion.

Rodney is driving me to Marie's on Thursday. He will return home on Friday, then come up again on Sunday and bring me back at the crack of dawn on Tuesday.

Ethel had a Christmas card and letter from Speed Bentham yesterday. It was a very nice letter and let me know he was married in church. He doesn't like Moose Jaw or instructing and has even asked to come overseas again. He sounds happy and I am quite content too. Hearing from him didn't bother me at all, in fact I was pleased.

Life is reaching a panic pace. [She had had my proposal.]

Saturday, Dec. 25, 1954

Daddy, you don't know how welcome your nylons are. I was clean out and the British stockings really can't compare. They never fit as well . . . Mum, your ties are so novel, Ethel has asked if she can take them to her office to show how smart our advertising ideas are. It was really a wonderful box, so attractively wrapped, and it made me quite homesick.

Friday, Dec. 31, 1954, 6:25 a.m. [added to above letter]

Waiting for bus to airport then plane to Paris. Weather very mild and dry. Last week pretty hectic. Your Christmas letter came yesterday.

Love, Ouida

[No mention of my marriage proposal which she had said she would "think about" over the next ten days. In the entry for Tuesday, January 4, 1955, her pocket diary has a single word, "Yes" underlined three times. That word alone was on a piece of paper she gave me in the office that morning.]

AFTERWORD

By Rodney Touche

In preserving six years of letters, Ouida's mother numbered the letters as they arrived and wrote on the outside the names of men she thought might be significant.

My name first appeared on the outside of a letter begun on October 12, 1954, but added to and not posted until October 20. Her mother wrote my name on the outside of three more letters. There had been no other names since May 1952.

I had joined the *Evening Standard* in early 1953 and sat at the long table occupied by reporters using the well-worn typewriters. Ouida was one of the few women reporters, none of the others outstandingly attractive. She wore lipstick, and I thought she was American—two strikes against her. Nor did I appeal to her, she said, because I wore glasses and was English. Perhaps she was through with Englishmen by then. She said that she did not want to marry one.

After eighteen months of ignoring each other, I invited her to come with me to the Russian Embassy, where I had been assigned to cover a reception.

Getting to know her revealed a unique, irresistible personality, so different to anyone I had known; nothing to do with the vodka.

Lord Beaverbrook gave her away at our wedding in 1955 and then invited us to stay with him at his country estate, Cherkley Court, twenty miles from London. Visiting it again in 2007, when it was open to the public, we found that his guest book still has the surname that she wrote for the first time: "Ouida Touche, May 1, 1955."

She wrote few letters to her mother after we were married. However, mail, not e-mail, was important to her. In her final twenty-five years in our apartment in Calgary, she would phone the front desk daily to see if the mail had been delivered. We put letters ready for posting on our hall table, and she would then take them to the postal box that she could see from our windows. Occasionally, I would see her watching for the collection to be made.

During winters when we visited the West Indies, mail arriving at the company's offices was too infrequent to be checked. She wrote few letters but she did write when she found a small shell or a strange bug that should go to a grandchild. Ouida also put down her thoughts and impressions in diary-style notebooks. She never showed me what she had written nor told me of her letters from England retrieved when her mother died. The letters were in a shoebox under her desk. The notebooks appeared for the first time by her bedside when she died.

One entry written Dec. 19, 1986, shows that I was lucky to marry her after six years of failure by other suitors. She had received a letter from a friend with a marriage problem. She had also been asked by a West Indian woman for advice on marriage. She wrote: "How can I be sitting on a small Caribbean island having my advice sought by women with troubled marriages? One by mail and one in person; from two ends of the economic scale, two cultures, two philosophies, two colours, yet the problems are surprisingly similar—indifferent men who expect service yet offer no rewards, no joy.

"My advice! Me, who backed into marriage at age 27 rather unconsciously when my energy was at a low ebb and my life devoid of challenges. Marriage loomed as a challenge. My whole life had been spent responding to challenges set by others. I analyzed neither my qualifications nor R's suitability. He was very positive and I did not manage to think up any negatives during my 10-day 'think about it.'

"I got 'flu instead in Paris. So I married."

The marriage was a success and lasted fifty-three years until her death in 2009.